God's Plan for Success
In Your Family Life

Irwin & Vijaya Lall

WIPF & STOCK · Eugene, Oregon

Wipf and Stock Publishers
199 W 8th Ave, Suite 3
Eugene, OR 97401

God's Plan for Success in Your Family Life
By Lall, Irwin and Lall, Vijaya
Copyright©2018 Apostolos
ISBN 13: 978-1-5326-6950-7
Publication date 9/23/2018
Previously published by Apostolos, 2018

"At a time when families are facing monumental challenges and in many cases are breaking down, this book is a breath of fresh air. Having known Bro. Irwin Lall and his wife Vijaya for many years, and having observed the blessings of their married life and the passion they have to communicate the same, I have no hesitation in recommending this book to couples of all ages so that as families one can serve the Lord."

Dr. Rajkumar Ramchandran, Executive Director, Logos Ministries

"Irwin and Vijaya Lall modeled a wonderful marriage and with their two daughters, a beautiful family. What you will find between the covers of this book is telling truths lived out in rich reality. You can pick up this book at any stage of your life and find divine principles to prevent problems and practical wisdom to resolve those that creep in. This book is a ready reckoner on family matters; it will never gather dust."

Dr. Samson Gandhi, Executive Director, Person to Person Institute for Christian Counselling

To Vijaya

My dream come true. The greatest gift to me, next only to the Lord Jesus Christ.

"Many women do noble things, but you surpass them all." Proverbs 31:29

Foreword

We think of marriage as one of the great institutions of our society. It's just always been around. It's something that we all take for granted.

And yet marriage is anything but an institution. The reality is that when two become one ... it's the becoming that is the hard part. The becoming is a frontier of human experience that every married couple explores, often without a map or a compass or the slightest clue as to the difficulties and challenges that will confront them.

As Irwin Lall writes in this amazing book, marriage either becomes heaven or hell on earth. Sadly, all too often, it is the latter. It's not that a man and a woman don't want to love each other. Of course they do! Their dream is to have a joyful, fulfilling, exciting, dynamic, life–long relationship. The thing that gets in the road of that dream, is that they simply don't know how to do that. This book is about the how.

Irwin and his late wife Vijaya's life's calling has been to share God's wisdom and insight into marriage and family relationships. I never met Vijaya, but she must have been an incredible woman. I see the love that is still in Irwin's heart for her. I hear the stories that he tells about their journey together. And each and every time that I have spoken at marriage and family conferences with him, I have so benefited from his incredibly practical and loving wisdom. A wisdom that comes from God.

Marriage relationships can be confusing, frustrating and downright agonizing. And that's even before the children come along and enter those challenging teenage years. In this book, Irwin lovingly and practically unpacks God's amazing wisdom for us, based on his years of experience in helping many couples through some of the most difficult relationships imaginable.

I don't think there is a single marriage, or a single family on this earth right at this moment, that wouldn't benefit from the godly wisdom in this book. Not a one. So with all my heart, I commend this amazing volume to you. May the Lord bless you, your marriage, your children and your children's children as you receive His Word into your heart. May He give you the power and the wisdom to love the most important people in your life with every fiber of your being. And may He unleash in your heart a love so profound, that you can't help living your life differently, sacrificially, humbly ... for as long as you draw breath. - *Berni Dymet, Bible Teacher and CEO, Christianityworks, Australia*

Acknowledgements

This book would not have seen the light of the day without the wisdom, anointing and empowerment of our Triune God, to whom all gratitude and glory accrues.

There are others that richly deserve mention. Starting with P. K. D. Lee who sowed the idea of penning our thoughts, to Dr. Sudhir Charles who relentlessly motivated and pursued us to get us into the writing mode. Our daughters Sruti and Preeti are always willing sounding boards, especially Sruti who has done a final and thorough edit of the book. She has even re-worked some parts of the manuscript, and her help and wisdom have been invaluable.

The editing team led by Kavitha David, together with Vijaya's sister Manjuvani, and Praneetha ably assisted by Joshua and Isaac deserve heartfelt thanks for polishing the basic manuscript and bringing in the soft-copy for the final edit. Kavitha has put in much effort and by now has the entire manuscript by heart. The husbands team comprising David, Vishwasanna and Anand contributed by minding the children and the homes in the absence of their wives. Thank you brothers for your part! To all our friends across the globe who have prayed and assisted to turn our dream into reality – we are very grateful to you!

Lastly, CEEFI, EFI, EMFI, The Haggai Institute International and National, Person to Person, Operation Mobilisation, EU & EGF, YWAM, YFC, YMCA, Christianityworks, many other Christian organizations and churches across the world in every denomination conceivable deserve grateful thanks for opening their doors for us to minister on the topic of the Christian Family. These opportunities have allowed us to learn and develop our teaching on marriage and the family, deepen our understanding on the subject and sharpen our skills.

Finally, we wish to again thank God, with a prayer that this book will bless its readers and bring Him great glory!

Contents

Foreword 6
Acknowledgements 7
Prologue 9
ONE: WHY IS THE FAMILY SO IMPORTANT TO GOD? 11
TWO: GOD'S DESIGN FOR MARRIAGE 33
THREE: A WRONG CHOICE CAN SPELL DISASTER 39
FOUR: KNOWING YOUR DIFFERENCES 55
FIVE: KNOWING YOUR ROLES 60
SIX: COMMUNICATION IN MARRIAGE 76
SEVEN: SEX AND MARRIAGE 90
EIGHT: FAMILY ALTAR 103
NINE: MANAGING CONFLICT 115
TEN: PARENTING 130
ELEVEN: DYSFUNCTIONAL FAMILIES OF THE BIBLE 159
TWELVE: HANDLING IN-LAWS & LIVE-IN PARENTS 174
THIRTEEN: HANDLING FINANCES 185
FOURTEEN: HANDLING FAMILY AND MINISTRY 200
FIFTEEN: HANDLING ABUSE AND DIVORCE 207
SIXTEEN: MARRIAGE MAKERS AND BREAKERS 215
EPILOGUE: OUR PERSONAL STORY 223
ENDNOTES 238

Prologue

"Thou hast made us for Thyself, O Lord, and our heart is restless until it finds its rest in Thee." Saint Augustine

Ecclesiastes 12:13 "All has been heard; the end of the matter is: Fear God [revere and worship Him, knowing that He is] and keep His commandments, for this is the whole of man [the full, original purpose of his creation, the object of God's providence, the root of character, the foundation of all happiness, the adjustment to all inharmonious circumstances and conditions under the sun] and the whole [duty] for every man." AMPC (Amplified Bible, Classic Edition)

Our God is beyond the limited boundaries of human intelligence. We can know Him only as much as He grants us to know and only as much as our comprehension can grasp, depending on our relationship with Him. Any discussion on the family should first focus on the Lord because He is the creator of this great institution. Our failure to do so has resulted and continues to result in untold misery.

There is so much that has gone wrong with the world today. Creation is groaning under the over-exploitation by man, with many species near extinction. We drink contaminated water, breathe poisoned air and eat adulterated food, making our bodies targets for many diseases and sicknesses. Violence and disregard to authority are at an all-time high. Gratification of our senses is the only mantra that we appear to appreciate. We seem to be on a roller-coaster ride to extinction. Our generation, as others gone before, is obsessed with wealth and pleasure, and families are unable to grapple with the challenges they face. Divorce courts are getting busier by the day, as marriage counselors have become powerless in patching up hurting marriages and families. As Vance Havner says in his book 'Just a Preacher', "We are smart enough to walk on the moon, but not safe enough to walk in the park."[i]

Yet in all this man-made muddle, there are some who seem to lead purposeful lives and appear delighted with their existence, despite facing the same challenges as their contemporaries. What is the difference? These people have discovered that God is the great "I AM," the Author and Perfecter, and "He who keeps Israel never slumbers." These are those who love Him and are the "apples of His eye," and He knows how to keep His own; those who wait upon the Lord will "mount up with wings like eagles." Unless God once again takes center stage in our lives, we are wasting our time and energies in a meaningless quest. He has made us for Himself and for His pleasure. Unless we recognize this fact and allow Him to lead and control our lives, life will never add up. God is alive and working. He is able to do beyond our wildest dreams to bring peace and purpose into marriages that are placed in His great hands. We are convinced that transformed, God honoring families are vital to domestic, social, national and global peace, and they can be change-agents in the purposes of God for a world aflame.

This book has been in the pipeline for over two decades. Earlier, we were perhaps more humanly motivated to write this book than being empowered by God the Holy Spirit. So it really never took off. In the meanwhile, God was ministering to us, equipping us through good and difficult times and using us to minister to families. He continues to work in and through us which is humbling. When we look back, we are more grateful for those difficult days, as our learning was greater, our joy deeper and our faith much stronger, as we saw Him fighting our battles. This book is about His vision, His teaching and also His dealing in our journey of faith with Him, through our failures and triumphs and the precious lessons we learnt in the process. Of late, He has been quickening us and we are convinced, that now He wants us to pen down the truths that He has taught us, not only in the context of the global family but also in terms of our own cultural setting. Through this book, our journey of learning continues and if His truths do not come out as clearly as they should have, we have probably not grasped them well. But, if they do come out powerfully, it means we have been sensitive to the leading of God the Holy Spirit. This book is about our great Triune God who has good plans for even bad people and their families. He is the one who can make the impossible, possible. "Family Matters" - tremendously to God, and as such, to us too!

It is our passionate desire, that as you begin to read this book, you would do so with a prayer, that this book would be His tool in your hands, to mold you and your family into His design. And it is our prayer, that you would not only discover His will, but Him primarily, and be very sensitive to His still small voice and be quick to obey all that He demands of you – at any cost! May He increase in this book as we strive to project Him and may you experience His presence in every page. Our prayer is that this book would be a tool in His hands to touch and transform you, so that through your transformed family, many more around the world would be blessed.

All glory belongs to our Triune God, thrice good, holy and loving.

Irwin & Vijaya Lall Secunderabad

ONE: WHY IS THE FAMILY SO IMPORTANT TO GOD?

"If you want to make enemies, try to change something." Woodrow Wilson

The first institution that God made was the family! God made man, found him to be inadequate and so created his mate. He put them in the best place and gave them a set of rules to live by. The interesting fact is that God never imposed His will (as He still does not), and asked the man and his wife to live by their choices. The devil made an entrance and the rest is a sad commentary of human choice—the consequences of which still plague us and will continue to do so till the Lord Jesus comes back.

Since then, the family has been a battleground that has seen the devil do his best to destroy this institution. Yet, the family has also been the recipient of the forgiveness and grace of God. It is worth noting that the devil does not question the legitimacy of the rules that God had given—he merely sows a doubt! That strategy of the devil still works extremely well.

One thought that occasionally crosses our minds is—why did God have to make a family through the institution of marriage? Could He not make just humans and have them co-habit? Genesis 1&2 elaborately tell us of creation, and 2:18–25 reveals how He created and brought the woman to the man. And then, in v. 24, God calls the woman "his (man's) wife." God in His infinite wisdom foresaw the fall of man and had to take into account his fallen nature and all the consequences. His image in the man and his wife was now marred with sin, and their loss of innocence and holiness went against their having any true and meaningful relationship modeled after the perfect relationship between the Triune God. Man had become selfish, self-oriented and self-pleasing. Choosing evil over good was now the primary nature of man.

He now needed redemption, which would come at the highest price—the death of God's own Son as an atonement for all humankind. Further he needed the image of God in his life to be recreated, and this work of recreation had to be accomplished within the boundaries of relationships.

God does nothing without a purpose, His plans and purposes are worked out in eternity. Isaiah 25:1 says, "Lord, you are my God; I will exalt you and praise your name, for in perfect faithfulness you have done wonderful things, things planned long ago."

God has a plan for the family in His scheme of things for humanity. This plan for the family is found in His Word.

This book reveals some facets of God's plan for the family as elaborated in His Holy Word. If the family is to accomplish His plan, we first need to have its blue-print, and then adhere to it.

Matt 7:24–27 speaks of a house that endures and a house that disintegrates. Wise families build houses that endure, whilst foolish families build houses that disintegrate. The difference is, the wise hear His word and obey, while the foolish hear and go their own way.

Anything that is manufactured, be it a car or a TV, must operate and function within its designed parameters. Otherwise it becomes dysfunctional. Similarly, families cannot accomplish the original purpose they were designed for unless they adhere to God's plan. In order to yield well-tuned individuals in families, God's Word provides a built-in flexibility in those issues which do not have to do with sin, or that transgress His laws.

Some families are either too rigid or too flexible. Rigid families are run by a schedule of do's and don'ts. There is hardly any room to either discuss behaviors or to make amendments. In such families, members feel that they are imprisoned, and long for freedom, especially teenagers. After much waiting and heartache, they realize that the rules are inflexible and not open to discussion, hence they wait for a suitable opportunity to either rebel, or at worst, run away. On the other hand, some families are so flexible, that there is no semblance of any law or rules, governing the behavior of the family members. Anything goes. The book of Judges reminds us, of the tragic statement, "there was no king over Israel and everyone did as they pleased." This gives rise to lawlessness and an unhealthy atmosphere in which to develop a family. The extreme approach in both cases is not the right one. The family has to operate within a specified framework which, while being flexible, is also functional, and able to accomplish God's plans for them.

It needs to be reiterated that a healthy individual, and a healthy home, will lead to a healthy church and society, which in turn leads to a healthy nation. Getting this one thing right really can have a global impact! But the work of change must begin on a micro-level and not macro-level. If you wish to change the world, then change your family first, because that is where the real change must begin.

TEN PURPOSES OF GOD IN MAKING THE FAMILY

Family has an important place in God's design for humanity. We have several wrong notions about the family, and such notions are colored by what we see in the lives of other married couples or families. We fail to fully grasp the plan of God regarding why He created families in the first place.

When my husband and co-author Irwin got his first job at the bank, his father broached the subject of marriage. Amongst various arguments in favor of getting married, the most important was that Irwin was earning well, and was well equipped to take care of a wife and subsequently raise a family. Very often life runs in cycles. When we believe that we are equipped to take care of a family, we get married. And then, the most logical sequence to follow is to have children. And then we go through the next cycle, of educating them, giving them stability in life, and when they are stable enough, we encourage them to get married. And this cycle goes on and on. But God is not as mundane as that! He has amazing plans for the family! The words of Jeremiah 29:11 can be applied to your family: "For I know the plans I have for you," declares the Lord, "plans to prosper you and not to harm you, plans to give you hope and a future."

Every enterprise starts with the concept stage, which eventually leads to the second stage, that of design. Accordingly, we will start in this chapter with the first stage: that is, concept of the family as envisaged by God. We will discuss the second stage in the next chapter.

One look at the world around us tells us that our God is not a God of random accidents. He is perfect and does the things in time which he has planned in eternity. In God's scheme of things, the family has a great purpose to accomplish!

It is interesting to see how different people understand the family in a variety of ways. If you were to ask some teenagers, they might say, "I can only visualize the bars of a prison cell where in my parents are jailers!" If you were to ask some housewives, they might reply, "My husband treats the family as a hotel. He remembers the family, only when he has to get his needs met!" Other couples treat the home as a boxing ring, where they are always struggling to see who is the boss of the home. Sadly, for some couples, the family is a convenient financial arrangement; nothing more and nothing less. In our years of ministry my husband and I have come across many husbands, who believe it is their job to provide for the family, but who do little else for their family. Those couples who come to us for counselling frequently illustrate this point. The husband thinks, that just because he has provided the family with a 42-inch plasma TV, the latest laptop, a three-bedroom apartment, and a good car, then his job as a father or husband is accomplished. He never stops and ask his family what they truly require of him.

So then, let's look at the 10 facets of a Christian home, from the Holy Scriptures.

1. A SHAPING COMMUNITY OF GOD

Irwin enjoys working with wood. It brings great excitement and pride to take a raw piece of wood, give it a shape, and then see the finished product. Similarly, since the family is an unfinished product—it always needs to be worked on. The family is a specialized community, empowered by God to shape every individual. 2 Corinthians 3:18 illustrates this point.

> And we all, who with unveiled faces contemplate the Lord's glory, are being transformed into his image with ever-increasing glory, which comes from the Lord, who is the Spirit.

Paul takes this imagery from Exodus, where Moses had the great privilege of going into the presence of God. As he spent time with the Lord, the Shekinah glory of God would shine on his face as he would begin to reflect the glory of God. This was a fearsome sight to the children of Israel, who were unaccustomed to it; indeed, it was so frightening that they would ask Moses to cover his face with a veil. Over time, however, this glory would begin to fade and perhaps in a few days the face of Moses would revert to its original form. Paul explains that as we take away the veil of unbelief, and consider the Word of God, it begins to act as a mirror reflecting us. It is then that the Holy Spirit begins to do something amazing. The Word of God never glosses over our blemishes and faults, yet as we look at the Word of God, the Spirit discovers blemishes that need to be weeded out, imperfections that need to be chiseled or reshaped and Scriptural truths that need to be hammered in. God the Holy Spirit is gentle, and will never force His actions upon us. But as we give Him permission, He gets to work upon us. As the divine carpenter, He starts the work of chiseling, sawing, hammering, and remolding us.

This process, while being painful and agonizing, will continue relentlessly, until the time when God the Holy Spirit looks at us critically and exclaims with delight, "now you look so much more like Jesus!" All this effort, the hard work, the pain, and the agony, is the handiwork of God the Holy Spirit to make us increasingly like Jesus with each passing day. God uses the work of the Holy Spirit through the family to recreate the image of Jesus in us.

God has many tools that He uses in this shaping process, be it the hammer of adversity, or the chisel of sickness. We would be happy if God the Holy Spirit Himself wielded these shaping instruments in His own hands. However, He hands over these instruments of shaping us into the hands of other people. For a husband, God hands over these instruments into the hands of his wife and his children and vice versa.

It is often seen that the most difficult people turn out to be the greatest blessing in our lives. When Irwin worked at the bank, one person there was extremely difficult to handle. Irwin began to dread the very thought of going to the bank every morning. He prayed for six months, asking the Lord to transfer this man away from his branch. At the end of six months, nothing happened. He continued to pray for the next couple of months. Yet there was no answer. It began to dawn on him that God was telling him, "Do you not realize, that I have put this man in your office to shape you, and to make you more Christ-like?" Once this truth dawned upon him, he began to see people as agents of change in his life. Proverbs 27:17 says, "As iron sharpens iron, so one person sharpens another."

Husbands are called to shape their wives in the image of the Lord Jesus Christ, wives are called to shape their husbands, parents are called to shape their children. After 35 years of being married, we have begun to appreciate that the larger calling of our life is to shape those around us. One day, as we stand in the presence of God on the day of judgement, we believe that God will look at Irwin and—if he does not resemble Jesus in some way—He will demand an explanation from Vijaya. He will then look at Vijaya, and if she does not conform to the image of Jesus Christ, He will ask Irwin why he failed in the mandate that God gave him to shape his family. In short, the mandate of every child of God is to make sure that his family is ministered to in such a way that he/she begins to reflect the image of God, so that in eternity when we all stand before God's throne, we shall all reflect the image of the Lord Jesus.

2. A SAFE FORTRESS FACILITATING TRANSFORMATION

Psalm 46 is a beautiful Psalm that describes our sovereign God as a fortress around us. Verse 1 says, "God is our refuge and strength, an ever-present help in trouble." The whole Psalm paints a visual picture of God as our protector and fortress surrounding us at all times giving us safety, security and comfort.

Yet since (in Gen 1:26) God created humankind in His image, we have to reflect Him even in the area of being a fortress around the people in our care. To be mature, we must reflect God's whole character in our lives—except, of course, for His omnipotence, omniscience, and omnipresence.

Irwin and I counsel many troubled families. Often parents request us to counsel their teenaged children who are not happy at home. They want to be out of the house all the time, mostly with their friends and in their friend's homes. When we talk to these children, they bring out their frustrations. They say that their parents are so busy making a living they have no time for their families. What I am talking about here is *meaningful time* where the children can open up and be understood in their own context. In this way, instead of the family home being a place of frustration, it becomes a place of refuge from life's troubles.

Irwin recalls that a long time ago, he took leave for one day and stayed home. Our younger daughter, Preeti, came home from school and as she came inside the house, he noticed that the little finger on her right hand was raised, and it appeared as if she was about to burst into tears. When he asked her why she looked so sad, she pointed to the little finger that probably was hurt. He just took the little finger in his hands and gave it a little kiss. That little kiss worked like magic and presto—the finger became fine. As far as I know, kisses have no medical value, but that did not matter—what mattered was that Daddy cared about the little things that bothered her.

If we do not demonstrate that the little things in our children's lives matter to us, we are in great danger of creating an emotional distance. Life comes around a full circle, and, as the saying goes, history repeats itself. When we grow old and need the attention of our children, we might just go to them, with our little finger raised, only to hear our children tell us that they are too busy to talk to us. It would be so tragic if this were to happen in our families, but sadly, this is the reality for many.

Alvin Toffler in his book *"Future Shock,"* mentions that the institution of the family is the giant shock-absorber of society. Irwin's job at the bank was very stressful. By the end of the day, his mind would turn blank and he would wait just to come home, expecting a hot cup of tea and a sympathetic shoulder to lean on to unburden himself. Thankfully, he recalls, "Vijaya was so loving and caring, she would meet all my expectations, easing my stress levels." Just imagine a similar scenario where a wife is unsympathetic, and instead of easing her husband's stress levels, launches straight into complaining about everything that had happened at home that day: the gas cylinder running out, the misbehavior of the dog, or the rebellion of the children. Of course, this works both ways, and at times the husband might have to be the shock absorber. There are a number of "shocks" that every member of the family will experience outside the four walls of the home. At such times, the home must be a place of refuge from the storms outside. But if the home itself begins to inflict shocks on individuals, where can they turn? Where else will they receive comfort, solace, and advice? Only when a home becomes a haven, sheltering and accepting, caring and comforting, can this transforming process of Christ-likeness take place.

3. A TRANSMITTER OF VALUE SYSTEMS

Life mimics an athletics stadium, where a relay race is taking place. It is said that the most crucial time of a relay race is when one team member passes on the baton to the succeeding team member. Any fumbling or miscalculation can cause the baton to fall, resulting in that team losing out.

In the 2008 Beijing Olympics, the American women's relay team dropped the baton and lost the race. If you see the photograph of the moment when the baton was dropped, you will notice a mixture of anguish, horror and dejection written large on the faces of the team members. This reminds us of a great truth from the Holy Scriptures as found in 2 Timothy 1:5, "I am reminded of your sincere faith, which first lived in your grandmother Lois and in your mother Eunice and, I am persuaded, now lives in you also." Paul had the privilege of seeing three generations of Timothy's family in action. Firstly, his grandmother Lois, then his mother Eunice, and then Timothy himself. Amazingly, he finds a common thread of an unfeigned faith in the three generations which was refreshing and rare.

In the book of Deuteronomy, chapter 6:2, God tells the Israelites through Moses, "so that you, your children and their children after them may fear the Lord your God as long as you live by keeping all his decrees and commands that I give you, and so that you may enjoy long life." In verse 7, God says, "Impress them on your children. Talk about them when you sit at home and when you walk along the road, when you lie down and when you get up."

It is clear that God is telling the Israelites the importance of passing on the tenets of their faith in God to future generations. They are not just to be taught, but to be taught diligently. The obvious inference here is to teach, to ensure obedience and further transmission.

Woodrow Wilson, once President of the USA was also the president of Princeton University. Addressing an auditorium packed with parents, students and professors, he said something very profound:

> I get many letters from you parents about your children. You want to know why we people up here in Princeton can't make more out of them and do more for them. Let me tell you the reason why we can't. It may shock you just a little, but I am not trying to be rude. The reason is that they are your sons, reared in your homes, blood of your blood, bone of your bone. They have absorbed the ideals of your homes. You have formed and fashioned them. They are your sons. In those malleable, moldable years of their lives you have forever left your imprint upon them.[ii]

These are great, but frightening, truths. It is apparent that we are in the process of leaving our imprints on our offspring and passing on the baton whether knowingly or unknowingly. Batons of either truthfulness, honesty, godliness, purity, and generosity or perhaps batons of greed, dishonesty, lust, disobedience, and rebellion.

This recalls the amazing true story of two individuals who shaped their dynasties. We could call it, "A Tale of Two Families!" It is about two different individuals who lived in the USA around the same period. The first was a man called Max Jukes; the second was Jonathan Edwards. Their posterity demonstrates amazing truths.

It is said that Max Jukes had 1026 descendants, out of whom:

- 300 were sent to prison for an average term of 13 years.
- 190 were public prostitutes.
- 680 of them were admitted alcoholics.
- Most of the family members were not gainfully occupied, they cost the state exchequer more than US $420,000.

The other person, Jonathan Edwards, had 929 descendants, out of whom:

- 430 were ministers or clergymen.
- 86 were university professors.
- 13 were university presidents.
- 75 of them authored good books.
- 7 were elected to the US Senate.
- 1 of them became the vice president of the US.

This family was illustrious, and did not cost the government one cent, but made the country proud with their contributions. What was the difference between these two people and their families? Why did they turn out so differently? It is a known fact that Max Jukes was an alcoholic and never encouraged his family to love God. On the other hand, Jonathan Edwards was a godly clergyman and always encouraged his family to keep God first. It is said that he would not let his family go to sleep at night unless they had family devotions.

What a difference! Wouldn't we love to be in the shoes of Jonathan Edwards! But this kind of posterity does not come about accidentally. It needs much prayer, much demonstration of godliness, much demonstration of love, and the teaching of precepts by example. To achieve what Jonathan Edwards did, we must choose godliness over worldliness and put our personal agenda aside. We must sacrifice in order to pass on the baton of godliness. It may be at the cost of personal gain or promotion, that our future generations follow the Lord wholeheartedly. But we must see this as a gain, not a loss.

4. A LABORATORY OF RELATIONSHIPS

The Bible has been described in many ways: The Word of God, Hammer, Sword of the Spirit, Water, Fire, Mirror and so on. We may also call it "'a book of relationships." It is all about relationships: our relationship with God and people. In Matt 22:35–40, a young lawyer asked Jesus what the greatest commandment was. Jesus answered, "'Love the Lord your God with all your heart and with all your soul and with all your mind.' This is the first and greatest commandment. And the second is like it: 'Love your neighbor as yourself.' All the Law and the Prophets hang on these two commandments." Thereby, Jesus summed up the whole content of the Holy Scriptures by signifying that our relationship to God and his people is paramount.

Therefore, we can say that the Bible is primarily concerned with relationships. We are all born into a family, and it is there we learn to relate to one another, and begin to forge characters and give shape to the image of God in each other.

A family is like a laboratory, where we may experiment and sometimes fail. Irwin recalls the times his school chemistry experiments would fail. His teacher would say, "Lall, do the experiment again, and do it better the next time!" What a tremendous truth lies behind this simple statement. When we fail in our family relationships, we go to God, expecting a rebuke. All He says is, "I understand! Do it again and do it better this time!"

There is a thought-provoking incident in John 21:15–17, which speaks about Peter. While Peter was an amazing man, we see him as short-tempered, emotionally volatile, and vociferous. He was prone to act before thinking, and very often his speech had to be reined in by Jesus. He was so volatile, that in the garden of Gethsemane he chopped off the ear of the high priest's servant. Jesus had to repair the damage, and perhaps saved Peter from being arrested on the spot along with Him. Peter even made grand claims that even if all the disciples would forsake Jesus, he wasn't going to be one among them. But we know, as the Bible unfolds the passion drama, that Peter ended up denying the Lord three times—even to the extent of using strong language in his denial.

In John 21, we find the post-resurrection incident where Peter and the disciples are confused about the events happening around them and the appearances and disappearances of their master and Lord. The suspense gets to Peter, and he decides to go fishing. Six other disciples join him, but they caught nothing and were no doubt discouraged. To their amazement, Jesus stood on the shore, and instructed them to cast the net again. This incident is a repeat of his original call of the disciples (see Luke 5:1–11). The catch is so huge that they are unable to haul it in.

Peter could not even wait for the boat to be brought ashore and in his eagerness to meet the Lord, jumped into the water and swam to where Jesus was. Then follows an interesting exchange between Jesus and Peter. Jesus asks Peter, "Simon, son of John, do you love me more than these?" Peter replies, "Yes, Lord; You know that I love you." Then Jesus says to Peter, "feed my Lambs." This exchange is repeated three times. It might suggest that Jesus is reminding Peter of the three times he had denied Him before His crucifixion. No matter what, Peter must have felt very guilty with an overwhelming feeling of failure, creeping into his heart. In his mind he would have concluded, "Jesus is reminding me of my failures." A cursory examination of the text would deem it so.

But in the original Greek text, we can understand more clearly why Jesus asked Simon Peter three times, whether he loved Him. There are three words generally used in Greek to describe love. The first being *agape*—sacrificial love, godly love, a love that would take us even to the cross, while expecting nothing in return. The second word (not used here) is *eros*—this is erotic love, used generally to describe love between a husband and a wife. The third word is *phileo*, which means, I am willing to love you, provided you love me back. Now in John 21, when Jesus asked Peter if he loved him, Jesus used the word *agape* for love. In response, Peter said that he loved Jesus with *phileo* love. Not satisfied with the answer, Jesus questioned Peter a second time if he did love him with *agape* love. Peter the second time, reiterates that he loved Jesus with *phileo* love. When the question is repeated the third time, we believe, Jesus brings down His expectation of love from *agape* to *phileo* love. How true it is! It is next to impossible, for human beings to demonstrate the truth of *agape* love in their relationships.

We have come across several husbands and wives burdening each other with demands that are impossible to meet. And when people around them fail to meet their expectations, they are written off as people who can never measure up. Teenagers, especially, feel the expectations of their parents to be so lofty, that no matter what they do, they always fall short of the yardstick of their parents. We believe that while in moral issues there can be no compromises allowed, in other issues, perhaps we need to lower our expectations and let others realize that we are willing to accept them, despite their failures. This would take away the great burden of "performance pressure" that makes a person feel that they are always under scrutiny and evaluation. Let people be what they are designed to be. That means understanding their limits and their gifts, and not flogging them to become what they were never meant to be.

The other truth of the story is that we all fail! This brings us to yet another incident involving Peter in Matt 18:21–22. Peter wanted to know how often he needed to forgive his brother. Now even before Jesus could answer, Peter blurted out "seven times?" Jesus replied, "seventy times seven." What Jesus means of course, is "every time."

In Matthew 6:8–15, Jesus makes this issue clear, making it mandatory for us to forgive the transgressions of others as they are linked to the forgiveness that God would accord to us for our transgressions. Verses 14 & 15 say, "For if you forgive other people when they sin against you, your heavenly Father will also forgive you. But if you do not forgive others their sins, your Father will not forgive your sins." Forgiveness is essential. It must become a lifestyle for everyone who loves and obeys the Lord. Many people ask, "if we keep on forgiving people, will we not be taken for fools?" The answer is that obedience to God is paramount, and what other people thinks of us is inconsequential. We are commanded to forgive, and so we must forgive.

Thankfully, God never keeps count of the number of times we seek His forgiveness. Accordingly, as His children, created in His image, we should not count of the number of times we have forgiven somebody. To forgive is to be godly. But not only does God forgive, in Isa 38:17, the prophet says, "you have put all my sins behind your back." Again in Jer 31:34 the Lord declares, "For I will forgive their wickedness, and will remember their sins no more." David says in Psalm 103:12, "as far as the east is from the west, so far has he removed our transgressions from us." When God forgives our iniquities, He also forgets what we had done to grieve Him. What a comfort!

Sadly, though most of us are willing to forgive, we continue to remember the wrongs done to us. These incidents become the fuel that ignites many fires which threaten to consume our married life. What is required is to forget them and never bring them up again. When God casts our sins in the deepest seas, who are we to dredge them up? Many of us have well maintained diaries in our minds, and the moment we have an argument with our spouse, these mental diaries are opened. Dates are meticulously recalled, old incidents reopened, and old hurts revisited.

Corrie Ten Boom was imprisoned in a Nazi concentration camp in World War Two, with her sister, Betsy. Women were routinely raped and killed in these camps. Corrie survived, but her sister did not. In one of her many books she recalls a certain incident when, after a Gospel meeting, people were lining up to shake her hand. As she was about to grasp an outstretched hand to shake it, she found—to her utter horror—a prison guard from the concentration camp, one of the most vicious tormentors of the inmates. As all her hatred came welling out from within her, she did not want to shake the hand of a man who had tortured her. But, as her hand touched the hand of this former Nazi, she found a sort of current flowing between their hands. She found herself crying and saying to the man, "I forgive you my brother, I forgive you." She recalls, it was a strange sight where the former prisoner and the former prison guard were holding hands and crying together, experiencing the grace of God. Corrie Ten Boom made this very profound statement, "I realized on that day, that to forgive is to set a prisoner free, and to discover that the prisoner was really you!"[iii]

Somewhere along the line, when we refuse to forgive people, we begin to carry a heavy baggage which hurts us more than it hurts the other person. When we choose to forgive, we free ourselves from the tyranny of an unforgiving spirit and realize the power of the statement, "burdens are lifted at Calvary." There are many husbands and wives who are carrying on with this baggage of an unforgiving spirit, and deeply hurting within.

We once had a neighbor, a woman who was married to a person who treated her cruelly. This lady had great faith and persisted in prayer for her husband. She prayed for 25 long years, when most of us would have given up. After 25 years, the Lord brought about an amazing change in her husband, who turned around and became a new person in Christ. He even became a pastor! This proves the power of forgiveness, and that no one is beyond salvation. God can change anyone, anytime, anywhere. But we need to understand that God's timetable is different from ours. The sooner we understand this, the sooner we give over the reins of our life into the hands of a sovereign God for whom nothing is impossible.

Dear reader, if God is speaking to you about an unforgiving spirit within you, take time to ask the Lord for help to forgive whoever has hurt you: your spouse, children, parents, or anyone else. When you do this, the grace of God will come flooding into your life, release you from the burden of bitterness, and turn the situation around in such a way that it will bring glory to God. A wise teacher once said, "great marriages are the union of two great forgivers."

Forgiveness reiterates the following truths:

- People do mess up. No one is perfect.
- Sometimes we must lower our expectations.
- Forgiveness is a stepping stone to renewal and progress.
- We may still remember the hurt, but we do not have to revisit the feelings of betrayal, anger, disappointment and injustice. As we do this, God's grace covers us and the memory begins to diminish and ultimately gets buried.

The family is like a laboratory. When we fail, forgiveness allows us to start again—and succeed!

5. A CENTRE FOR TRAINING

> Train up a child in the way he should go, Even when he is old he will not depart from it. Proverbs 22:6

Many young people are under tremendous pressure to perform (whether academically or in some other area), just to please their parents. When they are small, they somehow try to please their parents; but the moment they start growing up they will rebel against such expectations. Some will even run away to avoid the pressures of home. Parents may have unfulfilled dreams. When they marry and have children, they try to fulfil their dreams through the lives of their children. For instance, if a parent has not been able to learn music or play the keyboard, he or she encourages his or her child to pick up music, sometimes becoming obsessive about it and forcing the child to learn music, even if the child is not found to have any aptitude towards music. Other parents who dreamed of becoming doctors or engineers, might try to ensure that at least one of the children becomes a doctor or an engineer; and so on.

A closer look at Proverbs 22:6 reveals that we must "Start children off on the way they should go," not the way you would like him/her to go. As parents we are stewards of our children; God has entrusted them to our care, and it is our prime responsibility to make sure that the child becomes what he or she was originally destined to be by God.

Jeremiah 29:11 says, "For I know the plans that I have for you." This means that God has plans for everyone—including our children. There is nothing wrong in making plans for our children, but we must have the humility to submit our plans into God's hand, and to have His plans work out in the lives of our children (even when the two don't match). In addition, our children might begin to form plans for their lives. So now, we have to consider three sets of plans at the same time: the plans of the Lord; our plans; and the plans of our children. It is obvious that since God knows our future, and as He has designed us and created us for His glory, His plans are best for us.

It then becomes our responsibility to ensure that our children are so guided that they understand the plan of God for their lives, wholeheartedly endorse them, and work hard to become what God wants them to be.

6. A STEWARD OF GOD'S NATURAL RESOURCES

> Psalm 104:24 How many are your works, Lord! In wisdom you made them all; the earth is full of your creatures.

God has given us the privilege of travelling extensively across the world and we have enjoyed the awesome beauty of God's creation. We have seen natural wonders of the earth, as well as amazing animals, birds and ocean creatures. We have been rendered speechless by the sheer beauty and the perfection of God's creative powers.

Yet, there is an underlying sense of sadness and foreboding at the thought that perhaps these may not exist for long. The last great wildernesses are disappearing, the dense rainforests are shrinking, the glaciers melting at an alarming rate, the ozone cover depleting, making the earth hotter and hotter with each passing year. Hurricanes and tsunamis are frequently battering us. The weather patterns have gone haywire! Many animals are almost on the verge of extinction! A time is coming when we will be able to see wild animals only in our zoos and not in their natural habitat. Water is getting scarcer with each passing year as monsoons are failing to arrive and deliver their life-saving bounty.

All this destruction can be traced back to the irresponsible and selfish greed of humankind for acquiring wealth. Humanity is bent upon exploiting the resources of God to further its own ends. And, believe it or not, worse catastrophes are around the corner if we do not wake up and take immediate remedial measures. We believe that the home, as the change-agent it is designed to be, must play a great role in the preservation of ecology and ensuring that the creation of God is dealt with responsibly for our future generations to enjoy!

We suggest that families commence the task of teaching and enlightening their children about our shared responsibility to preserve and care for the natural world. We can develop in children a sense of awe and wonder by helping them discover the natural wonders of the world, the beauty of the animal world, the birds, and the fish. Discovery and National Geographic channels are simply wonderful tools to educate them. Planet Earth is a BBC series that is available in DVD format and is a must-see for every family.

We must help our children form a respect for nature. Teach the children to observe the beautiful wild-creatures and birds in your area. Visit the local zoos at least once a year and teach children to appreciate these animals and develop a wholesome curiosity about them. Small acts of kindness such as keeping bird-houses and water troughs outside your homes will help children develop a sense of responsibility for God's creation.

Promote keeping pets at home. It is scientifically proven that dogs have a beneficial effect on our health. Apart from this, having a pet at home makes us more caring and appreciative of God's wisdom in creating these wonderful creatures for our enjoyment. We have had the joy of having two dogs live with us and we have learnt so much from them.

Plan your holidays to make time for visits to forests, hills, or oceans; whilst there try to observe animals, birds and fish in their natural habitat.

Teach children to enjoy foliage, and encourage them to plant trees and flower-plants. Discourage them from plucking leaves or flowers, and from uprooting plants.

Teach them also to conserve water and electricity. Lead the way by using simple energy saving devices (such as energy efficient lightbulbs) at home.

Apprise children of the natural disasters happening all around us, their probable causes, and how they can help in their own small way to prevent them.

Get involved in movements that promote healthy use of resources and protection of ecology.

Explain the alarming rise in pollution levels, and how we can best bring them down. There are many excellent sites on the internet giving extensive information on this issue.

As a family please pray that the destruction of the ecology will stop, worldwide. God cares for His creation and you will see the positive results in time to come.

Please make sure that your family understands God has given us stewardship of His creation; we must give an account of our stewardship to Him. Many organizations which work hard to save the environment, but change must happen at the grass-roots level, which means, in your family! Every family that can bring about a great change—starting today!

7. A BULWARK AGAINST INJUSTICE, EVIL AND APATHY

> Matt 5:13–14 You are the salt of the earth. But if the salt loses its saltiness, how can it be made salty again? It is no longer good for anything, except to be thrown out and trampled underfoot. You are the light of the world. A town built on a hill cannot be hidden.

"If you don't stand for something you will fall for anything." Peter Marshall

Nothing describes our times better than the opening passage of the novel *"A Tale of Two Cities"* by Charles Dickens. "It was the best of times, it was the worst of times, it was the age of wisdom, it was the age of foolishness, it was the epoch of belief, it was the epoch of incredulity, it was the season of Light, it was the season of Darkness, it was the spring of hope, it was the winter of despair, we had everything before us, we had nothing before us, we were all going direct to Heaven, we were all going direct the other way – in short, the period was so far like the present period, that some of its noisiest authorities insisted on its being received, for good or for evil, in the superlative degree of comparison only."[iv]

We are troubled by what is happening in our cities, to our people and to our leadership. Terrorism, murder, and sexual violence seem to fill our TV news reports. Often, passersby are unwilling to get involved, and remain silent spectators. Take for example the accident victims that lie on the roads untended, while people shamelessly take videos of their suffering to upload them on YouTube, rather than helping them. While in India I saw news of a woman TV reporter being raped in the presence of many men who heartily encouraged the molesters rather than stopping them. Friends, remember, tomorrow that woman could be our wife, our daughter, our sister, or our mother!

Have we ourselves been silent spectators looking the other way when gross injustice is meted out to someone else? Jesus calls us to be the salt of the earth! Salt makes a difference everywhere, in every nook and corner. We cannot look the other way and remain silent spectators, or else God's judgment will overtake us! James 4:17 says, "If anyone, then, knows the good they ought to do and doesn't do it, it is sin for them."

In his Gettysburg Address, Abraham Lincoln quoted Dante in saying that "the hottest places in hell are reserved for those who in times of great moral crisis, maintain their neutrality." Let us not be one of those people who stand on the walls and wait. The only place where this issue can be addressed is in the family. We need to teach our children never to remain silent or neutral when injustice and sin prevail—even if it means to pay a heavy personal price. Let us teach them to do the following:

- To take preventive action if they see any other person being harmed. This can mean either personal intervention or raising an alarm for help from others including the authorities. To help the victims in any manner they require help.
- To be willing to help the authorities in identifying the culprits, even if threatened.
- To stop and help accident victims and provide them with first-aid.
- To go to the courts as a witness if need be, ensuring that offenders are meted out proper punishment.
- To stay away from corruption and rather discourage and curb it in others. If need be, to report it to the respective authorities.
- To reach out to victims and their families, pray for them and treat them with love and care.

We are asked to be the light of the world, banishing the darkness of injustice and sin, and we will certainly be judged for failing to do this.

On the other hand, make no mistake, love begets love, kindness begets kindness and one good turn deserves another. God forbid, we could be victims tomorrow and someone who has read this perhaps would reach out to you. Our families must become a defense against injustice and evil—it is the only hope for tomorrow.

8. A SHELTER TO SHARE GOD'S LOVE

> After these things he left Athens and went to Corinth. And he found a certain Jew named Aquila, a native of Pontus, having recently come from Italy with his wife Priscilla, because Claudius had commanded all the Jews to leave Rome. He came to them, and because he was of the same trade, he stayed with them and they were working, for by trade they were tent-makers. Acts 18:1–3

> Do not neglect to show hospitality to strangers, for by this some have entertained angels without knowing it. Hebrews 13:2

There are many needy people who need to experience the love of God, and our home can be a place that affords rest, recuperation, and a balm to those who are genuinely in need of restoration. Aquila and Priscilla had one such home. They opened their doors to a stranger named Paul who was so blessed in their home. Their home also became one of the first recorded home churches, and many found a Saviour and worshipped in their house. What a privilege! As discussed later in this book, all our resources are meant to be used in ministering to others, and showing hospitality is essential for every Christian home. However, the following guidelines that may be helpful:

While hospitality is essential, your house must not become a free-for-all-and-sundry.

There are many—even Christians—who enjoy nothing more than free food and lodging. Your home should not become an easy target for such people, who just descend to enjoy a good holiday. Your home is not a 'Holiday-Inn'. We have had people in the ministry, who at times wanted to overstay, and we feel this should be discouraged.

Your hospitality should not be to the discomfort of your own family. The whole family should be happily involved. Otherwise it can sow discord in the family.

You can only lodge people if you have enough room in your house to do so without impinging on your personal privacy.

You need not go overboard with hospitality in terms of food—visitors can share the food you generally eat at home.

This hospitality should be strictly need-based and for a short time only, more to afford mental or spiritual healing. Apart from offering food and comfort, it is also important to minister through the Word of God, prayer, and counsel.

You may often find servants of God passing through your city requiring a place to stay overnight. It could not only be a blessing for the family to have them over, but you may draw tremendous spiritual benefit from such people, as we have.

There are some young couples needing discipling and mentoring. Having them stay with older couples on a short visit could benefit them greatly in their spiritual walk. We have had many couples needing counselling who have stayed with us for a short time. This gave us an extended time with them and an opportunity to help them. But I must stress that these couples were known to us before we opened our homes. Also, rather than singles, it is preferable to have couples stay at your home. Having singles over should be avoided unless essential.

It is not advisable to have people with addictions staying over in your house – you could be putting yourself and them at risk. You may have the heart to help them, but you will be of greater service to them by getting them rehabilitated at a proper de-addiction center.

Although Hebrews 13 mentions being hospitable to strangers, keeping the present times in mind, it may not be a wise idea to have strangers *stay* with you. Rare exceptions can be made in cases that are highly recommended by close friends who can vouchsafe them (preferably for a shorter stay).

You could even think of inviting children from orphanages or women from rescue shelters during either summer or Christmas holidays for a short time, and share God's love and comfort with them.

Finally, these acts of kindness should be for the glory of God and blessing people and not with a motive to develop contacts that will be beneficial later.

Paul says to the church in Philippians 3:17, "Join together in following my example, brothers and sisters, and just as you have us as a model, keep your eyes on those who live as we do." This act of hospitality can help people observe you and learn to passionately love Jesus!

9. A PREVIEW OF EITHER HEAVEN OR HELL ON EARTH

We meet many friends who, when asked how they are doing, either say, "We are fine, thank you!" or, "Oh, we are going through hell!" Strange but true! There are many families that are happy and contented despite difficulties, sickness, and troubles. On the other hand, there are many families who, despite affluent lifestyles, seem to be living in sheer misery. We believe that God allows us a brief glimpse of heaven and hell right here on earth.

The family of Eli, the High Priest of the Lord at Shiloh, was judged because of the wickedness of his sons, Hophni and Phinehas (see 1 Sam 2:27–36). Eli had honoured his sons above the Lord by failing to rebuke them (see 3:13) for their wrongs. He tacitly participated in their wrongdoing by eating of the sacrifice the people offered to the Lord. Eli also failed to make sure that his sons had a personal experience of the Lord, besides failing to teach them the customs of the Priests (see 2:12, 13). Because of this, God said both of Eli's sons would die in one day, and the priesthood be removed from his family line, bringing them to abject poverty—a taste of hell on earth.

Are our homes a preview of heaven or a preview of hell? The choice is ours – if we make sure our family is godly, we make sure of a heavenly existence even on earth despite all kinds of difficulties. On the other hand, if we fail to develop godliness, we exist in hell on earth. Life is all about the choices we make!

10. A WITNESSING COMMUNITY OF GOD

At times, we may wonder who we are and why we are here. Remember, our great God is not a God of random accidents. He is a God of purpose. God has placed us wherever we are in time (Acts 17:26) for a very specific purpose. We believe that no matter who we are, where we are and what we do, we are firstly God's emissaries to a lost world. So, our families are to be witnessing communities of God.

The best Scriptural example of a witnessing family is that of Aquila and Priscilla (Acts 18:1–26; Rom 16:3–5; 1 Cor 16:19). This couple are always mentioned together as if they were inseparable. They lived together, ministered together, and risked their lives together. They were a hospitable couple whose home was open to people who needed shelter and comfort. Acts 18:1–4 tells us that they took in a stranger whose name was Paul; and in Acts 18:18–19 we read that they accompanied Paul on a sea voyage to Syria, and later settled in Ephesus while Paul continued his missionary journeys.

Sea voyages in those days were perilous, yet Aquila and Priscilla never shied away from risks for the sake of the Lord. From Acts 18:24–26, when they met Apollos, they knew the Word of God very well and could easily discern theological errors. Having said that, they never made a public outcry, but took Apollos aside and explained things to him. They were gentle yet uncompromising. The Bible also tells us that they had open doors for the gospel and fellowship in their home (Rom 16:3–5; 1 Cor 16:19). The gentile converts were grateful to them for their labour. This is an outstanding example of a family that stood together and worked together to bring glory to God; they made a difference wherever God placed them.

Every minute in my home country of India, 16 people pass away into a Christless eternity. How many of us are concerned about their souls, and care about where they are headed? Since we are "the salt of the earth," and "the light of the world," no matter where we are placed, we must be agents of change, dispelling darkness, showing the way, and making a difference.

But how can the world recognize the presence of Jesus amongst us? In Ps 133:1–2 we read, "How good and pleasant it is when God's people live together in unity! It is like precious oil poured on the head, running down on the beard, running down on Aaron's beard, down on the collar of his robe."

In the post-Egypt wanderings of the children of Israel, there were more than 600,000 men of war, with women, and children, and perhaps 2 to 3 million people wandering along with Moses and Aaron in the desert. How could this huge number sense the presence of the high priest amongst them?

Before Aaron went into the assembly of God's people, he would deck himself with the high priestly robes, after which a container of perfumed oil called the perfumer's blend, would be poured on his head. This then would cascade down from his head onto his beard, then onto his robes and come down his garments through the hem of his robes.

When I was a boy in India, my mother had a small bottle of perfume called 'June' which was imported from England and very expensive. This bottle was taken out on just a few occasions during the year. It was suitably hidden in a large trunk filled with clothes etc. It so happened that once my mother called me and sternly asked if I had meddled with the perfume bottle. I had not, and said so. But the reason mother suspected me was the fact that no matter where one went in the house, every corner of the house reeked of the perfume. When mother and I opened the box, we discovered that the perfume bottle was broken, and the smell was wafting out of the large steel trunk filled with clothes. You can well imagine the strength of the perfume and its ability to permeate everything around it.

So you see, as Aaron entered the assembly, following his anointing with perfumed oil, people just had to take a deep breath to know that Aaron was now amidst them. The same imagery is taken a step further by Paul in 2 Cor 2:15, where he says, "For we are a fragrance of Christ." Paul says that no matter where we are, when we pass by, people should be able to smell the fragrance of Christ in us. When can this happen? Psalm 133:1, "When God's people live together in unity." It is only when we exist together in unity and harmony as His children, can the world recognize the presence of Jesus amongst us.

Our mentors Warren and Ruth Myers who served the Lord through Navigators in south-east Asia, had an interesting story from their early missionary days in Hong Kong. As they could not afford expensive housing, they had to take a house on the outskirts of Hong Kong which was sandwiched between a pig slaughtering/canning factory on the one side and a perfumery on the other side. It did not take them much imagination to understand which way the wind was blowing!

There is a great spiritual parallel here. If we dwell together in love and harmony, we become the fragrance of Christ attracting people towards Him. If we live lives fraught with strife and suspicion, we take on the stink of Satan. There is always a choice, either to live in harmony or to live in disharmony.

St Francis of Assisi put it so meaningfully: "preach the gospel at all times, use words if necessary." The home affords a platform that can either promote a silent witnessing to the Lord, or provide an occasion to articulate the gospel.

How does your home measure up in terms of the ten concepts for the family that God has mentioned in the Scriptures?

The next chapter will deal with God's design for the family. And the remaining chapters of the book will focus on the aspects of maintaining a God-honoring family through effective communication, handling finances and strife wisely, developing a meaningful, devoted, Christ-centered life, and more!

† † † † †

TWO: GOD'S DESIGN FOR MARRIAGE

"As God by creation made two of one, so again by marriage He made one of two."
Thomas Adams

Genesis, the first book of the Bible records the beginning of the family. Proverbs 18:22 says, "He who finds a wife finds what is good and receives favor from the Lord" and Proverbs 19:14 says, "house and wealth are inherited from parents, but a prudent wife is from the Lord." Obviously, a prudent husband is from the Lord too! Genesis 1 and 2 give us an operational framework—a divine design to govern the institution of marriage, so that it functions smoothly, performs flawlessly, and progresses spiritually. We will now examine this basic framework.

When we read the account of creation in the first chapter of the book of Genesis, at the end of each day God said that it was good. But on the sixth day when He made humankind in Gen 1:31, it reads, "God saw all that he had made, and it was very good." However, in Genesis chapter 2 God said, "It is not good for the man to be alone; I will make a helper suitable for him." And so God made woman and brought her to the man. This passage conclusively tells us that marriage is God's design and not ours. If marriage is God's design, it is obvious that unless we follow the instructions given by Him regarding marriage, our marriages will never function properly and cannot sustain themselves.

The Hebrew word for helper is *awzar*, which means among other things, "to surround". It is such a revelation to understand that God wanted the wife to surround her husband as an integral part of his life, a partner who is involved in everything he does and able to help him in achieving God's best for them and for His kingdom. Husbands, please do not exclude your wives from any areas of your lives, rather involve them in as much as possible, so that you can draw from their God-given wisdom, counsel, and guidance.

Genesis 1:27 states, "God created mankind in his own image in the image of God he created them; male and female he created them." Since both man and woman were made in the image of God, both are equal in worth. Some men presume they are superior to women, and find it very difficult to accept this statement, as they believe that man was made the head and the woman his subordinate. But the truth is that as both are made in the image of God, both are made equal and God sees them as partners. In Genesis 1:28, God calls them, blesses them, and says to them, "Be fruitful and increase in number; fill the earth, and subdue it. Rule over the fish in the sea and the birds in the sky and over every living thing that moves on the ground." They both share an equal responsibility in governing over all His creation.

In Genesis 12:1–3 God promised Abram, "all peoples on earth will be blessed through you." In this way we see that God created the institution of marriage and family to carry out His plans and purposes for all mankind, and to be a blessing to the families across the globe. We also find from Rev 4:11, that God created all things for his own pleasure: "You are worthy, our Lord and God, to receive glory and honor and power, for you created all things, and by your will they were created and have their being." God created mankind and family to bring pleasure and happiness to God through our heartfelt and holy worship.

Gen 2:24–25 elaborates God's expectations in marriage:

> That is why a man leaves his father and mother and is united to his wife, and they become one flesh. Adam and his wife were both naked, and they felt no shame.

From this passage God gives us four principles to follow, to make sure that our marriages are satisfying and fruitful for His glory.

- LEAVE
- CLEAVE
- ONE FLESH
- NAKED AND NOT ASHAMED

LEAVE

Genesis 2:24 says that a man is expected to leave his parents and cleave to his wife. This principle is twisted out of its context, with many advocating every newly married couple to leave their parents and begin their newly married life together separately. We do recommend that a newly married couple live separately from their parents for some time in order to understand each other better, and also to grasp the dynamics of building their own home. However, this in no way means that the moment they are married the couple should divest themselves from their responsibility towards their parents. In fact, in 1 Timothy 5:8, God says that he who does not take care of the members of his own family is worse than an unbeliever.

Sometime ago, we got a midnight call from a friend who had been married for over 20 years with three teenage children. He'd had a heated row with his wife. As we spoke to them we found that while he was very loving, he was still very attached to his parents, especially his mother, taking her advice constantly and was incapable of taking decisions on his own as the head of the family. This was causing all the trouble.

We counsel a lot of young people contemplating marriage, urging them to understand that after they get married, the leader of their home should be the husband. This cutting away from the leadership of their parents is very vital for a new couple in building their own home. While we do acknowledge that parents are wise and loving, they can in no way be allowed to influence the new couple, except with their total agreement. Many parents find it too difficult to relinquish control over their married children and begin meddling with their decisions, which becomes the root cause that prevents a newly married couple from understanding the dynamics of God-given roles within marriage.

An apt analogy here is that of a child in its mother's womb, who is nourished through the umbilical cord. Once the child is born, the umbilical cord becomes a hindrance to the freedom and well-being of the child and has to be cut, allowing the child to grow outside the womb. Similarly, many men and their parents never cut away the umbilical cord of emotional dependence, even after marriage.

"Leaving" also has another aspect to it. The newly-weds bring their own baggage of their past, cultures, backgrounds, accomplishments, pride of the family and much more. This baggage prevents them from having a truly intimate and meaningful relationship with their spouse. Often, one spouse thinks his or her family is better than the other's. In such a scenario it is no surprise that each spouse is fiercely protective of their lineage, and the moment their family is compared derogatorily, their bristles stand-up and a fight ensues. It is important that once they get married, all negative baggage should be left behind and only those attitudes that contribute to the building of a healthy home should be retained as a common treasure, to be cherished and passed on to posterity.

CLEAVE

The Hebrew word for cleaving is *dabaq*, which means being glued together like two papers which are inseparable once glued. When we try to separate these two glued papers, we will only be tearing both, and destroying them. This is "cleaving", an inseparable lifelong bond which can only be dissolved by the death of the spouse. This is a permanent bond and God does not allow us to tamper with it in any way as said in Malachi 2:16 (note), "I hate divorce." There is no provision for divorce in the perfect plan of God for mankind. Jesus when questioned about divorce, in Matthew 19:4–9, said "But it was not this way from the beginning." He also says that "Moses permitted them to divorce only on the grounds of adultery, that too because of the hardness of their hearts."

However, many couples live under the same roof with no relationship between them. They may seem like a happily married couple, but for all practical purposes, they are divorced, mentally, physically and emotionally. They are staying together only for the sake of their children or to avoid the stigma of divorce.

Cleaving means not only being attached to your spouse, but also to your marriage commitment. Dietrich Bonhoeffer, writing to a newly married couple from the confines of his prison cell in Nazi Germany says, "It is not the love that will sustain your marriage, but from now on, it is your marriage that will sustain your love."[v] How true! Over time, love can fade, lose its gloss, or diminish in its excitement. One begins to wonder, "Where has the love gone?" It is precisely at such times that we need to hang on to the promise made to our spouse in the presence of God and His people, that we would continue to remain married, faithful, and supportive. God honors such a commitment and you will find that as you stick to your commitment, God begins to work and make your marriage beautiful in such a way that people will look at you and give glory to God. Greater and deeper love shall be reborn, and flourish to strengthen your marriage. As said earlier, cleaving is like two papers glued together so there should be no room for anything to come in between—especially a third person! This could be disastrous!

ONE FLESH

Most of us infer this to mean sex. This is only partially true. Plain simple water, also known to us as H_2O, is a mixture of two parts of hydrogen and one part of oxygen. When these two elements, distinctive on their own, are combined, they yield water. One cannot look at water and identify where hydrogen begins and where oxygen ends. Both these elements are mixed together to form one single entity. A wise man once said, "As in creation, God made two out of one, in marriage God makes one out of two."

This is the beauty of marriage—that two individuals, distinctly different, become one. In the analogy of the human body, God says in 1 Cor 12:26, "If one part suffers, every part suffers with it; if one part is honored, every part rejoices with it." If this be true for the body of Christ, how much more for the family, especially the couple. They are not two, but one.

Another prominent source of contention is "ownership." There was a husband who constantly threatened his wife and children saying that he would throw them out from "his" house. He always saw their house, as "his" house, their money as "his" money and everything was either "his" or "hers." They were married, but not yet become "one flesh." Another couple once came to us with a complaint that the husband had to pay the electricity bill, but as he was falling short of money that month, he could not pay it, and the electricity department disconnected the power supply to their house. Although the wife had the money to pay the bill, she preferred to live in a house lit by candles, rather than pay "his" bill. As a result, it was the children who suffered the most. Such attitudes drive the wedge deeper between family members and promotes an individualism which is detrimental to the well-being and health of the whole family.

From the day you get married, nothing remains "his" or "hers." Everything must be treated as "ours." It is such a joy where everything is shared and every member of the family has a sense of joint ownership. Such families are happy, contented and practice selfless sharing of all resources, often sacrificially.

THEY WERE NAKED AND WERE NOT ASHAMED

Before the fall of man in the Garden of Eden, the man and his wife were naked. Sin had not yet come into their lives, so their consciences were not marred and they were not aware of their nakedness. But soon after the fall, their eyes were opened to the fact that they were naked, and they had to cover themselves to hide their shame. However, this verse points to a much deeper truth that there was nothing hidden between them, and as a result, they had nothing to be ashamed of. One word that describes this is TRANSPARENCY.

A lady once complained to us that after her husband came home from work, his phone would ring, and he would quickly go out of the house to speak to the caller. This led to suspicion, resulting in arguments and strife at home. The wife logically said that if her husband had nothing to hide, he had no reason to receive the call privately. Many women regularly check their husband's cell phones and computers to check who has been calling or mailing them. God help the man whose wife finds other women on their list of callers! It is true that some husbands too keep a check on their wives. Life becomes complicated and difficult when the atmosphere at home is charged with this kind of suspicion, mistrust, and anger. Hiding something from one's spouse in no way contributes to the building of their relationship. No matter what, there should be absolute transparency between the couple.

One of Vijaya's friends who took voluntary retirement from the bank and received retirement benefits, asked Vijaya how she had invested her "black money." Vijaya was surprised, and said that we did not have any "black money" in our family. Her friend laughed and explained, "of course you don't, but I have. My *black money* is the amount I have kept away, without my husband knowing!"

Unless there is a spirit of acceptance, transparency cannot find a place at home. For instance, a father who is unwilling to accept his children as they are can never promote transparency in his children. He will always be seen as a dictator. A person who is always in perfection mode and makes no allowances for failures cannot encourage transparency in his/her spouse. Vijaya had another friend in the bank who would always complain about her husband. Vijaya found her unreasonable, and sympathized with the husband, much to the irritation of her friend. On one such occasion, when she was moaning about her husband, Vijaya asked her if her husband was caring, loving, and generous in his dealings with her and the children. She said, "yes," but she blurted out, "but my husband is not like your husband." Finally, the truth was out: this woman was comparing her husband unfavorably with others she had seen. She was focused on his negative and not his positive qualities. Vijaya said to her, "thank God, your husband is not like my husband!" Her friend was quite shocked and gaped in disbelief. Vijaya explained to her, that God designed her husband just for her, as He did with every couple. Comparing one's spouse with others only results in frustration and strife. God uniquely creates every person to reflect Him. When we begin to look at the positives, compliment them, and look for ways to have them exercise their God-given gifts and talents, life would take a turn for the better. Every person also has negatives which need to be worked upon. The best person to work on these is God the Holy Spirit. He is the only one who can touch every person deep down in their innermost being and bring out "streams of living water."

We can learn an important truth from the story of the "Beauty and the Beast." Underneath the gruff and ugly exterior of the ferocious beast lay a tender heart. As the girl began to see the beautiful person under the seemingly ugly exterior, she began to fall in love with the beast. Frankly speaking, we are all like "beasts" until the touch of the Holy Spirit transforms us. God is in the business of changing people. His work is perfect and lasts all time and eternity.

So let us strive to be transparent, even if it means to be vulnerable. Let us accept our spouses, children, and parents for who they are with all their warts and blemishes. Of course, that does not mean that we accept them with their moral and spiritual failings. We need to understand that moral and ethical issues have to be dealt with in the light of God's Word and with a sense of deep forgiveness. But as we begin to encourage people to dwell more on the positives and less on the negatives, we begin to progress on the highway of reconstructing our families for His glory.

THREE: A WRONG CHOICE CAN SPELL DISASTER

"By all means, marry. If you get a good wife, you'll become happy; if you get a bad one, you'll become a philosopher." Socrates

The second most important decision, after the decision to accept Jesus as our personal Savior, is the decision of marriage. Unlike salvation, where there is one option which you either accept or reject, the decision of marriage presents a whole variety of options which need to be mixed and matched to arrive at a decision. Hence, making this choice is quite tricky. We can understand the complexity of this decision from the following real-life experiences. While these are real life stories, the names, places, and occupations have been changed and any resemblance is purely accidental.

Dave was a young man, from a good family, and with a lucrative job. Hence, he was considered a prize pick for any family's marriageable daughter. Diana, a postgraduate in science, also had a good job. She belonged to a Christian family in a small town. Her father was in the ministry and had brought up his children with love and good values. But as is common, she was finding it difficult to find a suitable match for marriage. Dave appeared just such a match. He was suave, well read, and polished, and bowled over the girl's family. Everyone was pleased when they announced their engagement, even though they had not known each other for very long.

After the wedding, it took some time for Diana to discover deep problems in her relationship with Dave. Diana was at heart a simple girl, who dressed modestly, but Dave expected her to wear more revealing clothes. He was also addicted to watching pornographic movies as well. While visiting some of Dave's relatives, Diana discovered that Dave had actually been engaged to someone else, but it had not worked out. Her marriage to Dave ran into trouble, and they ultimately ended up in court, seeking a divorce.

Mark was brought up in a respectable Christian family. He was a good student did well at school and college and eventually got into a good government job. Life was good and running smoothly until he visited his friend's house and bumped into his friend's sister, Amber, a pretty, vivacious girl, with a charming personality. Mark fell for her like a ton of bricks and could think of nothing else but to get married to Amber. The trouble was, that Amber was from a different faith. Mark's parents, his friends, and all his well-wishers tried to reason with him but Mark was certain that this was God's will for his life and presumed that somewhere along the line, Amber would accept the Lord and be a part of His kingdom. Amber's parents too were unhappy and tried to dissuade her. To cut a long story short, they got married both in church and in a temple. As they began to settle down in their marriage, Mark discovered that although they were very much in love, they began to disagree on some major issues of life. Amber did sometimes go to church with Mark, but she was an unwilling participant. Little by little, major disagreements began to surface. The use of money, time, resources, priorities, goals, children, parents, and friends—almost every aspect of life began to bring about arguments, sometimes bordering on the violent. Not long after, Mark began to understand that he had made one of the biggest mistakes of his life. Amber felt the same. Life just came apart, and stood still, with just no way out but a painful divorce.

These are just two of the many stories we have come across in our counselling experience. Mistakes like these are painful and avoidable. Marriages like these, entered into without serious thought, *can* work out so long as these families can live in harmony. But this calls for a serious desire to seek God's wisdom and a willingness to change. Change, however, takes a long time. Much of the heartache in marriage is because of the wrong choices made in the first place. We make the mistake of choosing our spouse first, and only then trying to bring God into the picture for His approval.

But before we can discuss ways in which our choices can be guided by God, let us mention some things that we come across in our churches with alarming regularity.

It is a trend that is often repeated in Christian circles in our home churches in India. Frequently, in families today, both parents are employed and find little time to bring up their children. They tend to appease their conscience for not spending much time with them by indulging them or buying them costly gifts. As children grow into adolescence, they pass on from being Sunday school students to being members of the youth fellowship of their church. They also get into singing, worship, and music; boys particularly are fascinated with playing the guitar or the drums. They pester their parents to buy them these musical instruments, and are preoccupied with them. While these extracurricular activities may add to their all-round development, they may also prevent them from achieving academic excellence. Eventually, they turn out to be average students and do not measure up to the standards required for professional courses. But they can articulate well, perhaps sing well and can play an instrument or two. This is a very powerful combination that attracts the opposite sex, apparently very gullible and impressionable in their youth.

Girls, on the other hand, are more often studious, work hard, and are less distracted. In general, they do better academically, and many graduate from university. It comes as no surprise that it becomes very difficult for these girls to find suitable life partners, and in India today there are large numbers of highly qualified Christian girls looking for suitable grooms in the church. As they become older, the number of suitors become fewer, and the level of frustration grows. Naturally, some bring down their expectations in marriage and get married to a Christian man who may be less suitable than they had hoped. Others, upon not finding a suitable match, begin to look outside the church and compromise their faith by marrying boys from other faiths.

This situation may not be exactly reflected in the West, the circumstances in India bring us back to our earlier premise, that the choice of a person's life partner needs to be made after much prayer and consideration. There may be other prevailing trends amongst the youth of our church which are creating hurdles for them finding a suitable match for marriage.

SOME PRE-CONCEIVED NOTIONS ABOUT MARRIAGE

In addition to the above, there are some *preconceived notions* that can negatively affect our marriage choices. Dreams are part of our life, and the stories we hear fire our imagination. Every young girl reading the fairytale of Rapunzel believes that a handsome prince will one day come and they both will ride off into the sunset on a white horse. Most young people get so carried away by this story, that they begin to think that, post marriage, life will mimic the legend: "and they lived happily ever after." This is far from the truth. After the sweet honeymoon period, the dark side of their personalities surface, and the drudgery begins. The once handsome prince now appears as a self-serving, bullying tyrant, and the beautiful princess a mean and nagging hag.

Another fairytale, "The Frog Prince" leaves a deep impact upon young minds. Girls believe that every boy is like the frog waiting to be kissed by a ravishing princess, and the kiss transforms him into a dashing young prince. Sadly, the reverse often happens! The frog remains a frog and many times the ravishing princess also turns into a frog, and it takes long and painstaking effort to bring about the needed personality changes.

For all the young people reading this book, we would earnestly advise you to make your marriage choice after the prospective spouse has passed the test of being emotionally, logically, socially, and Scripturally sound; and most importantly once the will of God becomes clear to you.

SOME REASONS WHY WE "MISS THE BUS"

Irwin and I both had spinster aunts. These aunts were highly qualified, good-natured, and good-looking. For the casual onlooker, it seemed a mystery why these good ladies never got married. It was not because they had some "call" from God to remain single; it just did not happen. Not just spinsters alone, we also find some men who are well settled, who remain bachelors for no apparent reason.

Here are some reasons as to why some people remain single all their lives despite many efforts to get married.

WAITING FOR THE PERFECT PERSON!

Above we warned of setting our standards *too low*, but some of us may set our standards *too high*, so that it is difficult to accept prospective spouses who have the slightest imperfection. Perhaps they are not good-looking enough, not earning enough, does not dress well, cannot articulate well, has a boring job, and so on and so forth. This list can be endless.

As we travel, we come across many eligible young men and women who are ready for marriage. Many Indian parents used to ask Vijaya to look out for their children and get back to them if she found a suitable match for marriage. Vijaya would always ask these parents what, in their opinion, was a suitable match for their son or daughter. Most of the time, the parents would begin by saying, "all we want is a God-fearing person," but they would slowly come out loads of supplementary requests. "Well, if the girl holds a good government job, it would be ideal," or "My girl is quite tall, so the boy has to be at least 6 feet." This is hilarious, but sadly it illustrates how some young people (and their parents, who in Eastern cultures have big say in who their children marry) are looking for *the perfect person*.

We remember watching a very interesting Hollywood movie, "How the West was Won." Gregory Peck, the male lead who plays gambler Cleve Van Valen, comes across Lilith, a pretty casino entertainer played by Debbie Reynolds. Cleve falls in love with Lilith and proposes to her. Lileth turns him down, telling him that she was looking for the "perfect man." Cleve is heartbroken and moves on. Many years later they again meet in a casino, and to Cleve's surprise he finds out that she is still single. When asked why she was still unmarried, Lilith's reply is classic: "I found the perfect man, but the perfect man was looking for the perfect woman." So finding a perfect man or woman is a figment of our imagination - they do not exist!

SCARED TO TAKE THE PLUNGE

Many young people think that marriage is an unknown domain which can change their lives irrevocably, and are vehemently opposed to 'plunge' into the unknown. We must remember that God ordained marriage, and so it is good for us. We need to exercise our faith in this good God and His good plans for us, and step into marriage with a leap of faith.

HAUNTED BY A TURBULENT OR GUILTY PAST

Perhaps some young people, as children, have witnessed the turbulence in their parents' marriage. For others, their contemporaries—through bullying or name-calling—give them a bad self-image which creates hesitation towards marriage. Failed romances can similarly result in an aversion to getting married. To those who are haunted by bad experiences, here are four important Bible passages to help you lay these devastating memories to rest.

> Therefore, if anyone is in Christ, the new creation has come:[a] The old has gone, the new is here! (2 Cor 5:17)

> "Come now, let us settle the matter," says the Lord. "Though your sins are like scarlet, they shall be as white as snow; though they are red as crimson, they shall be like wool." (Isa 1:18)

> I, even I, am he who blots out your transgressions, for my own sake, and remembers your sins no more. (Isa 43:25)

> Forget the former things; do not dwell on the past. See, I am doing a new thing! Now it springs up; do you not perceive it? I am making a way in the wilderness and streams in the wasteland. (Isa 43:18–19)

If we have made a mess of our lives and we turn to God earnestly with true repentance, He is willing not just to forgive us but wipe out our mistakes. He also instructs us not to look back and He makes us new (as if we had never sinned), and promises to do something so good, so impossible, that it will be hard to believe. What a God we serve! What a Father to come back to! On the other hand, if we are victims of circumstances, or the abuse of others, God reassures us that He is in the process of birthing a new chapter in our lives and bids us not to recall the injustice meted out to us. God can turn those bad experiences into good for his glory, for Romans 8:28 says, "And we know that in all things God works for the good of those who love him, who have been called according to his purpose."

TOO BUSY BUILDING SUCCESSFUL LIVES

In the process of pursuing success, some are satisfied with "one-night stands" and see marriage as a nuisance. This has been labeled, "affluence intoxication." However, much later, when age catches up and the downside of such a lifestyle begins to trouble them, these people realize the value and comfort of a home built up painstakingly over decades.

While some people remain unmarried, there are some who get married for the wrong reasons.

WRONG REASONS FOR MARRIAGE

When young people "miss the bus" and as age advances they become frustrated and desperate to get married. This leads some of them get married for the wrong reasons. Some of these reasons are listed below:

- Getting older by the day.
- All my friends are getting married.
- Daily badgering by relatives, friends, and well-wishers for "good news."

We have heard of parents resorting to emotionally blackmailing their children into getting married "because they are getting old and want to see them settled before they die." We advise young people not to succumb to this emotional blackmail and to gently remind their parents that God has a plan and a time-frame for their marriage. Waiting for God to have His perfect will would be in their best interests too.

Sometimes Christian parents bulldoze their children into looking at prospective grooms or brides even when the young people are not fully prepared for marriage. In such cases children do not like to hurt their parent's feelings. As a result, some have consented to get married at the cost of their own comfort and happiness.

- What if I don't get married?

Many young people are terrified to imagine a scenario where they may not get married at all. This creates a panic situation often resulting in their jumping onto the marriage bandwagon.

- Escape from their own dysfunctional family.

Some young people come from dysfunctional homes rife with negative criticism, violence, and abuse. This leaves them with a longing to escape from their tragic existence into marriage, thinking they would be able to leave all the bitterness behind and go into a fairyland existence. Such people, expecting marriage to be a fairytale, discover that married life has its own challenges and needs a lot of work before it can resemble a fairytale and hence become disillusioned post-marriage.

- Escape from loneliness.

Some young people think marriage is the cure for their loneliness and plunge into marriage. In the end they discover that the cure is worse than the disease.

- Way to "easy" happiness.

Some young people think marriage is an easy way to happiness. And when troubles come their way, they get disillusioned.

In sum, we see that getting married for the wrong reasons fully justifies the saying, "marry in haste, repent at leisure."

GUIDELINES FOR CHOOSING A PARTNER

Marriage is definitely very important to God, as it was the first institution created and ordained by Him. Gen 2:18 tells us that post creation, God looked at Adam and He said, "It is not good for the man to be alone; I will make him a helper suitable for him." Accordingly, God made them both in His image to rule and to be fruitful and multiply and fill the earth and subdue it.

It is apparent that God expects every person to discover His image in their spouse. It is also apparent that God wanted both Adam and Eve to jointly carry out His mandate to govern creation. This mandate can be jeopardized through three aspects of the human behavior.

- LONELINESS

- IMMORALITY

- INDEPENDENCE

With His creation of marriage—companionship—partnership—progeny, with a single stroke of His wisdom, God brought in to human relationships a stability and attitude which reflects God (loving, caring and sacrificial). Certain passages of the Holy Scripture bring these truths to the fore. Read through: Gen 2:18, Gen 2:24; Heb 13:4; 1 Cor 7:2–5, 9; Gen 1:27, 28; Ps 127, 128; Prov 22:6.

In the Holy Bible, God gives some basic principles and guidelines that govern and control the institution of marriage. This has also been dealt with at great length in our chapter on "Marriage: God's Design." However, we would like to list them here in this chapter as well. These principles are found in Genesis 2:22–25:

> And the Lord God fashioned into a woman the rib which He had taken from the man, and brought her to the man. And the man said, "This is now bone of my bones, and flesh of my flesh; She shall be called Woman, because she was taken out of Man." For this cause a man shall leave his father and his mother, and shall cleave to his wife; and they shall become one flesh. And the man and his wife were both naked and were not ashamed.
>
> You have heard that it was said, 'You shall not commit adultery.' But I tell you that anyone who looks at a woman lustfully has already committed adultery with her in his heart. (Matt 5:27–28)
>
> So they are no longer two, but one flesh. Therefore what God has joined together, let no one separate." (Matt 19:6)

THE PRINCIPLES SET BY GOD FOR MARRIAGE

- To leave father and mother — primarily financially and emotionally.
- Cleave to one another — be joined as one till death parts them.
- Become one flesh — one in interdependence, finances, one single indivisible unit.
- Have intimacy — sexual, emotional, and spiritual as well.
- Intended to be monogamous — one husband and one wife as a single unit that demands physical and mental faithfulness and purity.

Putting all these mandates together, you will realize that God is giving you a recipe for a happy and a fruitful marriage. Follow it and you will never regret it. We would like to highlight the fact that God intended one man for one woman for their entire lifetime. It is not a matter of experimentation — whichever way you make a choice, you will have to live with it for your entire lifetime.

> You shall not commit adultery. (Exod 20:14)

This verse speaks of God's absolute standards of moral purity and that adultery is abominable to him - whether physical or mental.

GOD'S EXPECTATIONS FROM MARRIAGE

Before you can frame your own expectations in marriage, you must know

God's expectations in a marriage. They are:

Make sure that post marriage, your priorities change and your spouse takes precedence over every other relationship, except God.

Make sure that post marriage, your intimacy with your spouse will reflect largely your intimacy with God.

Make sure that you are faithful to your spouse - whether physically or mentally, regardless of any argument against it.

Make sure that you understand completely and adhere strictly to the fact, that your marriage must last all your lifetime.

Make sure that your family understands and lives by His will and purposes.

WHAT TO LOOK FOR WHILE CHOOSING A PARTNER

There are non-negotiable and negotiable aspects to look for in choosing a life partner. The non-negotiable traits are essential and cannot be compromised, whereas the negotiable traits are merely guidelines to enable us to find the ultimate leading of the Lord. First, let us understand those traits that are non-negotiable.

HE OR SHE SHOULD BE A BELIEVER

This is one trait that cannot be compromised upon. There are two passages that deal with this important characteristic, 1 Cor 6:14–18, and Neh 13:23–30. God the Holy Spirit forbids us to be unequally yoked or bound together with unbelievers. The unthinkable and unmatchable comparison given here is clear.

Believers	Unbelievers
Righteousness	Lawlessness
Light	Darkness
Christ	Belial (Satan)
Temple of God	Idols

God also mentions that if we take Him for His Word and do not intermingle with unbelievers He will welcome us, be our Father and we will be His sons and daughters. This denotes a special and preferential relationship with God.

MARRYING A BELIEVER HAS CERTAIN INBUILT ADVANTAGES AND BLESSINGS

Faith brings a common platform and makes life easier to live out. Faith becomes a compass to guide them through the maze that we call life on a day-to-day basis in our practical living. Faith sets a common path to tread and reach the common goal that God reveals to us.

We would like to add and clarify that marrying a believer alone is not enough. Make sure that the fruit of the Spirit is evident in your lives:

> But the fruit of the Spirit is love, joy, peace, forbearance, kindness, goodness, faithfulness, gentleness, self-control; against such things there is no law. (Gal 5:22–23)

These days there are too many pseudo-believers in the church, so make sure that their conversion, faith and walk with the Lord are genuine. If we fail to do this before marriage, it will lead to great dismay and perpetual regret after marriage.

MARRYING AN UNBELIEVER THROWS UP UNFORESEEN CHALLENGES

Marrying a non-believer not only goes against God's will, but also throws up many unpleasant challenges that can be insurmountable. Differences may crop up in the following thorny issues of life.

- Tithing, giving and generosity (even when the going is not good).
- Bringing up children in the physical and spiritual area.
- Discipline of children - when, how, and how much?
- Pointing children to the ultimate God-ordained goal in life.
- Protecting children from the lure of worldliness.
- Inculcating in children the love for God and for people rather than being self-centered.

MARRY SOMEONE WHO IS BALANCED, YOUR EQUAL IN EVERY WAY

The one we plan to marry should be our equal spiritually, intellectually, and financially as far as possible. While an exact match in all these areas may be impossible to find, it is worth the effort to find as close a match as possible. We in India, have grown up on a staple diet of Bollywood and other regional movies with the time tested "fall in love" formula, wherein either the hero or the heroine from a very poor background, falls in love with someone coming from a very rich background. They either bump in to each other in college, or there is the hero-saves-heroine-from-clutches-of-the-villain scenario. Then, they fall in love, are rejected by the rich parents and ultimately (through many nail biting twists and turns) get united in the end. While there can be exceptions, we are yet to see these kinds of scenarios become a happy reality in our 30 odd years of ministering to couples. Often, it happens the other way, and the couple finds out to their great and irreversible discomfort that this marriage should not have taken place at all.

CONSIDER ONE'S PERSONALITY CHARACTERISTICS BEFORE TAKING THE PLUNGE

The next attribute to look for in a potential spouse is their general demeanor and character. Abraham Lincoln once said, "Character is like a tree and reputation is like the shadow. The shadow is what we think of; the tree is the real thing."

The following are 12 character traits that can indicate the soundness of the individual while considering marriage:

- HUMILITY (John 13:1–7)
- SEXUAL PURITY (Heb 13:4)
- DEVOTION TO CHRIST (Phil 1:21)
- RIGHT PRIORITIES (Matt 6:33)
- RIGHT BELIEFS (2 Tim 1:12)
- COMMITMENT TO THE CHURCH (Heb 10:24–25)
- A LOVING ATTITUDE (1 John 4:20)
- SELF-CONTROL (Prov 16:32; 23:20–21)
- HONESTY (Prov 11:3; 28:22)
- BEAUTY BELOW THE SKIN (1 Sam 16:7)
- RESPONSIBILITY (Gen 24:22, 35, 53)
- GOOD RELATIONSHIP WITH PARENTS (Eph 6:1–3)

In addition, some other character traits that can contribute to good marriage are: stability, patience, common sense, sympathy, cheerfulness, kindness, courtesy, thoughtfulness, cleanliness, humor, good health, and respect for people.

While all these seem overwhelming, it is not our intention to ask you to look for "perfect people," this is rather a guide to help you evaluate and choose the right kind of person you are going to spend the rest of your life with. If the person is a believer and loves the Lord and has the willingness to submit to the work of the Holy Spirit, it is fully possible that God can bring about changes bit by bit, smoothening out rough edges in people and making them eventually Christ-like.

PEOPLE TO AVOID WHILE CONSIDERING YOUR FUTURE SPOUSE

There are three kinds of people you should preferably avoid or at least consider with extreme caution while choosing a life partner.

PERSONS HOLDING A CRIMINAL RECORD

We have come across young people who are idealistic in their thinking with a tremendous amount of self-confidence. These young people think that by marrying people who have a criminal record, they will be doing them a great favor and eventually reform them. While there can be rare exceptions, this practically is not the norm. We have experienced that choosing such people can result in future difficulties and can side track your life from its original purpose.

PERSONS WITH KNOWN ADDICTIONS

People with addictions need professional help for long periods and often relapse into their old habits easily. We knew a very promising young girl who married a man who was handsome, and charming, but a drug addict. She believed in her ability to turn him around. Many years after marriage, she saw the futility in trying to reform him. Eventually this young man died after an overdose, leaving behind a shattered and disillusioned wife and an orphaned son.

PERSONS WHO HAVE SCANT RESPECT FOR AUTHORITY

Vijaya had a teacher at school, a nun, who would tell her class to look for men to marry (in future), who had great respect and love for their parents, because that foreshadowed how they would take care of their wives. Many young men who have scant respect for their parents, superiors, or the law. They are basically anti-establishment and rebellious in their relationships. Such people might seem nice in the initial stages of marriage but soon they relapse into their original behavior.

10 QUESTIONS THAT CAN HELP YOU DEFINE THE RIGHT SPOUSE

- What place does God have in his or her life?
- Do you like one another?
- Do you respect one another?
- Do you respect each other's families?
- Do you share the same value systems?
- Can you be friends as well?
- Can you talk easily and for long?
- Are you intellectually on the same level?
- Do you have common interests?
- How do you feel about common areas (children, church, cash, friends)?

If your answer is mostly "yes" to the above questions, you are probably getting much closer in identifying your future spouse.

WHAT TO EXPECT AS YOU ENTER THE STATE OF MATRIMONY

Here are some things that you will encounter as soon as you get married. Having a positive outlook on these aspects is vital for a stable and happy marriage.

- A spouse who is imperfect.
- A person who is different in nature - physically and mentally too.
- Anger, and quarrels (infrequent or frequent).
- Egos and power struggles.
- Interference from in-laws.
- Laziness.
- Criticism.
- A sharp tongue.

SEEKING AND FINDING GOD'S WILL FOR MARRIAGE

The most important facet of choosing a life partner is knowing God's perfect will in this matter. This is not always as easy as we think it is. The Greek word for "will" in the Bible is *thelema*. That simply means choice, desire, and pleasure. When used about God, it designates His "purpose or plan" that has been designed for humankind. No one knows the will of God like God Himself! The one who walks with Him consistently and works hard to please Him will have no difficulty in finding His will. Broadly speaking there are two facets of God's will:

Firstly, the revealed will of God. This has already been revealed by Him and the only place you find it is in The Bible.

Secondly, the will of God, that is yet to be revealed for specific areas, times, situations and people.

We have experienced and realized in our own lives, through our personal walk with the Lord and through our preaching, teaching, and counseling that if we are immersed with doing the revealed will of God, we will not struggle with the undisclosed will of God. It is such a tragedy that people who never bother to walk with God or to listen to His voice, suddenly one day realize that they need Him and His wisdom. They begin the arduous hunt to find God's will, to insure against future failure and heartbreak, and not really to obey him or to bring glory to Him.

We would also like to caution that seeking God's will is important but what is paramount is to make sure that we do His will. Many young people seek His will and on finding it, realize that the person who God wants them to marry is not the person of their dreams, so they try to find ways and means to wriggle out of their commitment to do God's will. We solemnly warn that this is very dangerous and can result in adverse consequences that last a lifetime.

As we prepare to seek God's will for our marriages, we will have to consider five basic ingredients that go into finding out God's will:

- MUCH PRAYER
- MUCH WAITING ON GOD
- MUCH WISDOM
- MUCH PATIENCE
- MUCH COUNSEL (from His Word and His people)

We would like to elaborate on the five ingredients and divide them into ten easy steps as mentioned below.

- RIGHT PRIORITY (Matt 22:37; 6:33)
- DIGGING INTO GOD'S WORD (Ps 119:105, 130)
- PRAYER (Phil 4:6)

- COUNSEL OF GODLY PEOPLE (Prov 12:15; 15:22; 20:18)
- PROVIDENTIAL CIRCUMSTANCES (Rom 8:28; Phil 1:12)
- INNER PROMPTING OF GOD THE HOLY SPIRIT (Ps 143:10)
- COMMON SENSE (Prov 22:3)
- INNER PEACE (1 John 3:21)
- RIGHT TIMING (Eccl 3:1, 8:5)
- FAITH (Ps 37:5; Prov 3:5–6)

These indicators are like lamp-posts guiding us and making sure that our path is illuminated so that we do not stumble. But the greater challenge is not in finding God's will but to do it in its totality.

DATING

There is a lot of confusion over this issue, with many logical and reasonable objections raised by those who don't subscribe to the benefits of dating. Many Indian people think it is a Western concept which goes against our social thinking and pattern. There are some who also label it as sinful, while others find it unnecessary.

We have, after much prayer and thought, and having considered all the practical and social aspects that govern our society, formulated some dos and don'ts in dating. These are pointers in an advisory capacity, and we leave it to the esteemed readers to formulate their own ideas on dating.

Dating is desirable, but again within cultural boundaries—the objective being to know each other better and to obtain clarity to decide. It needs to be done with the permission of parents, of both the girl and the boy.

SEX BEFORE MARRIAGE

We live in a sex crazed world, and this has seeped into churches and marriages. Many young couples especially when going steady or engaged may not hesitate to experiment with sex, justifying themselves by the fact that they are eventually going to get married. This is expressly prohibited in the Bible and the two words are used in this context: fornication and adultery. Fornication is a sexual relationship between unmarried people and adultery is a sexual relationship between two people in which at least one of them is married to someone else.

Consider these five passages in the Bible for a greater understanding of this issue.

- 1 Cor 6:9–11 says that fornicators and adulterers will not inherit the kingdom of God.
- 1 Cor 6:18 instructs us to flee immorality.
- Eph 5:3–4 says that immorality (*porneia*, the root from which the word pornography comes) is not to be even named amongst us.
- 1 Thess 4:3–5 says it is God's will for us to be sanctified and abstain from sexual immorality.
- Heb 13:4 says that the marriage bed should be undefiled, and that God will judge fornicators and adulterers.

Clearly, sex is permissible only within the boundaries of marriage.

THE BLESSEDNESS OF BEING SINGLE

We would now like to deal with a very unique situation that some people face—the call to remain single for a specific purpose defined by God. In 1 Cor 7:7–9, 32–35, Paul mentions three aspects of being single. It is a gift from God and is meant for specific and undivided service. This passage clarifies that married individuals are obligated to please and serve their spouses, whereas people who remain single will focus their energies to please the Lord alone. Their service and interests will remain undivided in serving the Lord. This passage also instructs individuals who find it difficult to curb or control their sexual instincts to get married rather than burn with passion which might eventually lead them into sin.

In Matthew 19:10–12, Jesus refers to a specific category of believers who were called to be "eunuchs" for the sake of the kingdom of God. He was talking about people who had voluntarily chosen to remain single to be better able to serve the kingdom of heaven. If some of you reading this book are convicted by God to remain single, we urge you to prayerfully seek His clear and specific will for your lives to remain single and serve Him meaningfully.

In conclusion, we reiterate that there are four important areas that need to be planned before stepping in to marriage: spiritual, mental, financial, and emotional. Prospective brides and grooms should make sure that they are mature in all these four areas and financially capable of supporting a family before they take a plunge. Someone has rightly pointed out that –"marriage is not as much as finding the right person than being the right person!" To those of our readers who are contemplating marriage, we pray that God would bless you with His wisdom and that your choice will be His choice resulting in a great blessing to you and a great impact to His kingdom.

FOUR: KNOWING YOUR DIFFERENCES

"In politics, if you want anything said, ask a man: if you want anything done, ask a woman." Margaret Thatcher

"And verily, a woman needs to know but one man well to understand all men; whereas a man may know all women and understand not one of them." Helen Rowland

This chapter is not supposed to be medically and psychologically precise, although we have tried to be as accurate as we could within our framework of knowledge and experience. This is just to highlight how different we are, but how we do not have to feel threatened by our differences, but rather bring them together as strengths for the benefit of our families and the kingdom of God.

Wives, do you often wonder why, after a hard day at work, your husband prefers to unwind with TV, a book, or a jog, instead of telling you all about his day? Or why no interruptions are entertained while he reads his newspaper, unless the matter is earth-shatteringly urgent? Or why he cannot relate an incident with all its itsy bitsy juicy details that you have been waiting to hear?

Husbands, are you annoyed when your wife is asking you to turn right, she is actually pointing to the left? Does it puzzle you that her handbag may be a jumbled mess, yet she knows exactly where to find things? Does it frustrate you when a seemingly casual remark makes her all upset and touchy? Welcome to the club! These questions have disturbed and frustrated many distraught spouses. However, despite our dissimilarities, God intends us to work out our differences, to complement one another and to live in harmony.

On a lighter note, Professor Henry Higgins in the musical, "My Fair Lady" exclaims, "Why can't a woman behave like a man?" If you have seen the musical, you cannot forget this outburst of Prof. Higgins when he finds that Eliza Doolittle, the flower seller that he has groomed to perfection to be able to pass off as royalty, has disappeared from the house. He is bewildered, angry, and somewhere deep down in love with her (which he never acknowledges). While this line is funny, it describes the frustration when the two genders try to fully understand each other. Of course, a woman is not created to behave like a man neither is a man expected to behave like a woman.

Understanding the differences between the sexes is one of the most difficult and perplexing topics. A lot of marital problems would not happen in the first place, or could be handled with great ease, if both men and women understood that they are made differently to take different roles. Nevertheless, we would like to briefly dwell on this topic and see if we might help create a greater understanding and acceptance by husbands and wives, that they are able to live together amicably and accomplish God's purposes in their lives.

God never intended to duplicate Adam. Genesis 1:26 tells us that God made man in His image. Many people think that only man was made in the image of God—which is untrue. Strong's Hebrew concordance (H120) defines the word used for "man" to mean the humankind as a species. So the Bible says, God created humankind, that is men and women in the image of the Triune God. When God created the man, He gave some of His masculine attributes to him and when He made the woman, He gave some of His feminine attributes to her. You may have noticed this to be true to some extent. That is why Genesis 1:26 points out, "male and female, he created them." And God expects us to maintain this dissimilarity.

In fact, God is so specific about maintaining this dissimilarity that even their garments were to be kept different (Deut 22:5). This is intended to make both the genders understand that this distinctiveness is to be maintained and respected.

Matthew Henry, in his commentary on the Bible puts it so well, "That the woman was made of a rib out of the side of Adam; not made out of his head to rule over him, nor made out of his feet to be trampled upon by him, but out of his side to be equal with him, under his arm to be protected, and near his heart to be beloved."[vi]

Irwin recalls that no sooner had we married, that he could not understand why I was so different from him. He admits he spent the first few years of our marriage trying to make me like him. He completely failed, of course, until God reminded him that I was not supposed to be a carbon copy, but a unique original, with a totally different design. Since then, much water has flowed under the bridge and we have little by little, understood how different we (and all men and women) are! We understand that God endows both with some of His attributes, specific to each sex. When they come together in a bond of love, these complementing attributes serve to reflect the glory of the Triune God.

There are four areas in which we need to understand the differences between men and women.

THE PHYSICAL AREA

Men, on average, are taller and heavier than women, and tend to have a higher muscle mass, giving them an edge over women in physical activity. The male hormone testosterone has been linked not just to man's sex drive, but also to his need for independence, dominance, and at times the need to express that he is the "alpha male." This results in his frequently showing more competitive and aggressive behaviors compared to women.

Women generally achieve puberty earlier than men, and as such become more conscious not only of their bodies, but of the gender differences that exist between them. Estrogen, the female hormone, regulates a woman's menstrual cycle resulting in hormonal, physical and emotional changes during each cycle, including diminished sexual desire. God as our creator knew a woman's vulnerability during this time, and hence in His wisdom, gave the husband a command to leave his wife alone during this period (Lev 18:19). Pregnancy is another period when a woman's body goes through a host of changes, when the body is making unusual amounts of hormones such as progesterone. While each trimester has its own challenges, let it suffice to say that common threads running throughout pregnancy include physical discomfort, exhaustion, and moodiness which can be overwhelming. It would help the woman a great deal if her husband could lend a listening ear, a shoulder to lean on, and take over some of the domestic responsibilities. Women undergo physical and psychological changes during menopause too. Hormonal fluctuations may lead to uncomfortable physical symptoms, mood swings, and diminished sexual desire. It can be a challenging period for the woman, and she needs an understanding partner by her side who can provide the necessary emotional support.

Sexually, men and women operate very differently. Men are more sight-oriented and may be easily aroused simply by looking at their wives. Men tend to associate sex with physical pleasure and release. Women however, are more romantic and emotionally oriented. They need to feel loved. For them, sex is all about emotional bonding and the need to feel that they are special to their man. This does not mean that men do not have the capacity to be passionate or emotional, and there are always exceptions to the norm. By and large, these different responses to sex tend to give rise to misunderstandings. For instance, a man may be ready for sex at the end of a long and tiring day, and may perceive his wife as being unresponsive, as she naturally takes a longer time to feel physically and emotionally ready. Being aware of these differences and being able to adjust and go with the flow can immensely contribute to intimacy between a husband and wife.

THE PSYCHOLOGICAL AREA

Men are said to be relatively more logical and analytical. One plus one equals two, no matter what! They are also said, generally, to have better mathematical and spatial skills. Men can think in a highly specialized manner where they use specific parts of their brains to accomplish a specific task, while giving undivided attention to it. Women on the other hand, are capable of thinking in a more diffused manner, using both hemispheres of their brain at once, and are thus better equipped to divide their attention between multiple tasks. While there is no difference in intelligence between the two genders, women tend to have a better capacity to relate different concepts together, and to relate previous experiences with their current learning. Owing to the "joined-up" way in which they think, women interpret ideas and experiences differently from men. We often find that men think in a "compartmentalized" manner, where they separate their experiences and emotions into boxes.

Research shows that women generally have better verbal abilities, which is why they articulate more easily and in much greater detail, which often exasperates men, who, not being naturally good listeners, prefer communication to be to-the-point. On a lighter note, Western data suggests that men speak an average of 15,000 words a day, while women average 24,000 words!

THE SOCIAL/EMOTIONAL AREA

Men generally like to keep their feelings to themselves; while women love to share their feelings with their husbands and their closest friends (they usually feel neglected if denied quality time and a sympathetic ear). Often, men feel that it is "unmanly" to cry, probably due to their upbringing or cultural taboos. In our experience, we have found that women are emotionally more resilient and can cope much better with difficult situations. The woman is the glue (under God) that keeps the home together, especially in times of crises. No wonder they are called home-makers!

Women tend to feel deeply, cry easily, but are also quick to seek remedy. They are security-oriented, and believe in deep relational bonds and family ties. As mentioned earlier, women de-stress through communication and discussion. Their emotional communication may often be subtle–too subtle for a man, who prefers things in black and white. A woman expects her husband to understand her without having to say a word. For men, this is one of the greatest mysteries of life, as their wives expect them to look beyond their words to read their thoughts and emotions. Men tend to de-stress through solitary activities. They prefer to jog, or disappear into their "man-cave" to watch television or play video games. Many women do not understand this behaviour, and badger their husbands to share their problems, and end up getting a curt answer that hurts. When they are under stress, men need to be left alone.

Women are more gifted with what we call "intuition." They can read into human nature better than men, and are also better able to gauge social and emotional dynamics in various situations more accurately.

THE SPIRITUAL AREA

A new analysis of survey data finds that women pray more often than men, are more likely to believe in God and are more religious than men in a variety of other ways. Even at the time of Jesus, we find more women following Jesus, whether at the cross or the sepulcher. These days, on any given Sunday, or during special spiritual programs, we find that women outnumber men.

In our own assessment through our counselling experience of over 25 years, we find that women have deeper faith in God, pray more, read the Bible more often, uphold the family in prayer and backing up their husband's efforts through prayer. The level of integrity is higher in women, and so are their moral standards. Be it praying or teaching the faith at home to the children, or even having daily quiet time, it is the woman who comes out a winner.

In many homes, contrary to Scriptural teaching, it is the wives who take an initiative to have family devotions and have to bully their husbands to participate. Again, by and large, as they walk their talk, they are better than their male counterparts. Please remember that this is our personal assessment and there are always exceptions on both sides.

Each gender has its their own gifts from God and is designed to be independent in some ways and interdependent in others, to supplement and complement each other for the glory of God. Remember, we are on the same side—what is good for one is good for the other, and what is bad for one is bad for the other. What one lacks, the other supplies; where one is weak, the other stands strong; where one is confused, the other's wisdom clarifies. It is only when we begin to look for weaknesses and faults and feel threatened by the gifts of our spouse that we come outside God's purposes and begin to wreck our marriages and families.

FIVE: KNOWING YOUR ROLES

Marriage is not a fairy tale, where Prince Charming comes on a white horse and rescues the princess from an ogre (parents?!) who has imprisoned her in a tall tower. As we start to live together after marriage, the real task of building the home begins—problems begin to erupt, and the real ogres emerge within us! This is what differentiates a great marriage from a mundane one. How one tackles these differences and takes on the challenge of building on them determines the outcome: marvelous or mundane!

Marriage is akin to driving an automobile. The two front wheels determine the direction of the car as seen in the picture below.

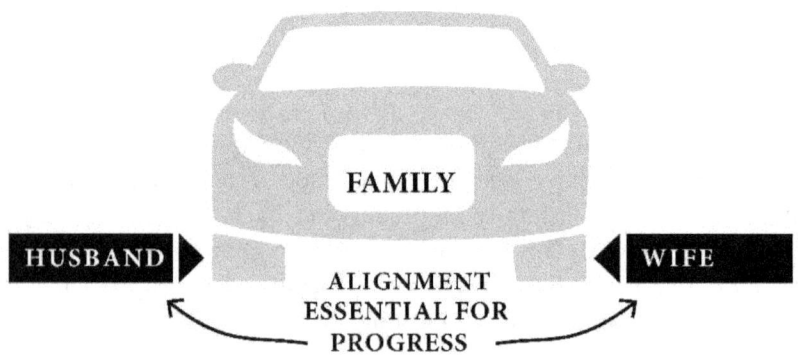

FAMILY ALIGNMENT IS ESSENTIAL FOR PROGRESS

When the front wheels of our car were out of alignment, they caused the tyres to wear out faster. The car was wobbling to such an extent that an accident was just waiting to happen. The husband and wife are the two front wheels in a marriage whose alignment determines the health and the direction of the family.

The Holy Scripture gives us a detailed insight on the roles of husband and wife, and playing the roles as per God's design makes the marriage healthy and fruitful. When we begin to operate outside this blue print, we invite trouble.

Often couples seeking counsel come with the following complaints:

- My spouse does not respect me.
- My spouse is unresponsive sexually.

- My spouse comes between me and the children when I discipline them.
- My children think I am harsh; I feel they are influenced by my spouse.
- I do not have the freedom to spend as I like.
- My spouse thinks that I am wasting time and money.
- My spouse thinks that I am more involved in my work than in my family.
- My spouse does not want me to keep my earlier friendships, especially with those of the opposite sex.
- My spouse does not give me the freedom to watch the television whenever I like.
- My spouse expects me do domestic chores and if I do not, nags me.
- My spouse does not allow me to spend time with my parents.
- My spouse does not respect my parents.
- My spouse does not initiate family devotions.
- My spouse is too engrossed in the lives of our children to pay attention to me.

Does any of this sound familiar? Welcome to the club of dissatisfied spouses! Before we begin to address these issues, let us look at what God says to both the spouses, the husband first and then to the wife.

As seen in the diagram below, God, as the originator and keeper of the family MUST be an integral part of every family. Without Him, we are wasting our time and effort. What God creates remains, the rest is only transitory. That is why Psalm 127:1 says, "Unless the Lord builds the house, they labour in vain who build it." Ecclesiastes 4:12 "A cord of three strands is not quickly torn apart." For a marriage to work effectively and consistently, it is essential for the marriage to consist not only of two individuals, but of God as the first party and the most important component. He should have prominence over every area of the family.

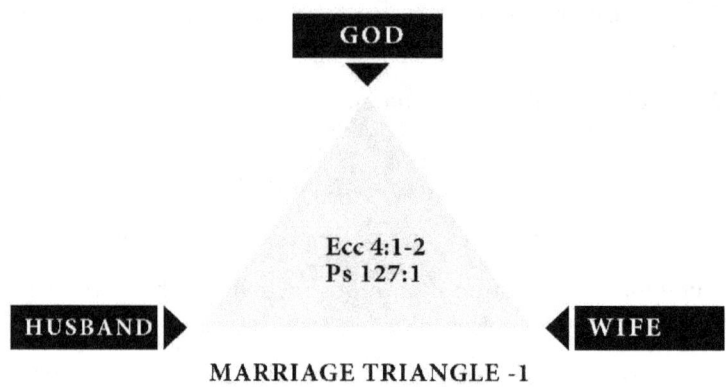

Further, the marriage triangle in the picture below demonstrates the importance of seeking the Lord together, as a couple.

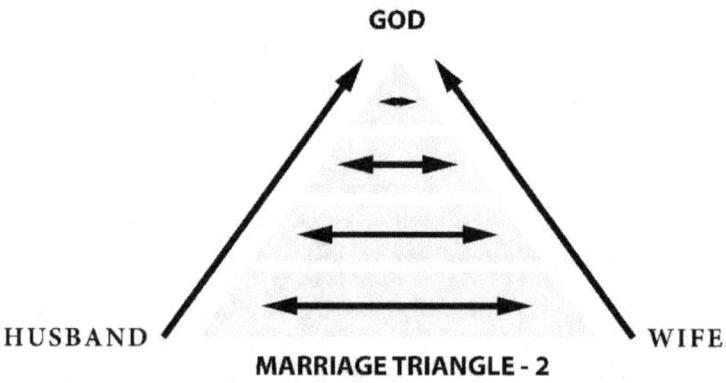

As both the husband and the wife seek the Lord together, they not only come closer to the Lord but to each other as well. Hebrews 3:4 says that God is the builder of everything. Any sane person will tell us that trying to build by deviating from the design of the architect would be dangerous. The designer needs to be involved at every level. It is a sad truth that many couples and families are trying to make their marriages work outside of the guidance of God's wisdom. While there are many insightful books available on marriage and family, none can surpass the Bible. It is God-inspired wisdom—there is no problem for which the Bible does not have a solution.

THE ROLE OF A HUSBAND

Ephesians 5 is a profound passage that deals with the roles of both husband and wife. So let us first examine the role of the husband in Ephesians 5:22–23.

> Wives, submit yourselves to your own husbands as you do to the Lord. For the husband is the head of the wife as Christ is the head of the church.

There are two things that the Lord is telling all the wives: 1) be subject to your husbands *(because)* 2) he is the head of the family. Yet whilst wives are exhorted to submit themselves to their husband's authority, at the same time Ephesians 5:21 exhorts the whole body of Christ to submit to one another. To understand this in the proper perspective, would mean that as the wife needs to submit to her husband, the husband also needs to submit himself to his wife; for they are both accountable to God.

FAMILY LEADERSHIP

"Servant leadership" is sadly missing in our times, as the "boss" style of leadership dominates contemporary thinking. Sadly, this concept has affected the thinking of many Christian husbands. This is a long way from the leadership example set by the Lord Jesus Christ in Mark 10:42–45:

> Jesus called them together and said, "You know that those who are regarded as rulers of the Gentiles lord it over them, and their high officials exercise authority over them. Not so with you. Instead, whoever wants to become great among you must be your servant, 44 and whoever wants to be first must be slave of all. For even the Son of Man did not come to be served, but to serve, and to give his life as a ransom for many."

Jesus said this immediately after James and John asked for special status compared to other disciples. Here, Jesus points to Himself as the epitome of servant leadership. Paul brings in this servant leadership model set by Jesus into the Christian home in Ephesians 5:25:

> Husbands, love your wives, just as Christ loved the church and gave himself up for her.

God expects husbands to be the representatives of Jesus Christ in their own homes. The tragedy is that many husbands behave like the devil at home and demand the respect due to Christ! We keep telling these men, "Behave like Christ Jesus at home and you will get the respect that Jesus would get from your family."

Jesus came to serve even to the extent of laying down His life for us. He exemplified this in John 13:4–20, when He washed the feet of His disciples, exhorting them do likewise (v. 14, 15). If this servant leadership needs to be practiced in the church, how much more in the home!

Husbands, would you be willing to serve your wives even as Christ served the church, His bride, to the extent that you would be willing to wash her feet? That would be Christ-like indeed! If you are not ready to wash the feet of your wife, you are not qualified to be her leader! You can wash her feet without loving her, but you cannot love her without washing her feet. However, washing our wives' feet is insignificant compared to what God says to husbands through Paul in Ephesians 5:25 (above).

Love is a generic term and it needs to be quantified and qualified. If we say that we do love our wives, it may be true to some extent. But God wants husbands to know that loving their wives cannot measure up, unless their love can be compared to the love that Christ had for the church – His bride! The depth of the love of the Lord Jesus was so deep and intense that He gave Himself, died for the church. Husbands, are you listening? God says, washing the feet of your wife may be a good idea, but the ultimate measurement of your love is when you are willing to give yourself up, yes, even die for her. This points to the sacrificial love which husbands need to cultivate for their wives.

Vijaya was suffering from renal failure that eventually required dialysis until a donor could be found for a kidney transplant. Irwin offered his kidney. This was turned down by the doctors, as Irwin's hypertension disqualified him from being a potential donor. When Vijaya's health began to fail, and transplant possibilities began to grow dim, Irwin pleaded daily with the Lord to add some more years to her life, *even at the cost of adding his remaining years to her life.* This is what being willing to "die" for your wife means. God is sovereign and did not answer this prayer. But Vijaya, the children and many others, were greatly inspired by Irwin's love for his wife, and his selfless and sacrificial attitude. Many people told us later, that this encouraged them to look at their own wives anew and renew their love and commitment to them, aiming to be Christ-like in their own families.

While a willingness to die for your wife is commendable, verse 26 goes on to say that Jesus died, "to make her holy." Sanctification is the process through which God the Holy Spirit makes believers holy, separated to God for His purposes (Rom 15:15–16; 2 Thess 2:13; 1 Pet 1:1–2). Husbands, God wants you to make sure that you labour and strive to have your wives sanctified by the work of the Holy Spirit, so that they can assist and willingly share with you in the ministry of building the body of Christ, starting with your families first. This is a priority to be addressed at any cost!

Sanctification is a process, and verse 26 mentions the steps that will be necessary in this process. "Cleansing her by the washing with water through the word." Husbands, ensure that your wives are nourished by the Word of God. This means, initiating a Bible study with your spouse, in addition to the regular family devotions; encourage her in her own spiritual walk, so she can grow into Christ likeness.

In verse 27 we read "to present her to himself as a radiant church, without stain or wrinkle or any other blemish, but holy and blameless." God wants the church to be glorious for Him. Desiring that the wife should be glorious and beautiful on the inside more than the outside is godly, and every husband should develop this attitude that his wife must be at her best – as God would want her to be. The godly leadership of the husband should enable the wife to maintain a holy and blameless life. Husbands should strive to become the epitome of all the qualities found in the Lord Jesus, to charm their wives into desiring Christ-likeness. Many husbands are so obsessed with the outer beauty of their wives that they never pause to appraise their inner beauty. They are more concerned about the wrinkles on the wives' faces than the wrinkles on their souls! But as vv. 28–29 make clear, husbands should nourish and cherish their wives, loving them as much as they love themselves.

Sadly, we have often observed a lack of reciprocity in the care husbands give their wives. For instance, when the husband comes home tired from work and with a splitting headache, everybody, the wife included, is expected to pamper him, serve him hot tea, massage his back, press his head and take care that he is not disturbed till the headache disappears. On the other hand, if he comes home to find that his wife is suffering from a severe headache, he is often unsympathetic and expects his wife to take an aspirin and lie down, till she gets better enough to cook the food and have the children complete the homework. The wife would be fortunate if the husband spares her from love-making that night!

Or perhaps in the morning, as the wife tries to get the children ready for school, struggling against the clock to prepare breakfast, wash dishes, dress the youngest, find dinner-money, and make sure they are at the bus stop before the school bus honks. Mum, with alarming regularity, wishes that she had eight pairs of hands and additional legs, not to forget more eyes. Dad in the meantime is sat reading the paper or checking his emails on his phone, throwing his wife some well-designed hints about making him a cup of coffee. She brings it to him, although her secret desire is to pour this scalding liquid on his head.

When the children are finally seen off, the wife is drenched with sweat, already tired and needs to relax on the sofa, on which her husband is sitting. Now, the husband gets into a romantic mood and puts his arm around his wife and says, "I love you" as a prelude to something more serious.

What happens next is not surprising as the husband gets what we call the "elbow treatment," a sharp jab in the side with the elbow. Invariably, the husband complains that his wife is unresponsive and rude, to the extent of hurting him physically, even after he specifically expressed his love for her! This illustration is purely hypothetical, and we sincerely hope no husbands reading this can recognize themselves here! But maybe you get the point!

It is our opinion that good sex begins in the morning. Now, we do not mean to say that the act itself must be indulged in, in the morning itself, but remind couples that husbands are "sight-oriented" whereas their wives are "emotion-oriented." The husband needs to demonstrate that he loves his wife by "doing things for her" and making her feel that she is very important to him, and display this in everyday living in practical terms. Vijaya always said that Irwin treated her like a queen, and you would see the stars twinkling in her eyes as she said this.

If the husband is responsive to his wife's travails in the morning, and takes charge of the children allowing her to finish cooking and other tasks, he would be proving to her that she is special and important to him. Remember, husbands and wives are partners in the grand adventure called life. If the husband fails to understand this, it results in the wife feeling that she is being "used" by her husband.

There is the story of a man who goes to a doctor complaining that his wife could not hear properly. The doctor asks the husband to conduct an experiment to find out the extent of hearing loss. As advised by the doctor, the man goes home in the evening and shouts right from the front gate, "Darling, what are you cooking for dinner tonight?" There is no response. He gets into the house and repeats the question in the living room. Ultimately, having heard no response, he finds her in the kitchen, cooking with her back towards him. He quietly slinks behind her, and shouts, "Darling, what are you cooking for dinner tonight?" The wife responds, "for heaven's sake, stop shouting! For the fifth time, I am making stew!"

Well, that is the story of most of us. We think we are fine, and it is the other person that needs to change! Someone wise said, "God change the world, but please begin with me!" Vijaya always says that God is in the department of change. Proverbs 16:7 says, "When a man's ways are pleasing to the Lord, He makes even his enemies to be at peace with him." As we concentrate on pleasing the Lord, He knows the desires of our hearts and begins to work on others as well, especially our spouses. Husbands, we trust the Lord has spoken to you. Are you ready for a change in your own attitudes without any strings attached? If you are, would you please take a moment to pray this prayer?

"Lord, thank you for my wife. I understand that she is the most precious and valuable gift given to me by you, after yourself! I understand that I have not been the leader you intended me to be and I wanted my wife to conform to my pattern. I promise you that I will sacrificially and selflessly love her even as you loved your bride, the church, and I will lead her spiritually and nourish and cherish her even to the last drop of my blood, without expecting anything in return. In the name of Jesus, Amen."

THE ROLE OF A WIFE

Many women are never able to fully grasp the privileged status that the Lord has granted them. Frequently husbands reinforce in the minds of their wives that they exist only to cater to their needs, be their child-bearers and domestic help. For some husbands, no matter how sacrificial she is, the wife is always found lacking and can never do enough. No matter how long-suffering she is, she has done nothing unusual or out of her way. Other women are confused about their responsibilities, which are generally defined for them by their husbands or children, not the Holy Scriptures.

But what is a woman's true status in her role as wife and mother?

HER STATUS

> And God created mankind in his own image, in the image of God he created them; male and female he created them. (Gen 1:27)

God made both men and women in His own image. If both are made in the image of God, the woman cannot be inferior to man. If the man and the woman are *both* made in the image of God, they both *have to be equal* in value as individuals. They only differ in their roles. Some husbands treat their wives as sub-standard citizens or lesser mortals, but this is in direct contradiction to God's creation purposes, in which both the husband and the wife are equal partners, in His mandate to:

> Be fruitful and increase in number; fill the earth and subdue it. Rule over the fish in the sea and the birds in the sky and over every living creature that moves on the ground. (Gen 1:28)

When God created man, He gave the man some of His dominant male attributes and when God created the woman, He gave her some of His dominant female attributes, and it is when they come into a bond of marriage and exercise their attributes and gifts, that they reflect the fullness of God.

Matthew Henry in his commentary of Genesis 2 states so beautifully, "That the woman was made of a rib out of the side of Adam; not made from his head to rule over him, nor out of his feet to be trampled upon by him, but out of his side to be equal with him, under his arm to be protected, and near his heart to be loved." Equal in status, but vastly differing in nature!

After marriage, Irwin often wondered why Vijaya was not like him, not knowing the fact that Vijaya *was not supposed to be like him*. Subsequently, God taught him the basic fact that God made his wife to supplement and complement him (and vice-versa). The figure of a clasped hand depicts the fact that when we clasp both our hands and intertwine our fingers we cover with our strengths, the weaknesses of our spouses.

A woman is perfectly designed to complete the personality of her man. In every man's heart there is a woman sized vacuum that can only be filled by his wife. In our bedroom, we had a dressing table with a sticker on its mirror reading, "No life without wife!" While this was funny, the underlying message is very valuable. Husbands, have you ever wondered how you can ever get along without your wife? Right from the early hours of the morning, to the time we fall asleep, we depend on our wives, who keep track of our needs and comforts, search for the stuff we've lost, care for the children, and give us sound wisdom. All this is done silently, selflessly and without grumbling. Praise God for such wives and mothers!

Wives are not only designed to be the helpers of their men at home, but also in the ministry. God has blessed our wives with many gifts and husbands would do well to notice, understand and capitalize on these gifts in attaining God's purposes for their families. Remember, God gave woman to her man, so that His work could be done efficiently and to perfection *by them together*. The Hebrew word for "helper" is "*awzar*," which means "to surround." So, if we apply this to the role of a wife, this would mean that the wife surrounds her husband. Now, if the wife surrounds her husband at all times, it implies that she is an integral part of all he does.

So many husbands compartmentalize their lives, even to the exclusion of their wives. Men, if you allow your wives to become an integral part of all that you do, you will be surprised at the wisdom of your wives. Sometimes they are wiser than you. Sharing your challenges with them enlists their support, wisdom, and prayers—and this becomes a very powerful platform to stand on in the battles of everyday life. God in His wisdom intends husbands and wives to be "allies" to assist, comfort, support and empathize with each other. Men, wives can partner with us, pray for us, and fight the battle with us!

Genesis 2:23 tells us that Adam, when he awoke from his sleep and looked at his gorgeous wife Eve, exclaimed "this is now bone of my bones and the flesh of my flesh, she shall be called 'woman,' because she was taken out of man." Adam instinctively knew that this creation of God was a part of his own body and life, and he proudly calls her "his woman." This statement is extremely significant in revealing God's mind, that the husband and wife are an integral part of a single entity, and while there is uniqueness in their individuality, there is greater uniqueness in their union, as it is a pointer to the Lord Jesus Christ and His bride, the church. This union is God-originated and ordained. It is permanent on earth and must be treated as a holy union, sanctified, blessed and sustained by God, for accomplishing His purposes on earth. Any effort to break this union shatters God's ordained law, and result in untold suffering, bringing dishonor to God. It is so sad to see couples operating only on individual levels and never together, thereby never experiencing the complete fullness that is theirs in Christ.

Genesis 3:16 declares God's judgment on Eve for disobeying Him, in which God clearly lays down the law that her husband will exercise authority over her. While the word originally used was "rule," God in no way wanted man to think that he could now be the boss of his wife. The word "rule" means "exercising authority," for it is logical to have a "head" of the family, lest "too many cooks spoil the broth." So, the wife should be under the authority of her husband and accountable to him, who would have the final say in the governance of the home.

HER ACHIEVEMENTS: THE VIRTUOUS WIFE (PROVERBS 31:10–31)

While our wives and mothers are highly accomplished in their own way, their achievements need to be measured against those of the *virtuous wife* mentioned in Proverbs 31:10–31. Wives, you would do well to study this passage for personal application.

The first thing about this virtuous wife is that her husband trusts her (v. 11). Trust is one of the major building blocks in marriage. It is a commodity that is getting rarer. Many husbands and wives try to keep tabs on their spouses, as there is lack of trust between them. Transparency alone can largely contribute to the building of trust between the couple. In our own marriage never once did Vijaya doubt or suspect Irwin, or keep any secrets from him. Our marriage was strengthened and deepened by our implicit trust in each other.

The virtuous wife never works any evil against her husband as long as she lives (v. 12). A couple once approached us with some major issues, and despite counselling, were unwilling to accept either their own faults or the need to work on their relationship. After a heated argument, the wife suddenly blurted out, "wait till you fall sick then I will show you your place." It was obvious that this wife was wishing to mistreat her husband when he was sick so she could prove her point. While there are always areas of frustration in any marriage, a virtuous wife would never think of this way of gaining an upper hand. Instead, verse 12 goes on to say that she will do him good all her life. She will be responsive to her husband's needs and do her best to meet them. Seven basic needs can be briefly stated: 1) Love, 2) Prayer, 3) Sex (1 Cor 7:3–5), 4) Admiration, 5) Domestic support, 6) Companionship, 7) Godly advice.

Verses 13 and 14 tell us that the virtuous wife is industrious, but more than that, she "works with eager hands." We have counselled several husbands who complained that while their wives worked very hard, they were always grumpy and perennially complained. We appreciate all the hard work women put in to bring up their families, but Christians must remember to work as unto the Lord without complaining. He who sees what you do in secret will reward you openly.

Verse 15 says that the virtuous wife is concerned about the needs of her whole household, including (in those days) the maids that were serving her family. She is an early riser, and begins to plan her day, using it to bless others.

Verse 16 & 24 highlight her financial acumen, as the wife plans the use of the family's resources. The woman who can work from home, or has an employer who sympathetically lets her fit work in around child care, then this is a great bonus, as she can add to the family income without compromising the time spent with her children.

Vijaya recollects the time when the Lord challenged her to quit her job at the bank. Firstly, to be available completely to the Lord for His work, but also because she wanted to spend much more time with both of our children who were getting ready to leave home for further studies. She recalls that after she quit her job, the time she spent with both of our children was some of the happiest times of their—and her—lives.

While we understand the need for mothers to work to ease the family's financial burden, do not do so at the cost of your children. If you do consider quitting your job, trust the Lord to provide all your needs. Quality time with your children is one of the greatest investments you could make in their lives. Irwin recalls the time when he was in school and his mother was a non-working wife/mother. His excitement would mount towards the last period at school, in anticipation of going home and sitting with his mother, who would have not just a hot cup of tea with something to munch alongside, but more than a listening ear, a caring heart and a fund of available time to listen to all his silly prattle and respond to all his doubts and fears too. A mother being home is like a shot in the arm for children, who grow up happy content and confident.

Verse 17 tells us how this virtuous wife understands that she is God's homemaker, which entails myriad demands of thinking, planning, and executing. This can be very physically depleting, so she girds herself with strength for all these activities. We often notice wives and mothers getting so busy and involved with homemaking, child rearing, husband-caring, that they begin to neglect their own health. As years roll by, this neglect begins to take a toll on their health. Some get into serious health problems, and this takes up most of their energy and the family resources to fight and overcome these issues. Wives and mothers, while it is important to take care of your families, it is also equally important to take care of your own health too.

This virtuous wife has a big heart and is generous in helping the poor and needy (v. 17). Generosity plays an important role in sharing God's love with hurting individuals and families. Children must be taught the value of generosity; we are accountable to God for all the resources He gives us.

The excellent and virtuous wife is a visionary. Verse 21 says that she is not scared of adversity as she has already planned and prepared for it. As the saying goes, "the fury of the storm displays the strength of the anchor."

Thus, times of deep distress or acute adversity bring out the real strength of the family, demonstrating their faith in a prayer-answering God. Again, we see that while the husband might be the leader, it is the wife who girds the family with strength and wisdom to tide over times of adversity. Verse 30 makes it very clear that this woman's strength and wisdom emanates from her fear of the Lord.

The virtuous woman also takes care of her appearance (v. 22). Vijaya observes that some women, soon after they become mothers, settle into the routine, and begin to neglect their appearance. For instance, in the mornings, busy as they are, they fail to notice that they are wearing a faded nightie, with uncombed hair and unkempt appearance. However, this does not escape the eye of the husband, who on reaching the office interacts with his lady colleagues who are dressed smartly and look good. Somewhere along the line he makes a comparison and begins to appreciate his colleagues more than his wife. Sometimes this can be a potential recipe for disaster. Wives, please understand that we are not suggesting that you look every inch like a film star right from the start of the day, but we suggest that you take good care of your appearance and look presentable, to preclude unfair comparisons in the mind of your husband.

Verse 23 states that a virtuous and godly wife becomes the cause for her husband to be well-known in society. Often, husbands prefer this to be the other way around. Sometimes we need to get used to the fact that God uses the gifts He has given our wives to bring Himself glory and bless us in the process.

An excellent wife is a great planner too (verses 24 and 25). Keeping the needs of the family in mind, she plans and makes things that can be profitably sold and used for the welfare of the family. Not only the husbands, but the wives as well are expected to be visionaries planning well in advance for the future, of course depending and trusting in the Lord for all their needs. That is one of the reasons for her to smile at the future and not be filled with apprehension.

Verse 26 tells us that this virtuous woman is wise, "she opens her mouth in wisdom," and she can impart wisdom and kindness through her teaching. Her children grow up to clinging to her sound, godly wisdom. This is very different from some of the wives that we have counselled who appear to be largely critical, loud and brash, and seldom speak in a way which edifies. Wives/mothers, on being heard, do your husband and children find your speech graceful, pleasant, and edifying? Remember, God expects us to use our speech to bless and not destroy (compare Proverbs 10:31, 32, 12:18).

A virtuous woman is not one "to eat the bread of idleness" (verse 27). The virtuous wife is never lazy; she is always busy doing something that will benefit the household. Wives/mothers, can you honestly answer the following questions?

> How do you use the time on your hands?
>
> How much time each day do you spend watching TV?
>
> How much time do you spend sleeping during the day?
>
> How much time do you spend on the telephone/mobile/internet/Facebook every day?
>
> How much meaningful time do you spend with your children/husband?
>
> Do you have a quiet time with the Lord each day and make sure that your family does too?

You will not be remembered by the dishes you cooked, no matter how delicious and wholesome, but by the legacy you leave behind, in terms of spiritual input, development of godly character in your children, and love for the Lord and His people. It is no wonder that the children of such a woman bless her, and her husband praises her (verse 28). This is the kind of praise that is spontaneous and is a great encouragement for this excellent wife.

Verse 29 proves the all-important truth that someone somewhere is always watching us. As we do that which is expected of us, we will be appreciated for our hard work. This appreciation sometimes might not come from husbands/children, but God who always watches will approve, and reward you.

All her good work, labour, wisdom, vision and attitudes come from one single fact—this is a woman who fears the Lord (verse 30). It therefore is understood that she does what she does primarily to please God and not her husband or children. Ladies, there are no shortcuts to spiritual life and the more you fear, love, follow, and serve God the more you will be known by the world, as there cannot be any better witness to your character than the work of your own hands (verse 31).

HER RESPONSIBILITY

We will need to look closer at Ephesians 5:22–24 to understand the responsibilities of the wife. Ephesians 5 clearly defines the roles of both wives and husbands. While the husband is to love his wife as Christ loved the church, the role of the wife is to submit to the authority of her husband, as to the Lord (verse 22). This submission is not out of fear or helplessness, but firstly out of love for the Lord and secondly out of obedience to His Word.

It should be clearly understood that the instructions to both husbands and wives found in the passage starting from verse 22 to verse 33 are UNCONDITIONAL. Nowhere does the Lord say, "wives, if your husbands are loving and kind, do this" or "husbands, if you're wives are submissive, do this." So, whether the husbands are loving or not, kind, caring, thoughtful, generous or not, wives are duty bound to be submissive to their husbands as unto the Lord.

This does not mean that the Lord assigns husbands a supreme authority which cannot be challenged or questioned, or that the wife has a subservient role to play. This is far from the truth. In many cultures, this is interpreted to mean that the wife has no say at home, and whatever the husband commands must be carried out. We have come across thorny practical issues, where unbelieving husbands demand illogical and unscriptural obedience from their wives, sometimes even to the extent of committing sin. Colossians 3:18 reads, "Wives, be subject to your husbands, as is fitting in the Lord." The original word that is used for "fitting" is *"anékó"* (suitable/proper). Thus this command can be understood to mean that wives are to be submissive to their husbands in a way that is suitable and proper in the Lord, subject to Scriptural boundaries. The following guidelines can be very helpful in understanding this command.

Wives, you should find yourself able to joyfully submit to your husband provided:

> He does not induce you to sin.
>
> His dealing is not in conflict with the Scriptures.
>
> His dealing is not in conflict with your faith in God.

HER ATTITUDE

1 Peter 3:1–6 sums up the attitude and behavior of the godly wife. She is: winning (v. 1); chaste and respectful (v. 2); not focused on outer beauty (v. 3); but rather focused on the development of inner beauty which is a gentle and a quiet spirit which God loves (v. 4); she is holy and hoping in God (v. 5); submissive and obedient to her husband (within scriptural boundaries); she does what is right without any fear (v. 6).

The ultimate result of all this is twofold: husbands are won over by observing their wife's behavior, without any spoken word (meaning – growing in favor with man); charm can cheat and beauty can beguile, but a wife who fears the Lord will receive praise from the Lord (meaning – growing in favor with God).

Wives, just remember these pointers, and you will go a long way in ensuring your perfect alignment with your husband, while allowing God to accomplish His purposes for you and your family.

SIX: COMMUNICATION IN MARRIAGE

"The single biggest problem in communication is the illusion that it has taken place." George Bernard Shaw

"The most important thing in communication is hearing what isn't being said. The art of reading between the lines is a lifelong quest of the wise." Shannon L. Alder

A combination of many ingredients goes into the making of a delicious dish. Likewise, it takes many ingredients to experience a great marriage. One such essential ingredient is effective communication. In any marriage, to achieve the "peak," the couple must pass through three crucial stages as shown in the diagram:

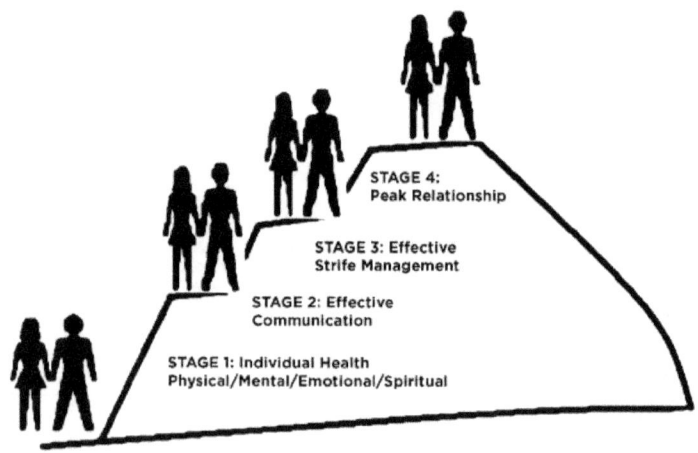

Stage 1 is the phase of the individual's physical, mental, emotional, and spiritual health. If any of these individual areas is affected adversely, it needs to be dealt with. Until remedial measures are initiated, and balance and healing are achieved, you cannot venture into stage 2, which is the area of communication skills. This is an essential component in assuring the well-being of the couple and for strengthening their marriage bonds. Once you grasp the secret of understanding your spouse through listening and speaking right, you are ready to handle stage 3, which is the conflict management stage. Only after scaling these three initial stages will you begin to sense the fulfillment and the satisfaction of the peak stage.

The mastering of these stages is a lifelong pursuit, and even then we continue at times to dither and meander through self-made mazes leading nowhere. But the rewards of effective communication are real and as they begin to come our way, pave the way for a desire, for a greater effort, to make our marriage the dream marriage that was intended by God originally.

In this chapter, we will look into the various components that combine into a communication process that builds a marriage. Later on, we will also deal with the aspect of strife management.

Norman Wright says, "Communication is a process (either verbal or non-verbal) of sharing information with another person, in such a way that he or she <u>understands</u> what you are saying."[vii]

THE FOUR PURPOSES OF COMMUNICATION

IMPARTING INFORMATION

When announcements are made over the PA system about the status of trains at a railway station, the announcements are general, addressed to all travelers. There is no relationship between the announcer and the listener. For various reasons, many couples remain at this stage in their communication; their marriage has not really matured or grown stronger.

DECISION MAKING

Suppose you need to purchase a new television, so you go to a dealer where a salesman helps you decide. He tries to be warm and friendly and shows you different models of televisions, explaining all their features. He tries to gain your trust through glib one-sided sales talk. Until your decision is made, you have not only received information, but have had a temporary kind of "relationship" with the salesman. Chances are that you will never see that person again; thus your communication is need-only based and does not go beyond that. Strangely, some couples are satisfied with this superficial stage, using communication only for making decisions.

DEVELOPING INTER-PERSONAL RELATIONSHIPS

If there is an important purpose to communicate, the participants involved are usually colleagues, neighbors, class-mates, business associates, doctors and such kind. There is a need to build a certain amount of trust, and so this level of relationship requires effort from both parties to make it meaningful. Even so, if this kind of relationship does not work out, you can drop out of it with the least amount of personal agony. This communication style goes beyond the above two stages and sometimes can result in life-long bonds. Between spouses, this kind of communication can help towards forging a purposeful relationship, provided we understand that we are dealing with people made in the image of God and we are placed in their lives not accidentally, but for His purpose.

BUILDING UP PEOPLE

This is the deepest and the most fulfilling stage of communication where you have the joy of seeing people change over time, as you continue to minister to them and help them achieve the purpose of God in their lives. The goal here is to develop the perfect relationship of the Triune God in these relationships. This can be a preview of the relationship that we will enjoy when we live in eternity. This level of communication demands a willingness to open ourselves in a way that promotes an honest, sincere, and life-transforming communication process.

Communication in marriage is achieved through three essential components: words, tone of voice, and body language. Experts tell us that words make up only 7% of our communication, with tone of voice making up 38% and body language a massive 55%.

So, for example, if Vijaya wants to communicate her love for Irwin by saying, "I love you," she will have to keep the above three communication components in mind, as explained below.

COMMUNICATION MERELY WITH WORDS

If she goes to him and says in a very dry and impersonal tone, seriously but without any warmth, "I love you," what would Irwin understand? Although the words are right, he would certainly not conclude that she is trying to communicate her love for him. In fact, he might just get the opposite impression!

COMMUNICATION WITH WORDS, ACCOMPANIED BY A MATCHING TONE OF VOICE

If she says the same thing with a slight smile, and with a warm inflection in her voice, he might infer that she does love him.

COMMUNICATION WITH WORDS, ASSISTED BY THE APPROPRIATE TONE OF VOICE AND BODY LANGUAGE

Finally, if she makes the same statement with a broad smile (suggestive), and a warm voice full of emotion, and then she puts her arm around him and hugs him while saying this, for sure, Irwin would be convinced that she truly loves him. Communication is not so much what you say, but what your spouse understands of what you say!

Communication is not easy to master, and there are certain blocks we must remove before we can effectively communicate with our spouses.

BLOCKS TO COMMUNICATION

THE RAT-RACE

We live in an ambitious world where many people's raison d'être is "get the maximum benefit with the minimum effort, and within the shortest time." This becomes such a driving force, that we appear to be on a rollercoaster ride to nowhere. We are so preoccupied with our obsession to "make it big" that we are prepared to sacrifice many things to achieve this goal.

It is pitiable to find our education system fully geared towards this end. We endlessly pressurize our children to achieve, rather than find goals that are in consonance with the mind of God. We have counselled many, many couples who work in shifts. The husband comes home after his shift and finds the wife ready to leave for work. This grind is relentless and ultimately takes its toll on their relationship. We were surprised to find out that many of these couples in their mid-30s did not have sex for months. Firstly, they had no time to themselves and what little time was leftover was either spent in catching up with their sleep or completing overdue domestic chores. Affairs in the office, even during office time, have been the frequent sad result.

KIDS

If you are not careful, children can become a major block in communication between husband and wife. From the time they are born until they leave home, it is natural that they need not just our time, but care, affection, and attention. Many wives, in their preoccupation to look after their children, tend to neglect their husbands. These husbands begin to breed resentment and dissatisfaction, and communication breaks down. When communication breaks down, the marriage is at risk.

When our children were very small, we realized that they would take up most of our time. We lived under the same roof, but hardly had any time to talk to each other meaningfully. Thankfully, Vijaya realized this danger and we found a solution. We accepted the help of Irwin's father and also helpful and caring neighbors who would babysit both our daughters for about an hour each evening, so that we could go for a walk all by ourselves, which gave us enough time to communicate heart to heart. Now we realize how important it was for us to take some time off just by ourselves to be able to hear and understand each other. This was one of the most powerful tools that built up our marriage.

MEDIA

Documented research tells us that urban husbands in the USA spend a minimum of 30 minutes in the morning reading the newspaper, and 2.8 hours watching television. In our own experience, it is not much different here. Just imagine, almost three hours are frittered away on activities that do not involve the family in any meaningful way. When both Irwin and Vijaya were working in banks, they would be amused to find their colleagues animatedly discussing marriages shown in the daily soap operas. They would minutely dissect these make-believe marriages and pass judgements on the actions of the soap opera husbands and wives. In all this time Irwin and Vijaya knew from their conversations, that their own marriages were going nowhere and were under tremendous stress. In fact, many of them were leading married lives just for the sake of their children, with hardly any relationship existing between the spouses.

THE 23rd CHANNEL

>The TV is my Shepherd, I shall not want.
>It makes me to lie down on the sofa,
>It leads me away from the Scriptures.
>It destroys my soul.
>It leads me in the path of sex and violence, for the sponsor's sake.
>Yeah though I walk in the shadow of my Christian responsibility,
>There will be no interruption, for the TV is with me.
>It's cable and remote control, they control me.
>It prepares a commercial before me, in the presence of my worldliness;
>It anoints my head with humanism, my company runneth over.
>Surely laziness and ignorance shall follow me all the days of my life, and I shall dwell in the house watching TV forever. (Anonymous)

Husbands and wives, while we do need relaxation, it cannot be at the cost of meaningful relationships with your spouse and children! For a change, try shutting off the television, and bring out some board games to play as a family; you will see the magic in getting together, kidding each other, laughing at each other, just being together and enjoying each other. It's bound to rejuvenate your relationships.

FATIGUE

It cannot be denied that we live in difficult times. In many major cities, people travel long distances to and from work. By the time we come home, we are exhausted and are in no mood to either listen to someone else or to engage in meaningful family activity. While this is commonplace, it takes creativity to make time to engage in relationship-building activities, despite the seeming lack of time or the energy to do it. Remember, you will always find time for something that you love and find rewarding in your life. Make sure each day to analyze your activities and see how meaningfully you can snatch some time from your daily routines, earmarking it to be spent with the family. Paramount amongst these would be the time to have family devotions.

FEAR OF CONFLICT

We have come across many couples whose relationship has either soured or become a drag for the simple reason that they have chosen not to share their hurts or fears. This is because one of them has become touchy and flies into a rage when these road blocks in their relationship are pointed out by the other person. This happens for two reasons:

> When one of them has a bloated ego and they have an "I-am-always-right" attitude.
>
> When they are unwilling, not only to accept that something is wrong, but are unwilling to work on these faults.

In such a scenario, the other members of the family conclude that it is meaningless to dialogue with this person as it leads nowhere. Hence the dirt constantly gets swept under the carpet only to explode at a later stage with much greater intensity, thereby damaging precious relationships. Some would also prefer temporary peace by stifling hurts, rather than temporary strife with lasting peace.

POOR LISTENING SKILLS

One of the major blocks in communication is poor listening skills. Often, husbands are guilty of this. Nothing irritates us more than finding out that while we were talking, our spouse's mind was wandering, and they were not listening to all that was being said. Once you realize that, you just lose the will to communicate.

OTHERS

There are many other blocks such as a criticizing spirit, lack of appreciation, lack of openness to understand the other person, etc. that could be potential causes for breakdown in our communication process.

DEVELOPING EFFECTIVE COMMUNICATION

Please be on your guard against the following four communication busters: 1) Lack of communication; 2) Improper/destructive communication; 3) Misunderstood communication; 4) Hypocrisy in communication.

Ephesians 4:29 says, "Do not let any unwholesome talk come out of your mouths, but only what is helpful for building others up according to their needs, that it may benefit those who listen." If you study this verse carefully, you will realize that this verse deals with two kinds of communication styles, the "negative" and the "positive."

NEGATIVE COMMUNICATION

The verse clearly says, "Let no unwholesome word proceed from your mouth but only such a word as is good." From this we understand that we need to avoid negative communication. Given below is a list of "negatives" that we would like to warn against.

NEGATIVE CRITICISM

Criticism can be both positive and negative; criticism that is positive is aimed at encouraging and bringing out the best in others. Negative criticism is more of an outburst of anger aimed at berating others and thereby bringing about guilt, in the hope that it will teach them a lesson. There are many children who are growing up with a feeling of worthlessness, because of the constant barrage of negative criticism from their parents and this behavior is generally repeated when these children become parents, deal with their own offspring in a similar manner.

NEGATIVE DEMANDS

Demands become negative when they are either ill-timed or impossible for someone to fulfil. For example, one's husband has been promising to buy her a dress for quite some time and has not gotten around to fulfilling his promise. The wife is upset and demands that her husband buy her a dress even though he has a large tax bill to pay that month. Or for instance, the husband turns romantic at the end of the day, but the wife is so tired by then (due to heavy demands on her time and strength), that she just wants to sleep. If he objects to this, the husband is making a negative, or unreasonable, demand. Demands must pass the test of sensitivity, do-ability, and sensibility in terms of its timing, logic and acceptance.

"YOU" LANGUAGE

Communication experts tell us that "you-language" is not generally well received, because it is seen more as "finger-pointing." For example, "you always let me down," "you never listen to me," "you always do this." Experts say a better way to say it would be, "I feel let down," "we are having difficulty communicating," or "I feel I am not being listened to." To make things better, it would be good to use, "we-language." For instance, "can we do something about this?" or "can we make listening to each other more effective?"

SILENT TREATMENT

Sometimes husbands, but mostly wives are the ones who adopt this attitude. They go into a shell and are not willing to communicate or discuss matters. This is a dangerous attitude. It is very frustrating, and difficult for the spouse to accept or tolerate. This can also give rise to unnecessary misunderstandings. It is better to talk it out, so that the matter can be resolved through open communication giving no place or foothold to the devil to create divisions.

SARCASM

This is another communication style that is extremely damaging to relationships. It involves saying the opposite of what you mean with the intention of hurting the other person. For example, a husband on seeing the report card of his son who flunked in mathematics says loudly to his son in the hearing of his wife, "Wow! Your mother is a brilliant mathematician, and thanks to her coaching, your marks in mathematics are awesome!" By saying this, the husband is not only insulting his wife and son, but laying the foundation for his son to behave in a similar fashion in his own family, when he has one!

NAME-CALLING

Parents sometimes call their children derogatory names like "fool," "idiot," "good for nothing," "useless," and so on. This is not acceptable. As we keep repeating these denigrating names, children tend to believe in their mind that they are not only useless, but can never measure up to our expectations for them. This creates a tremendous pressure on them to perform, and when they fail, it forces them into feeling guilty for not meeting expectations. Apart from this, their self-confidence and self-image take a nose dive and they become insecure about themselves.

UNFAIR COMPARISONS

Often we fall prey to the tendency of adversely comparing our children to others who are doing much better than our own. "Look at our neighbor's son, did you see his marks? He is such a brilliant boy, he works very hard you know, why can't you be like him?" Or "did you see that girl in the church? She is so smart, she is brilliant in studies, I won't be surprised if she gets a good job. You just don't seem to fit in, you just don't seem to work hard enough, you'll amount to nothing!'" Does this sound familiar? While constructive criticism is essential in shaping a child, destructive criticism can do just that—destroy them. Please understand that no two children are alike and God has a special plan for each of them based on the special gifts and abilities He has given them. Comparing them to others achieves nothing except breeding insecurity, and often resentment in them against you.

OFFENSIVE LANGUAGE

This is an absolute NO-NO! Nothing justifies the use of foul language. It is despicable, and leads to great harm. It also tends to belittle the one using this language in the eyes of others, causing a loss of respect. We have counselled many husbands who were so accustomed to using verbal abuse in their relationships that they completely lost the respect of their wives and children. The other danger of using offensive language at home is that we are also programming the impressionable minds of our children, who are taking in these offensive words. They will then emerge in their own conversation with others. Parents, please, never use words or even humor that is offensive or off-color. Someone wise once said, "let me know what you laugh at, and I will tell you who you are." Off-colour humor and dirty jokes too come under this category and godly families should steer clear of it.

POSITIVE COMMUNICATION

Having urged us to avoid negative communication, Ephesians 4:29 goes on to exhort us to adopt positive communication. Let us look at a few aspects of a positive communication style:

AFFIRMATIVE WORDS

The origin of the word 'affirm' is from Anglo-French *afermer*, from Latin *affirmare*, (*ad* + *firmare* = to make firm, or build up), meaning to confidently declare as true, and also to show a strong belief in something or somebody.

Affirmative words declare you believe in people around you, and build them up. They build up the self-confidence and self-image of people next to you, and in so doing, build your relationship with them.

POSITIVE LANGUAGE

By using only those words which are positive, you communicate your commitment to look at the positive side of people. You avoid the use of words like, "never," and "always," in a negative connotation. On the other hand, positive language makes use of compliments freely. Paying *genuine* compliments often to your spouse is necessary for a great marriage! Positive language can also be physical, the use of touch to communicate your affection to your spouse or your children. Your family can never ever misread this, and on the contrary, they read a message of your love in this touch. A hug a day keeps the blues away!

KIND WORDS

In times of stress or distress, people long for kind words that communicate empathy or sympathy. Sometimes we can become so insensitive that we fail to vocalize our empathy and miss out on an important building block of relationship. This especially is so true when someone makes a mistake. It can be so easy to find fault and berate them. But it serves no useful purpose, as people who commit mistakes generally pick up their lessons from the consequences that follow. A kind word is soothing and reaffirming.

ENCOURAGING WORDS

Stephen R. Covey says, "Treat a man as he is and he will remain as he is. Treat a man as he can and should be and he will become as he can and should be."[viii] Encouraging words go a long way in ensuring that people are inspired to do their best and be their best. This is a reality that can never be compromised, especially when dealing with children. Children tend to make mistakes as they are on a learning curve. Please allow adequate margins for this and prod them on with words that encourage and build.

HEALING WORDS

Proverbs 12:18 confirms the value of our language in bringing healing into troubled lives. It says, "The tongue of the wise brings healing." Proverbs 16:24 simply states, "Pleasant words are a honeycomb, sweet to the soul and healing to the bones." On the other hand, Proverbs 12:18 also mentions, "The words of the reckless pierce like swords." How often we have been guilty of damaging the self-respect and self-confidence of those around us, especially our own loved ones!

APPROPRIATE WORDS

We often fall prey to the attitude of saying the right thing at the wrong time, or the wrong thing at the right time. As we have seen, Ephesians 4:29 says, "Do not let any unwholesome talk come out of your mouths, but only what is helpful for building others up according to their needs, that it may benefit those who listen." This brings into focus the importance of an edifying word which is apt for the moment. Situational wisdom demands that we speak the right words at the right time; words that build people up.

As Proverbs 15:23 says, "A person finds joy in giving an apt reply—and how good is a timely word!" Positive communication:

- Strengthens the person rather than cutting them down.
- Is received well by the hearers.
- Becomes a source of God's life-changing grace.

Let us now talk about three kinds of therapies that infuse God's life changing grace to transform people.

LANGUAGE THERAPY

Proverbs 25:11 (NASB) says, "Like apples of gold in settings of silver is a word spoken in right circumstances." What beautiful imagery! The axiom, "an apple a day keeps the doctor away" can be adapted in language therapy to say, "a good word a day keeps marital strife away." Our language must be delightful and bring gladness and peace into the life of the listeners.

LAUGHTER THERAPY

Proverbs 15:13 tells us that "A joyful heart makes a cheerful face." If you are happy inside, it is visible on the outside for people to see. Humor plays an important part in building and cementing relationships, lightening up difficult situations and often diffusing volatile ones. It is so important to learn to laugh at ourselves and see the lighter side of life. However, a word of caution. When there is a serious disagreement that is being handled, humor can be detrimental in seeking a solution and should be avoided. It can give rise to a misunderstanding that the matter on hand is not being taken seriously.

LISTENING THERAPY

Listening is a very important aspect of developing healthy relationships. We are more naturally prone to speak than to listen. Listening is an art that needs to be learnt. Vijaya would often find Irwin inattentive when she was speaking. While there was "eye contact," and apparently "appropriate body language," yet Vijaya would be certain that he was not listening to her and his mind was wandering. Vijaya learnt the art of making sure that Irwin would be all ears when she would speak. In the middle of a conversation, Vijaya would suddenly stop and ask Irwin to relate the last couple of things she had just spoken. Obviously, and to his embarrassment, Irwin had to sheepishly accept that he had not been listening. As such, Irwin learnt the art of listening the hard way. This led to a deeper level of communication and better relational level between them.

Not listening carefully to the speaker leads them to believe four things:

- They are not important enough to the listener.
- The matter is not important enough to the listener.
- The listener has 'weightier' matters on his / her mind.
- The speaker feels belittled.

Sometimes, 'ventilation' of one's bottled up feelings can be a great therapy in relieving tension and strife. Often all that is needed are open and sympathetic ears, coupled with a closed mouth.

It is also vital to recognize the language of silence. Silence can either be deafening or can communicate great truths to those who have the patience to listen to its language. We must listen carefully, distinctly and responsively. In any home, we find a mix of different personalities. Some loud, some soft and some silent. The boisterous child manages to engage our attention by demanding it, while the quiet child smiles indulgently and silently. But we must pay equal attention to the feelings and needs of the quiet ones, whose silence can speak volumes. Never dismiss them with an affectionate pat on their heads, branding them as wonderful quiet children. We have in our experience seen such silent ones grow up to be extremely rebellious with destructive natures revealed much later on in life.

Proverbs 18:13 clarifies that, "To answer before listening—that is folly and shame." James 1:19 exhorts us to be, "quick to listen, slow to speak and slow to become angry." A wise man said that God has given us two ears and one mouth so that we could listen to twice the amount of what we speak!

The process of listening involves discovering not only a person's words but also the feelings behind them. Often, we listen to the words and either do not recognize their feelings or prefer to ignore them. It is essential that we not only to just hear the words but also try to delve into the feelings lurking behind these words. Our spouses want responses to their feelings rather than to their words. For instance, husbands will agree that wives often expect them to understand without any oral communication taking place between them. This can be very frustrating for men, if their wives expect them to understand their "unspoken words!"

Vijaya would sometimes get tired of cooking at home and would look for a "cooking holiday." However, it was beneath her dignity to tell Irwin that she was tired of cooking and would prefer a day off. The scenario would unfold as below:

> Vijaya: *I don't know what to cook this morning.*
>
> Irwin: *(After checking the fridge and finding some cabbage there)* "I see some cabbage; you could cook it with the beef and potatoes." *(Vijaya hates cabbage).*

Now, this makes Vijaya angry, not only because she hates cabbage, but also because Irwin has not sensed her true feelings and only responded to her spoken words. On the other hand, if Irwin responds with an offer to get himself something simple for lunch, this extra effort of responding to her feelings (rather than her words), constitutes meaningful listening. At times, our spouses can go into "silent mode." But their actions can speak volumes, like banging the door or throwing a dish down, or banging a book down on the table. They are communicating with their spouses with very loud "non-verbal language." If feedback from their spouse is not adequate or satisfactory, much worse is yet to come.

Lastly, let us conclude this chapter on communication by bringing up a very interesting aspect of our personal lives which can serve as a revelation in this area. Every time Irwin received a telephone call and had a long conversation with someone on the other side, Vijaya would hear a one-sided conversation which was obviously quite disjointed. Her presumption was that Irwin would come to her and update the entire conversation after finishing the call. But, to Vijaya's frustration, Irwin would conclude the conversation and go about his own business. In the meanwhile, Vijaya would become more curious with each passing minute, because she could hear a lot of "oohs" and "ahs." She would wait for quite some time expecting him to come and tell her about the call, but it would not happen. After some time, Vijaya unable to contain her curiosity would ask Irwin about the phone call and to her surprise Irwin would have already forgotten much of the conversation, saying, "Rev. so and so called me up, and asked me to preach in his church." This was quite baffling to Vijaya, because whenever she received a phone call, the first thing she would do after hanging up is to look for Irwin and relate the whole conversation (including every minor detail) to him. It was very irritating when Irwin didn't respond the way she usually did on receiving a phone call.

On one occasion, Vijaya heard a preacher talk about differing communication styles, labeling them as "painters" and "pointers." In every home, there are painters and pointers. Painters are those who love to describe every detail of an incident, whilst pointers are those people who speak in simple points completing a narration with the minimum of words. It is so amusing to see that in most couples, we find one painter and one pointer. When a painter speaks to a pointer, they should remember that the pointer gets easily bored with flowery and long descriptions and naturally their mind begins to wander. On the other hand, when a pointer speaks to a painter, his short, crisp and dry narration does not satisfy the painter who wants more details. So then, it is necessary to keep in mind that when a painter relates something to the pointer, long descriptions would be boring, and need to be kept short and crisp. On the other hand, when the pointer speaks to the painter, he would do well to paint at least a small picture of the event.

We trust that you will understand that we are designed to communicate God's life-changing grace to people with such passion that they will begin to understand the secrets of great relationships through words that heal, minds that perceive, and hearts that are tuned to words as well as silences.

SEVEN: SEX AND MARRIAGE

"Sex is the mysticism of materialism and the only possible religion in a materialistic society." Malcolm Muggeridge

We will now delve into one of the most difficult subjects to talk about especially in Christian circles. It is one of the most common aspects of human existence, but least talked about and rarely understood in its proper and God given context.

Sadly, for many Christians, marriage is a musical word, but sex is a five-letter word spelt DIRTY. Growing up in India, our parents discouraged us to talk about it or never tried to explain its physical and anatomical reality, or its spiritual implications. This kind of approach leads children to grow up with the idea that the subject of sex is taboo. As a result, when they reach adolescence, sex becomes mystical, and beckons young minds to experience, experiment and explore its forbidden territories. How tragic that much of what we learned about sex often was taught by our high-school classmates, not God's Word. Irwin once heard a story from his older classmates about a bodybuilder who had sex with 12 different women in one single night and died the next morning!

But sex is so important in the plan of God, that He starts talking about it from the first chapter in the Bible. Genesis 2:18 reveals God's plan for companionship, marriage, and sex. Then the Lord God said, "it is not good for the man to be alone; I will make him a helper suitable for him." This indicates two truths:

> Adam needed a relationship with one of his own kind.

> Adam needed assistance from one of his own kind.

With apologies to St. Augustine, we would like to rephrase his great statement to read as: "There is a woman sized vacuum in every man's heart and he is restless till he fills it up with a woman of his choice and size!"

Genesis 1:28 states, "God blessed them and said to them, "Be fruitful and increase in number; fill the earth and subdue it. Rule over the fish in the sea and the birds in the sky and over every living creature that moves on the ground." This passage indicates the four principles that God lays down for Adam and Eve together. Please remember, God calls them and says to them that:

> They had to physically procreate for mankind to proliferate on the earth.

> They had control over other creatures.

They had to govern wisely over His creation.

In short, they had to accomplish God's purpose for them and His creation.

It is more than obvious that this was not possible unless both Adam and his wife Eve would become one, physically, mentally, emotionally, and spiritually. We expand more on this in the following pages.

For this union to take place, God gives His next command in Genesis 2:24–25, *"That is why a man leaves his father and mother and is united to his wife, and they become one flesh. Adam and his wife were both naked, and they felt no shame."*

If we analyze this passage, we arrive at four conclusions:

- God calls Eve Adam's "wife," indicating the relationship of marriage existed between them.
- The call to leave and cleave indicates an exclusive relationship.
- Becoming one flesh indicates becoming a family, and so among other things means that the act of sex (necessary for building family) is blessed by God.
- Nakedness, without the feeling of shame, indicates purity in this union.

The passage mentioned above (Genesis 2:24–25) mentions the fact that Adam and Eve were joined as one flesh and were naked and not ashamed and this indicates the following four principles:

- Total union of two individuals.
- Total transparency between each other.
- Total submission to each other.
- Total discovery of each other.

Dwight H. Small says:

> Self-disclosure through sexual intercourse invites self-disclosure at all levels of personal existence. This is an exclusive revelation unique to the couple. They know each other, as they know no other person. This unique knowledge is tantamount to laying claim to another in genuine belonging ... the nakedness and physical coupling is symbolic of the fact that nothing is hidden or withheld between them.[ix]

God tells us in Genesis 4:1 that Adam *knew* Eve his wife and she conceived. Sexual relationship within marriage enables a couple to know each other in a way which cannot be experienced in any other way. To participate in sexual intercourse means not only to uncover one's body but also one's inner being to another. Therefore the Scripture often describes sexual intercourse as "knowing," the same word used in Hebrews in connection with knowing God.

Quite often, women accuse their husbands of "using" them to just satisfy their sexual needs. As a result, they begin to dislike the very act of sex itself, thereby causing the husband to accuse them of not being sensitive to their needs. Sex without getting to know the spouse more intimately is akin to just using the person for satisfying our desires and that does not glorify the Lord. God created sex for a much larger purpose.

SEX UNITES US IN THREE AREAS

1. PHYSICALLY

Apart from the fact of procreation through sexual union, sex also benefits us in many ways physically. Medical science has enumerated 10 benefits through the act of sex: it keeps our immune system working well; enhances our sexual drive; improves women's bladder control; reduces the risk of prostate cancer in men; lowers blood pressure in the long term; is good exercise; lowers risk of heart attack; improve sleep; eases stress; and releases substances called endorphins, which are also released when we laugh or are euphoric. This gives a feeling of bliss and happiness. (Courtesy: - http://www.webmd.com/sex-relationships/guide/sex and-health)

2. EMOTIONALLY

Self-giving and self-disclosing sex, with no inhibitions, serves to strengthen the emotional bond between husbands and wives. Emotional well-being contributes to physical and overall well-being.

3. SPIRITUALLY

May your fountain be blessed, and may you rejoice in the wife of your youth. A loving doe, a graceful deer—may her breasts satisfy you always, may you ever be intoxicated with her love. (Prov 5:18–19)

No other ecstasy (except the greater and higher ecstasy of the interface of man with God), matches the ecstasy of the enjoyment of sex between a husband and a wife within the holy and sanctified framework of marriage. It is holy, pure and an unselfish act of giving oneself totally in this God- given joyous act. Sex is God's gift to humankind; therefore, it is good, holy and for our benefit. That is why God gives detailed instructions and laws to regulate this vital area found in his instruction manual - the Holy Bible. So, let us first examine the laws that God has laid down to keep sex holy, blameless and a source of great joy to husbands and wives.

GOD'S LAWS FOR SEX

Married people must have sex only with their spouses:

> Marriage should be honored by all, and the marriage bed kept pure, for God will judge the adulterer and all the sexually immoral. (Heb 13:4)

Single people must not have sex with anyone; to do so would defile their bodies

> Flee from sexual immorality. All other sins a person commits are outside the body, but whoever sins sexually, sins against their own body. (1 Cor 6:18)

The Bible equates lust with physical sex (Matt 5:28); and reminds us that God will judge each person for the good or bad they do in their body (2 Cor 5:10). Only sex between human beings is permitted (Lev 18:23). Same gender sex is prohibited (e.g. Rom 1:26–27; Lev 18:22), as is adultery (Exod 20:14) and "coveting" our neighbor's wife or husband (Exod 20:17). This reminds us that adultery does not happen suddenly. It is always the result of looking at the forbidden, pondering over it with lust laden thoughts, and finally, when an opportunity comes knocking at the door, it happens. In addition, polygamy (having multiple wives or husbands) although common in the Old Testament, it was forbidden in the New (see 1 Cor 7:2).

THE PERVERSION OF SEX BY SATAN

Whatever is holy, pure, godly, edifying, uniting, joyful, and bringing worship to God, and automatically becomes the target of Satan. So it is no wonder that Satan has manipulated and distorted this holy gift of God, to lure away countless people from truly and rightly enjoying it and gratefully giving God the glory! Sex has become one of the strongest tools in the hands of the devil to destroy God's people.

How has Satan perverted this gift of God? We can find this right in the beginning of the Bible, in the book of Genesis 3:1–7. In the perfect garden, where two perfect human beings lived, crawled in slimy Serpent. He misled Eve, and both Adam and Eve disobeyed God, incurring His punishment. Verse 7 is very significant which tells how Satan managed to distort this great gift of God called sex.

> Then the eyes of both of them were opened and they knew that they were naked; and they sewed fig leaves together and made for themselves loin coverings. (Gen 3:7)

Notice: the eyes of both were opened, knowledge of evil came into their minds; they knew they were naked, and suddenly being naked (and thus sex) became bad; they sewed fig leaves together to cover themselves: the first cover-up began, as they made themselves loin coverings: the "knowing" connection got blocked.

God pronounced His judgment against the woman and caused her to be under the subjection of her husband. From then on, the battle for prominence and superiority has been raging between men and women. The natural woman does not willingly submit to the authority of her husband and likewise, the natural man feels threatened by this attitude and does his best to subdue her and to rule her, even if it has to be through destroying her personality through sex! We call it the "fig leaf complex!" This great divide continues to exist between men and women, rebellion versus forced domination. That is precisely the reason why God says in Ephesians 5:22, 25, "Wives, submit to your husbands" and "Husbands, love your wives" to the extent of giving up your life for her sake. God saw deep into the future of how this great gift of sex would be distorted and manipulated.

Dr. John Gottman, a psychologist at the University of Washington says, "Sexual harassment is a subtle rape, and rape is more about fear than sex. Harassment is a way for a man to make a woman vulnerable."[x] Rape is primarily an act of power and aggression, with the sexual aspect taking secondary role.

The devil knew the importance and value of sex, so he uses three strategies in the area of sex to take us away from God.

STRATEGY 1: Divide the Sexes (i.e.) Men vs. Women

The primary factor in dividing the sexes is to create "satisfaction substitutes" and can be achieved by sex-denial, or finding refuge in work, fantasies, power and mistrust. Each sex tries to be independent of each other.

STRATEGY 2: Distort the Gift

Sexual deviations like bondage, discipline practices, paedophilia, fetishism, incest, rape, animal sex, group sex, and distorted satisfaction through pornography etc.

STRATEGY 3: Destroy the Species

The repercussions arising out of strategy numbers 1 and 2, are: an increased distance from God and spouse, loss of ecstasy with one's spouse, extra-marital affairs, sexually acquired diseases, all of which find their root cause in sexual aberrations.

THE CHANGING FACE OF SEX, ADULTERY, AND RELATIONSHIPS

In the 1970s, my home country of India experienced a media explosion which brought the television to literally every urban household. The Western revolution of the Sixties had finally arrived there. Suddenly, the world started knocking at our doors begging to be let in. Glossy television advertisements featuring alluring products sold by handsome men and beautiful women took over the imagination of hitherto simple Indian minds. It was a game changer—India was never the same. New channels started sprouting up, vying for viewership. The aim was to capture the middle-class minds at any cost. Dozens of soap operas were being aired, and the Indian psyche had to grapple with adulterous liaisons which were sugar coated to appear harmless. Suddenly, adultery no longer looked dangerous or forbidden, rather it appeared to be attractive and satisfying.

Later, with the opening up of the Indian economy, money becoming the new mantra, and relationships had to take a backseat. Rising stress levels caused by money driven pursuits began to take a toll. Office flings became commonplace. Families earlier supposedly strong, began developing cracks. Joint family systems began to recede, taken over by DINK (double income, no kids) households. Naturally, as real-time relationships began to be cumbersome, the vacuum was being seamlessly filled by online relationships, casual sex, and viewing pornography on the internet.

CHRISTIANS, PASTORS, AND CHURCH: PORNOGRAPHY STATISTICS

A poll for Christianity Today suggests that 51% of pastors find cyber-porn a possible temptation; 37% say it is a current struggle (Christianity Today, Leadership Survey, 12/2001). 57% of pastors say that addiction to pornography is the most sexually damaging issue to their congregation (Christians and Sex Leadership Journal Survey, March 2005). With the internet explosion, porn is only a click away, all that is needed is a simple mobile phone or a computer with an internet connection and an eroded conscience. Filth is dished out by the barrel-full right into our homes. Although the statistics above may relate to the US, India is not far behind and we have come across this dragon breathing its fire into many homes and destroying many marriages.

SOME FACTS ABOUT PORNOGRAPHY

Psychologists say that conversation with men ranks among the top two emotional needs of a woman. This is easier via the internet, since the person we are talking to does not see us. The cloak of anonymity makes it easy to put lustful thoughts into action. Pornography is readily accessible on the internet, and there is little fear of being discovered by others. It is effortless—other communication is dependent on body language, tone, expression, but this is one dimensional. Many do not even seek counselling because they have not "physically" committed adultery. They think that just watching pictures does not amount to adultery. They forget what Jesus says in Matthew 5:8. Pornography dulls the senses and becomes addictive, opening us up to demonic and sinful behavior. It robs us of the sense of deep fulfillment that sex within marriage produces and leaves us with a deep-seated feeling of guilt. At the same time, it dissociates us from reality, making us incapable of handling actual situations in marriage.

MAINTAINING YOUR SEXUAL PURITY

God has called us to a holy living and instructs us in 1 Peter 1:16, "You shall be holy, for I am Holy." This is one of the most powerful challenges facing families today. We would like to touch upon certain aspects of how to maintain our sexual purity in a world that has gone crazy over sex.

HOW TO OBTAIN SEXUAL VICTORY

Paul says in 1 Thess 5:22, "reject every kind of evil." The KJV says "abstain from all appearance of evil." Please note, it is not just evil, Paul mentions even an appearance of evil. Even if it appears marginally evil, you cannot be a part of it.

> Flee the evil desires of youth and pursue righteousness, faith, love and peace, along with those who call on the Lord out of a pure heart. (2 Tim 2:22)

Three truths emerge from this verse. Firstly, we must "flee" or run away as fast as possible from sexual sin (cf. 1 Cor 6:18–20), as Joseph did when pursued by Potiphar's wife. Genesis 39:10 says, "And though she spoke to Joseph day after day, he refused to go to bed with her or even be with her." We must define sexual boundaries clearly and biblically, as Joseph did. This will prevent us falling into sexual sin. As we present our bodies on God's altar (Rom 12:1), we declare them dead to the world and alive to the Lord. He sanctifies them and that is one of the surest ways of preventing temptation and sin from entering our lives.

This means that we submit to the Lordship of the Holy Spirit every day afresh and walk in His power alone. Every morning when you wake up, lay your eyes, ears, mouth, your mind and heart, your hands and feet on the altar offering it up to God and making a covenant with Him to use them for holy purposes alone. As you do this, you will see a marked departure from the world and a new love for God and His kingdom. We must be watchful (1 Cor 10:12), because it is when we let our guard down and consider ourselves invincible, we fall.

As well as "fleeing" from sin, we must "pursue" what is right, faithful, loving, and peaceful; we must maintain fellowship "with those" like-minded and God-loving Christians. This helps us fulfil Romans 12:2, "Do not conform to the pattern of this world, but be transformed by the renewing of your mind. Then you will be able to test and approve what God's will is— his good, pleasing and perfect will." One of the greatest mistakes we make is to blend in wherever we are. Always remember that we are a royal priesthood, a holy nation, a peculiar people, a people for God's own possession (1 Peter 2:9). Our trouble begins when we forget this and try to be a part of this fallen world. As we begin to separate ourselves, God the Holy Spirit begins the work of regeneration and transforming our minds into Christ-likeness.

God's Word asks:

> How can a young person stay on the path of purity? By living according to your word. I have hidden your word in my heart that I might not sin against you. (Psalms 119:9, 11)

Hiding the word of God in your hearts and walking by it every day is a sure antidote to sin. Some unknown saint has aptly observed, "either the Bible will keep you away from sin, or sin will keep you away from the Bible."

Feeding our hearts and minds on the Word of God daily and living by it is like a vaccination against sin. Never neglect it.

> Turn my eyes away from worthless things; preserve my life according to your word. (Ps 119:37)

Turn your eyes from looking at vanity. We often try to put the onus of protecting us from sin on God alone, but do we understand our part in staying away from sin? When we do our part, we can be sure that God will do His! Job (a married man) wisely says, in Job 31:1, that he has made a covenant with his eyes not to look (lustfully) at a virgin. God loves such people and when He finds them serious about tackling sin, He leads them to the necessary resources to battle sin. By filling our minds with good things (Phil 4:8), we can avoid evil.

The Bible tells us that it is the fear of God that keeps us away from sin (Prov 16:6). Let us not take God for granted. It is high time we realize His awesome majesty in comparison to our frail helplessness. As we begin to walk with Him, trust Him and obey Him, we will realize that we develop a positive and healthy fear of Him which is a powerful deterrent to sin.

HANDLING SEXUAL TEMPTATION – A PRACTICAL APPROACH

Here are some practical steps to avoid or handle sexual temptation. They may sound old-fashioned but they work extremely well:

- Only develop close friendships with those of your own sex. Keep your social and work-life interactions with the opposite sex at a superficial/platonic level.
- Do not discuss personal matters with members of the opposite sex (except immediate family).
- Talk only when needed or essential with members of the opposite sex. Do not seek them out for the sake of conversation.
- If for some reason you find that you are alone with a member of the opposite sex for a brief period, have minimum interaction with no personal overtones.
- Stop daydreaming. Often you will find that our mind suddenly pulls away from what you are doing. This is dangerous and you need to aggressively curb it. Get busy by doing something, or reading something, or simply begin praying.
- Keep a tight watch over what you see. In conversation with those of the opposite sex, keep eye contact rather than admire their bodies.

- Discover and rediscover the uniqueness of your own spouse. A great marriage is one where you fall in love many times with your own spouse.

- Handle bad thoughts by shutting them out of your mind. In the musical, "The Sound of Music," we are exhorted to remember "our favourite things." If you make Scripture your favourite memory and begin to meditate on the Scripture, you will be able to snap out of the fleeting tendency to do wrong or commit sin.

- Know and pray for your weaknesses. Rebuke the devil in Jesus' name. James 4:7 says, "Submit yourselves, then, to God. Resist the devil, and he will flee from you."

- Always know and understand the situation, your response and its ultimate consequences. Had David thought of the horrendous consequences of his one night of pleasure with Bathsheba, we are sure that he would have run away from this temptation.

- Submit to the Lordship of God the Holy Spirit every day afresh, and obey implicitly.

- Run away from even the slightest appearance of evil. Do not fall into the temptation of trying to see where it might lead and how you could conquer it. It is best to run away. Someone has said that when you are on the road to sin, God always sends a lion on the way. The wise run away, and the foolish tear the lion apart and proceed on the road of sin and ultimately face ruin.

- Enlist the help and prayer support of your spouse or a mentor in this battle of handling temptations.

- Be accountable to your spouse, mentor, yourself, and God.

- Your daily quiet time should be a priority.

- Finally fear, obey, and love God passionately.

FACTORS NECESSARY FOR A HARMONIOUS SEX LIFE

Many couples come to us seeking advice about their sex lives in marriage. Here are some factors that contribute to a good sex life. Maintain good health. Good mental and physical health is essential for a good sex life. A person who is preoccupied in his mind or in poor health is likely to find sex less enjoyable and may even avoid it. It pays to ensure that we enjoy good physical and mental health. Even good emotional and spiritual health can contribute to a great sex life.

Develop a well-adjusted personality. We are what we think. If we have not dealt with our own insecurities and weaknesses, we will not be able to relate to our spouse honestly, openly, and deeply.

Live a life devoted to Christ and a desire to please God by holy living. Remember, God has a solution for every problem, including sexual ones. As we focus on pleasing God, every area of our will be in harmony with his will. We begin to genuinely admire and love our spouses more. This acts as the glue in our relationships and brings in romance, ecstasy in marriage and finally fulfillment.

Develop a positive attitude towards sex—relish it! Sex is not all about our own satisfaction. We should accept sex as one of the best gifts God has given us, and honor our spouse as a gift from God, mutually sharing ourselves in the act of making love. As our self-disclosure levels go up, the intimacy in the sexual act begins to get better. Remember, the older the wine, the tastier it is!

Accept the normal desire for children. There are many who think that having children does not contribute to a good marriage. You will be surprised at the positive changes that come sweeping in, as a child is born into the family. While there is hard work and depletion of energy levels, this is one of the most positive events in a couple's life. It makes us more caring, more tolerant, more sacrificial, more responsible, and more accountable. After the new arrival, couples can feel deeply enriched; parenthood has brought them closer, and this in turn can lead to a better sex life.

Understand the biological factors involved in sex. We should bear in mind that men and women are different: physically and mentally. Women especially undergo hormonal changes which husbands need to understand. Both of us generally suggest that a couple intending to marry or getting engaged buy a good book on sex written by a renowned Christian doctor. You will find many of them at Christian book stores.

Talk to each other openly about sex. This is very important, especially soon after marriage. Each one has their own idea of sex and their likes and dislikes which must be respected. Fallacies and misconceptions need to be understood and discarded. Make sure, that your spouse can fully enjoy the act. This cannot happen unless the couple communicates effectively in this area. The more the communication, the better the experience!

Maintain your privacy. It is obvious that privacy adds to freeing the couple in the act of sex. Hampered or poor privacy due to house-sharing arrangements can be very detrimental to your sex life!

Make a conscious effort to improve your sex life. Sometimes one partner can get so preoccupied in self-enjoyment that they forget sex is not just about "me;" it is also about their spouse. There should be a continuous desire to understand the dynamics of the sexual act and how it can be improved to ensure that both the husband and the wife get the deep enjoyment that God wills for them.

Maintain complete physical and mental fidelity. Nothing destroys your sex life as badly as marital infidelity, whether physical or mental. Take the case of a young couple who came to us for counselling. The wife complained that the husband was avoiding all physical contact. The husband was a busy executive and during counselling we discovered he was deep into hard-core pornography. The addiction was so bad, that virtual sex was more exciting to him than actual sex. This happens with alarming frequency these days, with more and more couples getting into the unhealthy habit of using TV and internet porn. Please stay away from any kind of pornography. Not only does it damage your relationship with your spouse—and of course with your God—in the long-run it damages your sex life.

Cultivate a desire to know and understand your mate intimately. This is the prerequisite to a good sexual life with your spouse. Sex is about giving, and giving improves with knowing, understanding, and loving.

Avoid internet/technology addiction. You would be surprised to know that such an addiction is causing divorces these days. When spouses get too caught up "catching up with friends" online or with constant texting, husbands and wives can feel neglected and threatened, some of them even initiate steps to walk out of the marriage.

Let us briefly examine a passage from Scripture:

> The husband should fulfill his marital duty to his wife, and likewise the wife to her husband. The wife does not have authority over her own body but yields it to her husband. In the same way, the husband does not have authority over his own body but yields it to his wife. Do not deprive each other except perhaps by mutual consent and for a time, so that you may devote yourselves to prayer. Then come together again so that Satan will not tempt you because of your lack of self-control. (1 Cor 7:3–5)

Husbands and wives must fulfill their duties in meeting each other's sexual needs, for our spouses have been given authority over our bodies by God. It is only for the purpose of getting into a season of prayer that we stay away from sex. Unless, of course, in the case of physical sickness, when it becomes our responsibility to respect the fact that our sick spouse will not want sex.

If we do not meet the sexual needs of our spouses, it gives Satan an occasion to tempt us, resulting in our falling into sexual sin. While this does not justify or excuse extra-marital relationships, we should understand and respect the fact that unmet needs can be dangerous.

Finally, remember, in its God-given form and within the holy bond of marriage between a loving, sacrificial, caring couple, sex takes on one of the many forms of worship we can give to God! And it is our prayer and desire that you, in your marriage would truly worship God in your sexual life with and through your spouse!

EIGHT: FAMILY ALTAR

"God didn't make the course and destiny of nations and of individuals dependent on the decisions of Congresses and Parliaments, nor did He lay this power in the hands of rulers and kings; but God placed it in the praying family! This is why the devil cannot ruin nations of men until he has destroyed the homes of prayer! That is why Satan hates the family altar." Norman V. Williams[xi]

In many Christian homes, we find a wall plaque that reads, "the family that prays together, stays together." The irony of the whole matter is that many of these families do not pray together. On the other hand, many parents approach us for counselling about their children who are going astray. The anxiety of the parents is understandable; they say, "we are praying so hard for our children, but God does not seem to answer our prayer." Again, the irony is that prayer and family devotion has not been a lifestyle with them, and is only seen as a quick fix in crisis situations. They feel that they can twist God's hand through prayer to grant their petitions. But beyond this, God is kept as far as possible from their family, because bringing Him in causes changes that are not acceptable to them.

Let us define what family devotions are, starting with some historical and Scriptural perspectives. In the Old Testament, family devotion is also called the family altar, where they worshipped the one true God, Yahweh. In those times, the father (usually the firstborn) was considered as the priest until this task was officially passed down to the tribe of Levi.

The worship was centered on the altar and this was designed to focus the family on four aspects:

- A realization of God's person and holiness.
- A realization of one's personal sinfulness.
- A realization of the fact that the way to God was through sacrifice (shedding of blood).
- A realization that this worship was a platform or a meeting place between God and man.

During the time of Moses, family worship became a time where every Hebrew parent was commanded to teach the commandments of the law and explain the real meaning of religious observations to their children:

> These are the commands, decrees and laws the Lord your God directed me to teach you to observe in the land that you are crossing the Jordan to possess, so that you, your children and their children after them may fear the Lord your God as long as you live by

keeping all his decrees and commands that I give you, and so that you may enjoy long life. Impress them on your children. Talk about them when you sit at home and when you walk along the road, when you lie down and when you get up. Tie them as symbols on your hands and bind them on your foreheads. Write them on the doorframes of your houses and on your gates. (Deut 6:1–2, 7–9)

Primarily, this passage speaks to parents. It simply says, "that you might do them." So, unless we do these things ourselves, we forfeit our right to teach them to our children. Without doing it ourselves, trying to teach others would be openly seen as hypocrisy. We cannot pass on something that we do not possess.

God is giving us a commission to accomplish three things. Firstly, we must *talk of them*: inside the house for the family to listen, observe and adopt; and outside the house for others to listen, observe and validate. We must do this *night and day*: God's word must translate into our daily lifestyles.

Secondly, we need *to bind* God's law *on our hands and our foreheads*, signifying that His Word must guide our actions and our thoughts.

Thirdly, we should *write them on the doorposts of our house and on our gates*. This simply means that all those who enter the portals of your house must be able to recognize the Lordship of God over your household, and these inscriptions serve to testify of His presence and power in family life.

Family worship also included the recital of a prayer called the "Shema." Jewish families quoted from three passages from the Pentateuch, each morning and evening.

    SHEMA: Deut 4:6–9 "the Lord our God is one."

    VEHAYAH: Deut 11:13–21 "obedience leads to blessing."

    VAIOMER: Num 15:37–41 "constant reminder to observe His commandments."

Families also considered it a part of their spiritual duty to go on a pilgrimage to Jerusalem. With this basic understanding of how family devotions evolved over a period of time, let us now look into the reasons why it is still essential to have family devotions regularly today. God says through Proverbs 4:23, "Above all else, guard your heart, for everything you do flows from it." So first and foremost, each one of us is to diligently watch over our spiritual life because that is where we find our bearing, sustenance, and purpose.

THERE ARE SIX BASIC REASONS TO MAKE SURE THAT WE HAVE OUR FAMILY DEVOTIONS EVERY DAY

GOD COMMANDS IT

> These commandments that I give you today are to be on your hearts. Impress them on your children. Talk about them when you sit at home and when you walk along the road, when you lie down and when you get up. (Deut 6:6–7)

God is reiterating a basic truth. First, you apply your heart to what is being said, and then second, when you speak of them and teach them, what you say will make sense to your children. Thus, you will facilitate their learning.

DESTINIES ARE SHAPED AT FAMILY DEVOTIONS

> Start children off on the way they should go, and even when they are old they will not turn from it. (Prov 22:6)

It is obvious that a child's future depends greatly on how he or she is taught Biblical principles at home. A sound foundation leads to a sound life. This aspect of family devotions is vital, and we would like to dwell a little more on it. God has blessed us with many ways of receiving inputs, and one of them, a very important one, is the gift of hearing. Right from our birth we keep on hearing voices. These voices continue to hammer into our mind the various facets and attitudes that govern our decision making and our actions. Given below, is a diagrammatic representation of what happens when we hear these voices, and how they form the value systems that govern us.

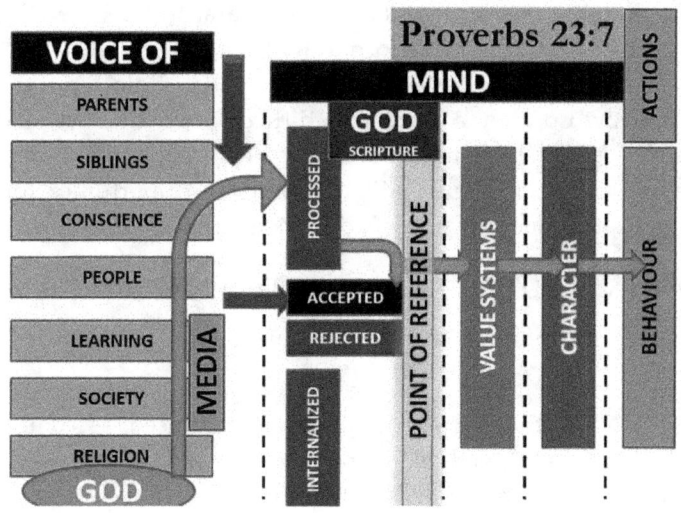

Proverbs 23:7 (note) says, "For as he thinks within himself, so he is," and as you can see from the picture above, from infancy onwards there are about seven different kinds of voices that we keep hearing all the time: parents, siblings, conscience, people (especially peers), learning, society (especially media) and religion.

As we continue to hear these voices, they are processed by our mind resulting in them being either accepted or rejected depending on the benchmark that everyone evolves in their thinking process over time. The voices that we accept are eventually internalized and shape our value systems. Our character is a sum of all our value systems; for out of this flows our behavior, which is seen by others.

Our task as a family, especially as parents, is to make sure that the voice labelled as "religion" is turned into the voice of God. This must be a grid through which every other voice must be filtered, sifted, and verified. *God's Word should become a point of reference* on which our value systems are based, resulting in a godly character, behavior and actions.

Andrew Fletcher, a Scottish writer and politician, makes a very strong statement, "let me make the songs of a nation, and I care not who makes its laws."[xii] How true it is! It is no secret that music and songs form the most potent platform to deliver philosophies of life that impregnate fertile young minds. Many modern songs urge young people to "do what you want, be what you want, go out and get what you want." When our younger generation feeds on these kinds of philosophies, the result is that they become self-centered, leading a life that is only interested in gratifying themselves, even at the cost of others. Discipline is a word that is frowned upon and those who try to instill it are seen as draconian. Given this context, the family altar is not only a platform but also a change agent to make God as the point of reference for every individual or child. As our children continue to grow up, they come across difficulties, challenges, and barriers that require wisdom to handle. If God is their point of reference, every challenge and every difficulty will turn into an opportunity for them to display the wisdom and power of God in their lives.

IT PROMOTES SPIRITUAL GROWTH OF PARENTS AND CHILDREN

> Fulfill your promise to your servant, so that you may be feared. (Ps 119:38)

We live in a society that is so technologically advanced, so comfort-driven, and so self-seeking that we have scant time or reverence for God. God says in Malachi 1:6, "A son honors his father and a servant his master. Then if I am a father, where is My honor? And if I am a master, where is My respect?" Proverbs 1:7 and 9:10 tell us that the fear of the Lord is the beginning of knowledge and wisdom. God is exhorting us to receive knowledge and wisdom by fearing Him and that must be the focus of family devotions, to make sure that our families fear and revere Him. By doing this we grow spiritually and get equipped to handle life.

IT PROMOTES HEALTHY COMMUNICATION

> then I can answer anyone who taunts me, for I trust in your word. (Ps 119:42)

Family devotions are also a place where we find answers and get equipped to communicate effectively with people.

IT REMOVES BARRIERS BETWEEN FAMILY MEMBERS

> Can two walk together, except they be agreed? Amos 3:3 (KJV)

The secret of walking with people is to agree together within scriptural boundaries! At the platform of the family altar, the family can learn from God's Word the secrets for developing healthy attitudes and relationships for happy living. If we give prominence to God and His Word, we will have no difficulty in agreeing even on the most disagreeable matters, thereby fostering an atmosphere to live amicably for His glory.

IT STRENGTHENS FAMILY BONDS

> Do not rebuke mockers or they will hate you; rebuke the wise and they will love you. Instruct the wise and they will be wiser still; teach the righteous and they will add to their learning. (Prov 9:8–9)

> A wise son brings joy to his father, but a foolish son brings grief to his mother. (Prov 10:1)

During family devotions we not only spend time with God hearing and communing with Him, but also with family members—especially our children—in the light of God's Word. The Word of God serves as an illuminating factor in bringing out our hidden flaws, and at the family altar, we have the privilege of assisting each other and addressing these flaws with godly Scriptural wisdom. That is why Solomon says that when we teach and reprove wise individuals of the family, they will love us and consequently make our hearts glad. This process fosters, repairs, and strengthens family ties.

PRACTICAL ASPECTS OF FAMILY DEVOTIONS

WHEN?

This is a very contentious issue. Some believe early morning is a right time to have devotions, while others feel the time just before we go to bed is the right time.

It is not the time that should dictate family devotions, but the other way round. By following a rigid program with many unwilling and unprepared family members, we gain little. The objective is not just to have family devotions but to make sure that every individual in the family relishes the presence of God and learns something they can take away with them. In the present context, with the pressures on time and energy whether be it long or different working hours of the husband and wife, commuting time to the office, study patterns, school timetables, it is a severe challenge to find a common time that is suitable to every member of the family.

Therefore, we would like to suggest something, without being dogmatic about it. Ideally, mornings give us a reasonably quiet time to sit for family devotions. But in families with one or two school-going children, morning could be a harrowing time! While the rest of the family is talking about God and scriptural principles, the mother's mind is on breakfast, lunch, getting children ready in time to board the school bus and also preparing herself to go to work. Schools also regularly saddle the children with a large quantity of home-work which often spills on to the next morning. Hence, the minds of children would also be hovering on the incomplete homework and the consequences that would follow at school if it is not completed. So, in such a context, family devotions would just be a matter of routine and not a matter of enjoyment.

Hence, before you decide what time to have family devotions, it would be best if every individual is consulted on a time that would suit them. Let a consensus emerge between all the family members, so that they will have no excuse not to actively participate in the devotion. In case consensus is not forthcoming, a common time suitable to most of the family members should be adopted. Alternately, there is always a possibility of splitting the devotion into two separate timings to make sure that everyone will definitely be a part of it. Make sure that this time that you spend forging an interface with God and with the whole family would have no distractions and disturbances that would impinge on the quality of the devotions.

WHERE?

Different families have different ideas on where or which place is the most suitable to have their family devotions. We would like you to ensure that the place you have chosen is free from distractions, and is not so comfortable that family members are tempted to go to sleep or feel lazy. As you will see later on, family devotions can also include a time of Bible study, requiring some writing. It would be good if it can be arranged around the dining table provided it is non- distracting.

HOW LONG?

In our seminars we generally ask families what is the suitable duration for the family altar. On one extreme, some say 1 hour and on the other extreme, 10 minutes. We reiterate that there is no yardstick to govern the amount of time you spend with the Lord as a family, but out of personal experience we would suggest a broad-based timeframe that can help you decide.

My wife and I both recall how dry and uninteresting the times of family devotion were in our childhood. Our parents were orthodox in their approach and insisted on having devotions just before bedtime. These devotions involved the reading of a small portion of Scripture followed by a long (seemingly endless) prayer mostly by the father, although with a great missionary zeal and a heart for the poor. This prayer would carry on till a long list was exhausted by which time most of the children were exhausted and would have gone to sleep. This however, did set the tone, and reinforced the importance of our own family devotions, and it played a very significant role in the spiritual nurture of our children. So we suggest that you experiment with timings, and then stick to the one that brings in maximum response from everyone, and maximum spiritual dividends.

We suggest that every family must have two separate sets of family devotions: one, where the husband and wife meet alone; and another where the whole family gets together. These can ideally last between 30 minutes and 1 hour. Time spent all together as a family can be more like 15–30 minutes depending on the tolerance level of all the members, especially the youngest members, of the family.

CONTENTS/INGREDIENTS

Family devotion can be flexible, yet work into it the following ingredients.

WORSHIP

> Serve the Lord with fear and celebrate his rule with trembling. (Ps 2:11)

Worship is where you focus on God, giving him the rightful place in your lives individually and collectively. Worship can consist of singing some worship choruses and songs, short prayers of worship stating who God is and dwelling on His attributes without getting into any personal requests. This can also include brief testimonies of what the Lord has done during the day, and praising Him for answered prayers and recalling His faithfulness and goodness. Each day a new attribute of God can be used to praise and worship Him.

SCRIPTURE

> All Scripture is God-breathed and is useful for teaching, rebuking, correcting and training in righteousness, so that the servant of God may be thoroughly equipped for every good work. (2 Tim 3:16–17)

This passage tells us that the Bible is vital in every area of our life:

- For doctrine: what we should know.
- For reproof: knowledge of where we have gone wrong.
- For correction: for course corrections when we deviate from Biblical norms.
- For instruction in righteousness: to understand the way to living right in the sight of God.
- Scripture makes us adequate, competent, and complete. It equips us for every good purpose that God intends to accomplish in our life and the lives of others too for His glory.

There are five ways to imbibe the Word of God: hearing, reading, studying, meditating, and memorizing.

Have a systematic plan to read the Bible every day. You can also use a Bible devotional everyday like, "Our Daily Bread," "Every Day with Jesus," or any other devotional that you find suitable for the whole family.

Have a systematic plan to study the Bible. We have used the three-point Bible study method devised by the Navigators which proved to be quite useful to bring out the Scripture's essential truths for any intellectual level.

Meditating is chewing and digesting what you read and study. It is a time of silence and concentration wherein you wait on the Lord to talk to you and explain the content of your study passage. This also involves applying lessons diligently to your everyday life. Without application, the study of the Bible only remains an academic pursuit and not a spiritual one.

Memorizing Scripture is equally important as Psalm 119:11 reveals, "I have hidden your word in my heart that I might not sin against you."

Remember the goal—it is basically to bring us closer to God to know Him better and to lead meaningful and purposeful lives.

INTERACTION

> And let us consider how we may spur one another on toward love and good deeds, not giving up meeting together, as some are in the habit of doing, but encouraging one another—and all the more as you see the Day approaching. (Heb 10:24–25)

Bible study is meant to stimulate us into becoming the kind of people that God wants us to be. We must consider one another—to promote doing good, knowing our time on earth is limited and His coming is nearer than we ever thought.

Make sure that everyone participates. One person can read the Bible, another can give a short testimony, someone else can pray, and someone else can give an interpretation of the passage. Everyone must feel involved and taken seriously. You will be surprised at the many gems and pearls of wisdom that come from the minds of small children during the time of family devotions.

PRAYER/INTERCESSION

Jesus gave a beautiful pattern for praying and interceding in Matt 6:9–13. Briefly, it can be stated in the following parts: adoration, thanksgiving, confession, and supplication.

Children generally consider prayer as a request letter to God for material blessings. They should understand clearly that prayer is a comprehensive, wholesome communication with our heavenly Father, with supplication or requests coming last in prayer. While this truth can be easily grasped by older children, it will suffice for the younger children to understand that God is their very personal heavenly Father, who is interested in them and who will answer them when they talk to Him. So our family prayer time should gently allow the children to develop their own personal prayer style. You should make sure that the children understand that it is not the language, but the heart of the one making the prayer that God is interested in. Help them to be simple, original, and sincere.

Make lists of prayer items, which would become praise items as the Lord answers them. This would help children to recognize the fact that God answers prayer. Our children should also be made to understand that sometimes God says "no" to a prayer request and at times we must wait for an answer. And when God says "no," it is for our best. God remains good all the time.

PERSONAL APPLICATION

> Your word is a lamp for my feet and a light on my path. (Ps 119:105)
>
> The unfolding of your words gives light; it gives understanding to the simple. (Ps 119:130)
>
> Great peace have those who love your law, and nothing can make them stumble. (Ps 119:165)

One of the most important facets of the family altar is personalized application of the Scriptures to govern our daily lives and transform us into the image of Jesus. Make sure that you help children to apply the Scripture that you read every day into their personal lives by giving personal examples and also living out the Scripture in your own life consistently.

ULTIMATE GOAL OF DEVOTIONS

These can be simply stated as completeness (Col 1:28); Christ-likeness (Gal 4:19); development of a godly lifestyle (Luke 2:52); and a vision for evangelism (John 4:35). This last point, evangelism, is important, for our children must see the need to proclaim the good news that Jesus can come into every life to give them answers, a purpose, a hope, a future, and power over circumstances.

As you develop your own family devotional style, the whole family must be able to remember and keep in mind the importance of three further factors:

> Be still, and know that I am God (Ps 46:10 KJV)

We live in busy times, and it is no surprise that this attitude of "being still" in the presence of God is in short supply. Our minds tend to run in a million directions. Many complain that as soon as they sit down to study the Bible, their minds run amok. So this practice of being still in the presence of God will have to be cultivated and deeply ingrained in the minds of all the family members. You will find this a very rewarding practice.

> To everything there is a season, and a time to every purpose under the Heaven (Ecc 3:1 KJV)

The whole family must learn to respect the value of time. The Bible exhorts us to make the most of our time, "because the days are evil." (Eph 5:16).

We find it very disturbing when families do not come on time for the Sunday morning worship services. It is also sad that no amount of cajoling or exhorting moves them. It is taken for granted that going late to church is acceptable. These people while going late to church, will doubly make sure that their children are on time to the school and they themselves will be on time to attend their offices and much earlier to board their flights. It just shows that they have scant respect or fear for God. Children learn from parents and if you do not respect God, you cannot expect your children to do so. Please make sure that the value of going on time to church is solidly ingrained into the minds of all your family members. This also includes appreciating the value of time and being on time everywhere.

> One thing I ask from the Lord, this only do I seek: that I may dwell in the house of the Lord all the days of my life, to gaze on the beauty of the Lord and to seek him in his temple. (Ps 27:4)

Our families must grasp this truth. Family devotions must become the focal point to behold the beauty of the Lord and to meditate on Him. We often find families in a great hurry, and devotions become very cursory. Please make sure that you are never in a hurry just to finish a passage each day and pray meaninglessly just as a formality. This time must be dynamic, meaningful and life changing.

FACTORS HAMPERING DEVOTIONS

There are certain factors that can hamper family devotions and keep us from enjoying them: the poor spiritual life and standards of parents; a lack of time; addiction to entertainment and media, especially the television; fatigue; unresolved problems; and many more.

If these factors operate in our family, we will either try to avoid having family devotions or have them more as a matter of routine without any real benefit accruing from them. Unless the above are taken care of, your devotions will remain devoid of that vitality that can only come when the Holy Spirit operates amongst us. Devotions should be looked forward to with anticipation and not anxiety. Occasionally, expect a dry spirit in people. At such times do not force them to pray. Rather pray with them and encourage them to quickly emerge from this and begin to enjoy the devotions.

It may not be possible to have devotions as a family each day. Try to have them as frequently as possible. Find out the reasons that are hampering them and find solutions. You may need to assess and reassess your family devotions frequently as a couple, and reorganize them if necessary.

IF JESUS CAME TO YOUR HOUSE

by Lois Blanchard Eades

If Jesus came to your house to spend a day or two…
If He came unexpectedly, I wonder what you'd do.
Oh, I know you'd give your nicest room to such an honoured Guest
And all the food you'd serve to Him would be the very best
And you would keep assuring Him you're glad to have Him there…
That having Him in your home is joy beyond compare.

But when you saw Him coming, would you meet Him at the door
With arms outstretched in welcome to our heavenly visitor?
Or would you may be change your clothes before you let Him in?
Or hide some magazines and put back the Bible where they'd been?
Would you turn off the radio and hope He hadn't heard?
And wish you hadn't uttered that last, loud hasty word?

Would you hide your worldly music and put some hymn books out?
Could you let Jesus walk right in, or would you rush about?
And I wonder if the Saviour spent a day or two with you,
Would you go right on doing the things you always do?
Would you go on saying the things you always say?
Would life for you continue as it does from day to day?

Would your family conversations keep up its usual pace?
And would you find it hard each meal to say a table grace?
Would you sing the songs you always sing and read the book you read?
And let Him know the things on which your mind and spirit feed?
Would you take Jesus with you everywhere you'd planned to go?
Or would you, maybe change your plans for just a day or so?

Would you be glad to have Him meet your very closest friends?
Or would you hope they'd stay away until His visit ends?
Would you be glad to have Him stay forever on and on?
Or would you sigh with great relief when He at last was gone?
It might be interesting to know the things that you would do,
If Jesus Christ in person, came to spend some time with you.

Meeting with Jesus must transform us, AND OUR FAMILIES TOO![xiii]

NINE: MANAGING CONFLICT

"Conflict is inevitable, but combat is optional." Max Lucado

Soon after marriage, Irwin wanted to know if Vijaya could cook a favourite dish which his mother used to make. He was delighted to find out that she could! At lunchtime, they sat down to eat and Vijaya expectantly looked at Irwin's face to know if she had passed the test. With the first morsel, Irwin's face showed that he was not really pleased with the dish. Irwin remarked, "This is not how my mother used to make it!" Obviously Vijaya was taken aback and promptly retorted, "But my mother made it that way!" And it was our first brush with marital strife. For a moment, we had forgotten that our upbringings in India had been very different! Irwin came from a Punjabi background, whereas Vijaya was from a Telugu household. That means we grew up with different cultures, languages, perspectives, viewpoints, and eating habits—all these things can contribute to misunderstandings and strife within marriages.

From toothpaste tubes to table manners, discipline of children to disobedience of teenagers, anything and everything has the propensity to turn our placid lives into battle zones. Often, when we counsel couples or families, we find that, misunderstanding, lack of forbearance and insensitivity stand out as major reasons contributing to strife. In all cases, each blames the other and vice versa.

Let us give you an outstanding quote from Zig Ziglar:

> "I have no way of knowing whether or not you married the wrong person, but I do know that many people have a lot of wrong ideas about marriage and what it takes to make that marriage happy and successful. I'll be the first to admit that it's possible that you did marry the wrong person. However, if you treat the wrong person like the right person, you could do well and end up having married the right person after all. On the other hand, if you marry the right person and treat that person wrong, you certainly will have ended up marrying the wrong person. I also know that it is far more important to be the right kind of person than it is to marry the right person. In short, whether you married the right or wrong person is primarily up to you."[xiv]

What a profound statement which cuts across all defenses of strife by underlining the necessity of being the right person yourself, instead of expecting that from your spouse!

Leo Tolstoy, the great writer says, "What counts in making a happy marriage is not so much how compatible you are, but how you deal with incompatibility." Billy Graham when asked about his secret of love, being married 54 years to the same person, says, "Ruth and I are happily incompatible."[xv] We would like to refer you back to the diagram titled "THE MARRIAGE TRIANGLE" in the chapter on communication. You will see that the attainment of "peak relationship" depends on crossing three different stages, the first one is managing the area of physical, mental, spiritual, and emotional health, the second is effective communication skills, and the third is effective strife management, to be able to go to the fourth and final stage which is the peak stage.

How we view and handle marital strife defines the happiness, contentment, and stability of a marriage in time to come.

MARITAL STRIFE - BANE OR BOON?

Almost all couples feel that strife is detrimental and is not normal. This misunderstanding can cause further damage to the marriage. We would like to give you some statements about marital strife that can be eye openers: strife is normal and inevitable; it does not mean absence of love, for love does not preclude strife; the fury of the storm displays the strength of the anchor.

Remember, how you handle strife determines the course of your marriage. Never regard divorce as an option (Mal 2:16). Having said that, violence is on no occasion permissible; nor is bad language. We believe that "real men don't hit women." Only weak and insecure husbands manhandle their wives. Compromise is a valid solution, as in many situations both sides could have validity. But compromise is never an option in handling issues concerning sin or those which contradict the Scriptures. Couples must recognize that seeking help at times is essential—failure to do so will damage your marriage. Every marriage has in-built needs and when these needs are not met or inadequately met, it can cause strife in the family. Here are some possible deficiencies or unmet needs:

- Lack of affection and intimacy.
- Lack of companionship.
- Different expectations about sex.
- Lack of and improper use of finances.
- Differing ideas and convictions in the upbringing of children.
- Lack of domestic support.

- Improper communication or the lack of it.
- Lack of transparency in relationships.
- Lack of respect and admiration for spouse.
- Lack of commitment to make the relationship work.

Dr. James Dobson, a renowned teacher on family life, lists a number of problems common in marriage: the absence of romance; in-laws; low self-esteem; problems with children; finances; loneliness/boredom; sexual problems; health problems; ageing; insensitivity; among others. In his expert opinion, Dr. Dobson says that among the above listed issues, low self-esteem is the one that is the biggest cause of marital strife. We totally agree with him that this is true regardless of national or cultural boundaries.

OUR NATURAL RESPONSES IN HANDLING STRIFE

It is not the strife, but your response that decides where the strife will take your marriage. There is a wrong way and right way to handle strife. Let us first deal with three natural responses we adopt to handle strife.

AGGRESSION: We have often heard that "offence is the best defense." Often we try to become aggressive in marital strife and try to win it either by bullying or hammering down our spouse into submission. It is also said that there are no winners in an argument. This response does not help in finding solutions, but can go a long way in suppressing emotions that can damage the marriage.

PASSIVITY/SUBMISSIVENESS: The second natural response to handle strife is to become passive/indifferent or submissive. We simply say, "If that's the way you want it, go ahead, I'm least bothered," or "I will go along with whatever you want."

RETRACTION: The third way is to retract completely and go into a shell. The fairer sex generally goes into what we label as, "giving the silent treatment." Not only does this not work, it infuriates the spouse.

Indeed, none of these methods work. On the other hand, they contribute to heightened resentment, anger, and bitterness.

Unless we get down to the roots of strife and handle it effectively, finding suitable solutions is next to impossible. From our experience in counselling, we are going to give you the tools to deal with strife and emerge out of it with your marriage and love intact. We would like to sound a note of warning here, that these principles, unless taken to heart and adhered to in totality, will not produce tangible results. This advice comes from our own experience in handling strife in a way that brings healing and glory to God.

ORIGINS OF STRIFE

As you can see, there are four quadrants in a circle, with each of them representing one area through which strife occurs in a marriage.

Let us examine them one by one.

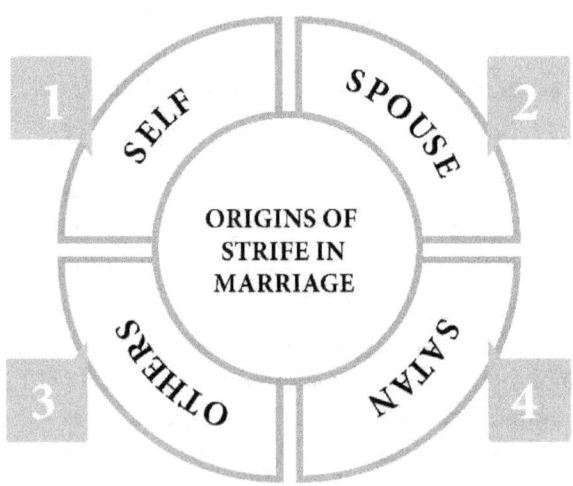

SELF

Dwight L Moody once remarked, "I have had more trouble with myself than with any man I have ever met." How right he was! Let us examine what the Bible has to say about strife and apply those lessons in our situations.

> For where you have envy and selfish ambition, there you find disorder and every evil practice. (Jas 3:16)

Time and again, we have come across people who, although married, live only for themselves. Their spouse exists only to cater to their needs and does not matter in their scheme of things. We often find wives who are so gifted and talented, that without meaning to, they outshine their husbands. Husbands in such marriages sometimes feel very threatened and begin to bully their wives into a subservient role that suppresses their talents. They forget that in God's sight they are one, and no matter who does well or excels, the glory belongs to God and the blessings come to them as a couple. It is very rarely that we find husbands encouraging their wives to bring out the best in them.

Vijaya was an introvert, preferring to stay outside the limelight. She openly admits and appreciates the role that Irwin played in bringing out her gifts, encouraging her to develop her teaching and counseling skills. In James 3:16, the apostle warns about the "Me orientation," which is defined by three attitudes: self-centeredness, self-gratification, and self-aggrandizement: "he that is of a proud heart (EGO) stirreth up strife." (Prov 28:25 KJV) EGO in its full form is: Edging God Out.

It is rightly said, "You cannot be right and married at the same time." If you are trying to be right and prove your partner wrong, you have stepped outside the marriage. The egoistic mindset can also be described in the following three ways: "I am the BOSS;" "I am ALWAYS RIGHT;" and "I am BETTER THAN YOU."

These are the kind of people who will never acknowledge that something is wrong with them. On the contrary, they think it is always their spouse who is at fault and needs to mend his or her ways. They do not like to seek help, because they think that nothing is wrong with them. God and His Word have little role to play in their lives as they continue to operate on the premise that they are above the rest of the people around them.

THE ANTIDOTE TO SELF AS FOUND IN PHILIPPIANS 2:1–8

So how do we handle such people? Are you one of them? You will find the antidote in the Bible:

> If therefore there is any encouragement in Christ, if there is any consolation of love, if there is any fellowship of the Spirit, if any affection and compassion, make my joy complete by being of the same mind, maintaining the same love, united in spirit, intent on one purpose. Do nothing from selfishness or empty conceit, but with humility of mind let each *regard one another as more important than himself;* do not *merely* look out for your own personal interests, *but also for the interests of others*. Have this attitude in yourselves which was also in Christ Jesus, who, although He existed in the form of God, did not regard equality with God a thing to be grasped, but emptied Himself, taking the form of a bond-servant, *and* being made in the likeness of men. Being found in appearance as a man, *He humbled Himself* by becoming obedient to the point of death, even death on a cross. (Phil 2:1–8 KJV)

C. S. Lewis says, "True humility is not thinking less of yourself; it is thinking of yourself less." Real joy is found in the acronym: J–Jesus first; O–Others next; Y–Yourself last. In the light of God's wisdom, if you take everything mentioned above seriously, you will come to the following conclusions:

- My spouse is more important than me.
- I must keep the interests of my spouse above my own.
- I must humble myself before God and before my spouse.
- If my spouse is talented (possibly more than me), it is something that God has blessed my spouse with. It is my responsibility to encourage my spouse to do his or her best for the glory of God and the building up of His kingdom. By doing so, I will please God and be blessed and honored by Him. Also this will make my spouse extremely happy in demonstrating my sacrificial love for him or her. We challenge you, dear readers to practice this without expecting anything in return and we assure you that you will reap rich dividends in terms of a peaceful, blessed and fruitful family.

SPOUSE

Most couples who come for counselling have a common accusation against their spouse, "I never thought you were like this," or "I never thought you could do this," or "you have surprised me and I am deeply hurt." This does not surprise us as we realize that these couples have failed to consider the following facts:

- Your spouse too struggles with the same fallen nature.
- You are both still on the same side (despite the strife).
- You either sail together or you sink together.

It is always the case that someone has to take the initiative and start the process of resolving the issue. Failure to resolve the issue amicably will hurt your family in more ways than you can imagine. To handle the attitude of our spouse, we need to deal with our own attitudes first in the light of the following Scripture:

> Above all, love each other deeply, because love covers over a multitude of sins. (1 Pet 4:8)

Antoine de Saint-Exupery says, "Life has taught us that love does not consist in gazing at each other, but in looking outward together in the same direction."

In your marriage, you must regularly practice forgiveness: keep short accounts. That means you need to regularly clean your memory bank of all the hurts and the pains inflicted on you in the past. It is not easy, but in obedience, as you begin to try this out by the grace of God, you will find it becoming easier and easier to practice this. In Matthew 18:22, Jesus said to Peter, "I tell you, not seven times, but seventy-seven times." Seventy times seven just meant as often as required. Keep in mind that forgiveness without "forget-ness" does not contribute to lasting peace. To forget is a conscious choice that we must make, and trust the Lord. As we begin to practice this, we will realize that although we may yet remember the feeling of hurt, the memory eventually becomes dimmer, and ultimately fades out. Jesus also said,

> If someone slaps you on one cheek, turn to them the other also. If someone takes your coat, do not withhold your shirt from them. Luke 6:29

If we are asked to turn our other cheek to someone who slaps us, and be willing to give more than what is asked to people outside the family, how much more it applies to those who are within the family! Similarly, if we take to heart the words of Paul, "When we are cursed, we bless; when we are persecuted, we endure it" (1 Cor 4:12). We will practice this in family life. Human nature is always to mete out what has been given to us. Tit-for-Tat. But a godly response dictates that we meet a blow with a blessing. In so doing we prove to be the children of God.

Notice how Jesus also says:

> And if anyone wants to sue you and take your shirt, hand over your coat as well. (Matt 5:40)

As a rule, we are averse to people taking advantage of us and treat them with derision and contempt. Jesus wants us to go an extra mile, even to the extent of perhaps suffering a loss. Proverbs 25:21–22 says, "If your enemy is hungry, give him food to eat; if he is thirsty, give him water to drink. In doing this, you will heap burning coals on his head, and the Lord will reward you." The Lord who watches your response will recompense you more than adequately.

We believe that if you practice the above principles relentlessly, that is, love without expecting anything in return, forgive unconditionally, suffer patiently and silently, endure by blessing others, and give where not expected to, you will reflect your heavenly Father's attributes and contribute to building up a peaceful and loving home.

OTHERS

The third factor involved in marital strife is the category of 'others.' By others, we mean the following three categories, primarily: children, family and friends, and in-laws.

Here is an ACTION PLAN to help you understand and handle others:

- Be united as a couple (remember you are on the same side).
- Keep communication lines open-be a good listener.
- Focus on the problem, not on people, to ensure that you keep the past/prejudices out of the ambit of the present strife.
- Understand the issue from both sides.
- Keep in mind what is best for the family and not you alone.
- Understand the mind of the Lord; keep your focus on Scripture, the Holy Spirit and divine wisdom.
- Seek help if needed from godly counsellors. Proverbs 11:14 says that, "For lack of guidance a nation falls, but victory is won through many advisers."
- Initiate suitable remedial action with the following reference points: listen, reflect, discuss, decide changes required with the concurrence of your spouse, monitor progress and make course corrections if need be.

To sum up, let all be harmonious, sympathetic, brotherly, kindhearted, and humble in spirit. not returning evil for evil, or insult for insult, but giving a blessing instead; for you were called for the very purpose that you might inherit a blessing. (1 Pet 3:8–9)

Here, Peter is especially addressing husbands and wives. This passage highlights the simple fact that our reactions determine our relationships. Life is all about reactions; if our reactions are godly, the people around us will be happy and relationships become godly, strong and life changing.

SATAN

The last causative factor for marital strife is our arch enemy, Satan, who loves to break-up families. He is aware of the potential of healthy families to produce godly saints and great leaders who could turn the course of history and bring glory to God. Therefore, Satan loves to hit at the family.

> For our struggle is not against flesh and blood, but against the rulers, against the authorities, against the powers of this dark world and against the spiritual forces of evil in the heavenly realms. (Eph 6:12)

That is why God instructs us in Eph 6:13 to "Therefore put on the full armor of God, so that when the day of evil comes, you may be able to stand your ground, and after you have done everything, to stand."

While some people are quick to attribute all the ills of our society to Satan, we forget that much of it also comes from our fallen nature inherited from our forefather Adam. Nevertheless, Satan is a reality and can be a tangible source of marital strife.

As Paul draws his wisdom from the Roman soldier's armour, we too can learn some important ways to fight Satan, from the once powerful Roman legions. The Roman legions were a formidable fighting machine and their march into battle is legendary. There are five lessons that we can learn from the marching Roman legions, as seen in the picture below.

STAY CLOSE Husbands and wives, and children, walk in love and forbearance and close to each other.

CLOSE GAPS Do not give the devil a foothold, mostly through unresolved conflicts, unforgiveness, bitterness, hatred, walking away from God and in failing to use His resources for victory.

STAND UNDIVIDED Be of the same mind, reconcile differences quickly.

STAND FIRM Let nothing divide you or threaten you, stand in the confidence of God.

OBEY COMMANDER (GOD) Be implicit in your obedience.

James 4:7 admonishes us, "Submit yourselves, then, to God. Resist the devil, and he will flee from you." Before we can resist the devil, we must submit to God. We need to submit totally to His Lordship, leading, power, sovereignty, and control of our life in an attitude of total obedience. Failure to do so will only result in an inability to resist or fight Satan.

After we have submitted to God, He gives us His protection and power for victory. Satan will continue to attack but to no avail. He will not be able to breach the defense that God puts around us. On the contrary, we will have the authority in the name of Jesus to command him to leave us and our family alone.

SOME PRACTICAL WAYS TO HANDLE STRIFE

One of the most practical and logical ways suggested by the Bible on handling strife is found in Eph 4:26, "In your anger do not sin": Do not let the sun go down while you are still angry."

God says that all our tussles and arguments should be settled before sundown. Let us explain this more clearly through the conflict graph that you see on this page.

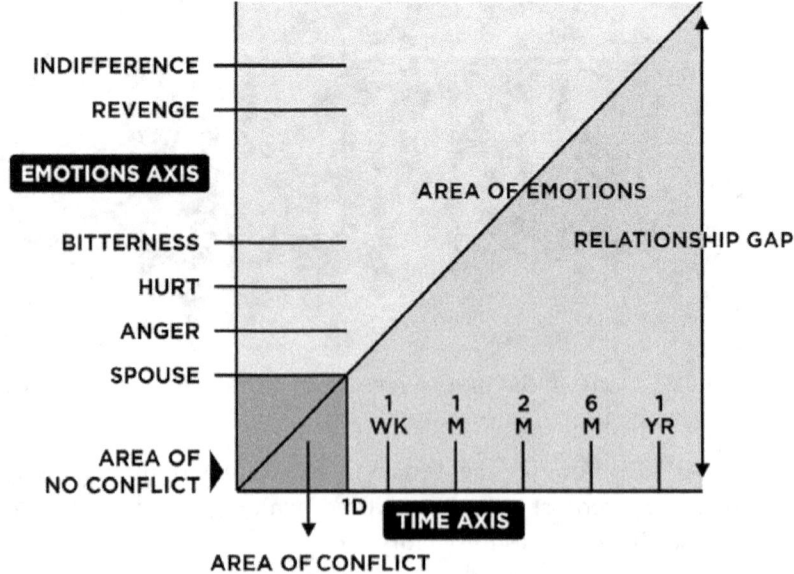

Horizontally, you have the time axis, whereas vertically you find the emotions axis and from the point they meet, you find a tangent going up. The time axis represents the progression of time taken from the start of a quarrel or argument, to the time that elapses without reconciling the issue. The emotions axis represents various progressive emotions that we experience starting from anger, hurt, bitterness, feelings of revenge, and ultimately indifference. The progression of these emotions varies from person to person, but in every case, leads to the final stage of indifference. This is the most dangerous stage in marital strife. As long as you keep arguing or fighting, it denotes a healthy response to make things work despite differences. The day you reach the stage of indifference, it signifies that you have accepted the fact that this strife cannot be settled amicably, and secondly, that you have lost the drive or the interest to make your relationship better and workable. Where the two axes meet on the lower left-hand corner, you find "area of no conflict." This is not the place where no conflict exists, but the starting point of a new conflict. As both time and emotions progress, the conflict line escalates. As the tangent starts to rise, the relationship gap begins to widen. At the beginning, this gap is very small, but with more time elapsing, this gap becomes larger. The larger the gap, the more difficult it is to settle the issue. Therefore, it is no wonder that God instructs us to handle the strife before sundown, where the relationship gap is minimal.

You will also find that the area of emotions is much larger than the area of conflict. Generally, when couples come for counselling, the issue always appears to be amplified and clouded by emotions. When we sift through the emotions to find the real cause, often the initial conflict is very mild and easily solvable. But by not handling it properly and in time, we risk complicating it, coloring it, twisting it, and making it all the harder to address it and achieve peace. The obvious thing is to reduce the strife from the area of emotions to the area of conflict, which then become easier to sort out.

FOUR PRACTICAL WAYS OF HANDLING STRIFE

There are four practical ways to handle strife.

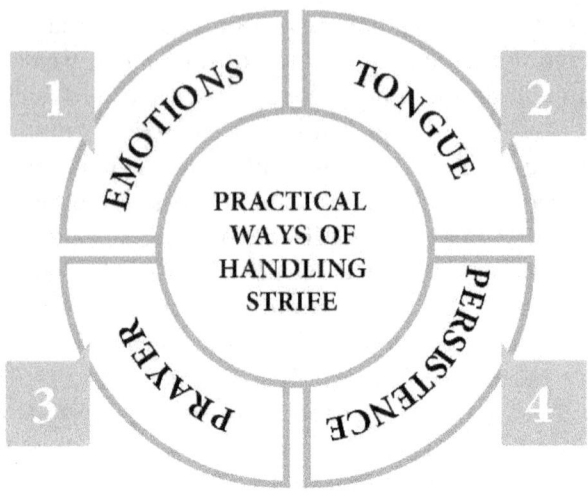

1. By controlling our emotions.
2. By controlling our tongue.
3. By handling it through prayer.
4. By handling it through persistence.

Let us examine these one by one.

BY CONTROLLING OUR EMOTIONS

When we get into an argument with our spouse, the first thing that happens is our emotions get charged. Until these are quietened down, we can never sit at the discussion table to settle the issue. Some guidelines to calm down and control our emotions are discussed here.

The first thing to do in an argument is to lower our voice. Psychologists tell us that when we are emotionally charged, our voices automatically rise in pitch and volume. This only serves to aggravate the situation and your spouse. In our experience, we have noticed it is generally the husbands who go ballistic in their decibels. If you are one of those, even if you happen to be the wife, please consciously reduce the volume to non-threatening levels.

To further calm your emotions, the best solution is for the one who is angrier and louder to leave the place for a brief period. Please inform your spouse that you need to leave the place for a short time to cool down and control yourself. We have found this to be generally acceptable by the other partner as it helps them to cool down too. Psychologists also suggest some practical ways to calm yourself down if you find yourself in a heated argument:

- Go outside and do some deep breathing exercises, or go for a short walk.
- Leave the place of conflict and go to a quiet place to listen to some soothing music.
- Start counting backwards from 100, this occupies your mind and does not allow it to ponder over the matter causing strife.
- Go and visit a friend or a relative you are fond of, for a short while. This is only to soothe you and not to share about the strife and gain their sympathy.
- If you have a mentor, call them, and pray with them.
- Never ever talk about this with anyone with an intention to gain support by belittling your spouse.
- If the strife threatens to escalate or is getting more difficult to solve, seek the help of a godly counsellor.
- Once both of you have calmed down, either get back to discussing the issue to find a solution or set a time to discuss later and settle it.
- In the meantime pray, seeking God's wisdom and His will in this situation.

BY CONTROLLING OUR TONGUE

From our counselling experience of the last 25 to 30 years, we have come to certain logical conclusions, that the way we use our tongue either ignites a strife, makes it worse, or helps solve it.

Proverbs 17:9 says, "Whoever would foster love covers over an offense, but whoever repeats the matter separates close friends." Two things are implied here. Firstly, spouses who habitually complain about their husbands or wives to other people make matters worse. As the famous saying goes, "never wash your dirty linen in public." Never speak about your problems with anyone except the Lord and godly counsellors from whom you regularly seek wisdom and solutions to your problems.

Secondly, we would like to advise husbands and more so their wives in the light of Proverbs 17:9, not to repeat something over and over with their spouse. There is a very apt word in the English language that describes this kind of behavior—"nagging." Nagging accomplishes nothing except infuriating your spouse, who often feels cornered and unable to handle it. Nagging can be like a buzzing mosquito in the middle of the night. We have a golden rule: "do not repeat a matter more than twice." Even if the matter is urgent and requires your spouse's attention, repeating it continuously will negate its importance. It is better to let them learn from experience and draw their own lessons and conclusions. Wisdom dictates that for a marriage to have any chance, every day at least six things should go unsaid.

Ten things the Bible says about handling our situations well using our tongues.

KEEP WORDS FEW (Prov 10:19)

SPEAK ACCEPTABLE WORDS (Prov 10:32)

ANSWER GENTLY (Prov 15:1)

WORDS MUST BRING HEALING (Prov 12:18)

BE QUICK TO HEAR, SLOW TO SPEAK/ANGER (Jas 1:19)

TRY UNDERSTANDING OTHERS (Prov 18:2)

KNOW THAT SWEET WORDS ARE PERSUASIVE (Prov 16:21, 23)

DO NOT BE REPETITIVE (Prov 17:9)

LET THE LORD BETHE JUDGE (Prov 21:2)

KNOW THAT YOU ARE ACCOUNTABLE FOR YOUR WORDS (Matt 12:36)

HANDLING MARITAL STRIFE THROUGH PRAYER

The third and the most important segment of handling marital strife is through prayer. James 1:5 says, "If any of you lacks wisdom, you should ask God, who gives generously to all without finding fault, and it will be given to you." In chapter 5:16, James tells us that the effective prayer of a righteous man can accomplish much. Putting these two verses together, we can understand that God is willing to generously give us His wisdom as we come to Him in fervent prayer, coupled with righteous living.

We have come across complicated cases of marital strife which elude understanding and solution. We fall back always on the time-tested method of praying, and encouraging the couple to pray and seek the Lord earnestly. As they go to the feet of the Lord, the couple finds their relationship mended, love restored, and their marriage kept intact—or made better than before. As said in Isaiah 9, our God is a "Wonderful Counsellor, the Everlasting Father and the Prince of Peace."

HANDLING MARITAL STRIFE THROUGH PERSISTENCE

Another practical way of handling strife is to be persistent in finding solutions and mending relationships. Some thoughts on finding solutions through persistence are listed here:

- Persist in knowing the truth and your spouse better.
- Persist in seeking God in the issue.
- Persist in gentle behavior and language.
- Persist in bringing the matter to its conclusion—even if it is later.
- Persist in seeking lessons that God is teaching you through the strife and apply them in your marriage.

Every strife teaches certain lessons prompting some lifestyle and behavioral changes. Such an attitude of recommitment becomes essential if we are to avoid unpleasantness in the future and put our marriages on a sound footing.

Accordingly, re-covenant to live by your marriage covenant:

> for better-for worse,
> for richer-for poorer,
> in sickness-in health,
> till death do us part.

That means renewing your covenant between God, yourself, and your spouse.

Live by God's Word and Spirit. Remember where the Spirit of God is there is peace (2 Cor 3:17). Meet each day for spending time in God's presence; live unselfishly; spend quality time together; accomplish the plans of God for your family and for God's kingdom together; please God in everything; settle your issues before sunset; forgive and never carry grudges forward; be open to counsel and change.

It is our prayer that these suggestions would help you handle strife positively and help you to rebuild your marriage on Christ the solid rock.

TEN: PARENTING

"We cannot always build the future for our youth, but we can build our youth for the future." Franklin D. Roosevelt

"The best thing a father can do for his children is to love their mother." John Wooden

Psalm 127:3 "Children are a heritage from the Lord, offspring a reward from him." Different people see children differently. Some see them as a reward, a gift from God, some as a natural consequence of procreation, yet others see them as obstacles in their pursuit of materialism. No matter how you see them, children are a result of God's instruction to Adam and Eve to multiply and fill the earth. As everything that God created is just right and perfect, even children are just right, perfect and part of God's Holy purpose.

There are two extremes in the way children are handled. While on one hand children are pampered, mollycoddled, received with thanksgiving, and brought up with great love, affection, care and protection, on the other hand they are abused, violated, maimed and treated as a commodity. Trafficking of children is a well-organized crime whether for the sake of using them for prostitution, pornography, or for fighting in wars. It is disgusting to see how low humanity has sunk in treating these precious gifts and bundles of joy that God gives us. Thank God that He is faithful and does not withdraw His promised blessings based on how humankind treats children.

Today, even functional and healthy families are being subjected to tremendous stress and unhealthy influences. In homes where children witness or experience abuse or violence, the result can be fear, frustration, anger, withdrawal. Children may even become abusers themselves, and in this way the cycle of abuse can continue through generations. Mental health experts speak of the increase in children suffering from depression or otherwise unable to cope with the difficulties of life. Those responsible for the criminal justice system are desperately looking for ways to prevent children entering that cycle of crime. Police, judges, or even governments are not able to do what parents have the privilege of doing. We must not sidestep our responsibility for the moral training and supervision of our children. We must, of course, teach them by rules and precepts—but most of all by example. We need to provide our children with homes which offer order and loving discipline. There is no substitute for the essential elements of parental and moral guidance: lots of time together, doing chores, playing and reading, or doing homework together. As parents we must take responsibility to patiently explain the way the world works and how people ought to live, as well as how they sometimes fall short.

The truth is that our children are the product of our own homes. They are primarily what we make them. Blaming others for the misdemeanors of our children is sheer stupidity. It is high time we realized that we have a large role in shaping our children into whatever they become.

Even in seemingly healthy families, you will find dysfunctional children; while on the other hand in dysfunctional families, at times healthy children emerge. It brings us to conclude that while there are no set formulae in handling children, neglecting to heed the Holy Scriptures will make sure that we fail as parents. The Bible has much to speak about parenting and we will try to examine and draw some lessons that could help us in this vital and God-given responsibility.

Primarily, parenting has certain pre-requisites, as found in Deuteronomy 6:4–8:

> Hear, O Israel: The Lord our God, the Lord is one. Love the Lord your God with all your heart and with all your soul and with all your strength. These commandments that I give you today are to be on your hearts. Impress them on your children. Talk about them when you sit at home and when you walk along the road, when you lie down and when you get up. Tie them as symbols on your hands and bind them on your foreheads.

While we do understand that God is instructing us to make sure that we teach His precepts to coming generations, we often forget that He is first asking us to love Him, bind His word on our heart and then teach our generation. So there are three principles that God is giving us through this passage in terms of impacting our generations to come.

PERSONAL DEVOTION (Deut 6:5)

God is asking us to examine our own life and walk with Him before we can teach others. So, let us as parents first learn to fear, obey and love the Lord and then we will be able to pass on our personal walk to our children.

FORMAL TEACHING (Deut 6:7a)

This simply means teaching Scripture at many levels, like in family devotions, Sunday schools, church services/seminars. Enabling a systematic learning of God's instructions is vital.

PERSONAL EXAMPLE (Deut 6:7b–8)

This simply means teaching through living the message. Teaching Scripture systematically to our children does not make a difference unless they see the Scriptures being lived out every day in our lives. The creed of modern parenting is, "do as I say, don't do as I do." This does not work, as our children can easily spot the dichotomy of our lives. Once they experience our dual standards, they close their minds to our instruction. Some wise preacher said that the principles of God are more easily *caught* by children than *taught* to them. This has much to do with the kind of parenting style you adopt, as we will discover in this chapter.

PARENTING STYLES: FIND YOURS!

Psychologists agree that there are four distinct parenting styles that we adopt in bringing up our children: the big boss parent; the puppet parent; the perennially busy parent; and the balanced parent.

Let us examine the pros and cons of each style and see where we fit in.

THE BIG BOSS PARENT

CHARACTERISTICS

Psychologists also call this style a "dictatorship" style. These parents are strong on discipline and are fond of keeping a tight control over their children. They have many unreasonable rules that are not open to discussion or negotiation. These parents are also low on warmth and affection, and do not provide enough emotional support to the child. They generally resort to shouting and threatening; they criticize freely, blame and might even beat their children. In some homes with this type of parents, we have come across both mental and physical abuse. These parents do not give freedom for the child's unique individuality to emerge – they impose their own ideas/opinions onto the child and expect them to comply without questioning. Anything short of this brings about severe repercussions.

CONSEQUENCES

Children growing up in such families develop low self-esteem and are unable to relate to their peers. Since these parents keep tight control and are unwilling to trust their children to do something on their own, these children lack initiative. They are just content to obey orders given by others and left on their own they generally become unproductive. As they begin to grow and discover other happy and healthy children and families, they draw parallels into their own existence and ultimately reject their parental value systems.

These children may also harbor a lot of anger which can manifest in unproductive, sometimes destructive ways. They also need to lean on someone as they have not been able to build up their own character and value systems, hence look to others for leadership.

THE PUPPET PARENT

CHARACTERISTICS

In this family, rules are non-existent, and mostly it is the children who control and manipulate their parents, who ignore misbehavior and are content to let someone else either control or discipline the children. For instance, if their children misbehave at home, they end up complaining either to their teacher at school or even Sunday school, expecting them to handle and address the issue of the disobedience or misbehavior which has its roots in the home.

While these parents are high on warmth, they are low on discipline, and may indulge the child too much. There are no clear rules for children, who need a structured environment, especially in their formative years. Children recognize the absence of courage or determination on the part of the parents to handle them and never see them as leaders in the home.

CONSEQUENCES

Children in such families often get confused because of the lack of strong leadership from their parents. Often, in such homes it is the children who rule and parents who obey! As a result, they are easily influenced by other children or any other influence strong enough to impact them, whether wrong or right! These children lack a clear sense of identity as there is no exemplary leadership at home that can give them anchorage. They grow up to be spoilt, self-indulgent, and are not open to change.

THE PERENNIALLY BUSY PARENT

CHARACTERISTICS

In this family, both parents are working, so they are financially and materially strong but do not have time for parenting. Some companies operate on shifts and sometimes both parents work on different shifts. When the father is coming in, the mother is going out for work or vice-versa. The only time they meet is on a weekend, when there are too many things to do on the home front and too little time to complete them. By the time they are through with housework it is already a new week and this vicious cycle goes on and on. Children in such homes are generally brought up by baby sitters and so pick up the value systems of the babysitters rather than the parents. There was a shocking incident in India of such a couple who left their infant daughter with a babysitter. One day they bumped into a woman begging on the streets with a small baby in her arms. To their horror they discovered that baby was their own daughter who was left with the baby sitter! The baby sitter was hiring out their toddler to the beggars for money.

These busy parents, even when they come home, bring a part of the office along with them and work from home. And even if they have some time for themselves, their minds are pre-occupied. Even if some of them succeed in making tons of money, live in palatial homes, and have holidays in exotic foreign locations, they remain emotionally depleted, physically tired, and perennially dissatisfied. They lack the wisdom to exit this rollercoaster that generally becomes a monster gobbling up their family.

As these parents are unable to spend time with their children they live with massive guilt. On one hand, they know that they need to spend more time with their children but on the other hand, they have gotten themselves deeply enmeshed with the desire to succeed, to make it big in the world and be recognized for their success. This is a web that is very difficult to extricate oneself from. As they feel helpless to tear away from their careers, they try to compensate for their absence by indulging their children and spending a lot of money instead of time. The children are pampered with costly toys; every desire of their children is lavishly met and they succeed in quelling their children's cry for attention by smothering them with gifts.

Another fallout of being busy is their inability to keep up their promises to the children. The children might want to visit the zoo on a weekend, and the parents readily agree. But something pressing comes up and the parents let their children down by not taking them to the zoo. On the other hand, sometimes, when the time comes to keep the promise, they are extremely tired and the very thought of going out and doing something with the children is unwelcome. Again and again their promises are broken.

CONSEQUENCES

The first fallout is that the children begin to feel they are unwanted and unloved. Children are very perceptive and they can easily see that the parents are prioritizing their jobs over them. The second fallout is that children stop trusting their parents because they have been repeatedly let down. They begin to reconcile themselves to the fact that they must fend for themselves.

As they feel unloved, it often happens that they begin to seek love elsewhere. The vacuum of love left by the parents is filled by either someone else or by something else. Either they fall into the trap of unhealthy relationships or veer off into addictions. Children of these families develop low self-esteem as they feel they do not matter in their parents' scheme of things, or not worthy of love.

Often in seminars, some of the dear ladies very apologetically introduce themselves as homemakers. We feel that the most important calling of God for women is to be wives to their husbands and mothers to their children, even if it means sacrificing their careers for the sake of the family. The argument most often heard from working mothers is that they are trying to provide a better life for their children. This is a dichotomy. The "better life" that they think they can give their children by earning more is denied to them by their absence. We hope that the Lord would speak to many busy parents so that they see the importance of spending as much time with their precious children before they leave home, perhaps never to return.

THE BALANCED PARENT

CHARACTERISTICS

Psychologists often refer to these parents as the parent-coach combination. These parents provide a happy home for their children. By this we do not mean that there are no troubles or issues at home. Every home has its own specific turbulence, but happy homes are not rocked by the turbulence, rather it strengthens them. These parents make sure that they spend a lot of time with their children. They are self-disciplined, and keep their promises at all costs, except in the rarest of cases. Their parenting style is high on warmth, but is also balanced by a good level of discipline. They teach primarily by setting an example and lead from the front. They encourage children to be independent, confident individuals who can make sound decisions.

Being coach-parents involves a lot of sacrifice in terms of energy, lost income, lost career opportunities, and emotional drain. But this adds to the investment into their children, by producing happiness, love, confidence, and good health too.

CONSEQUENCES

As the children watch the self-discipline of their parents, they too learn to be disciplined. As the parents are basically coaches, teaching life, the children learn to respect their limits and understand their limitations as well. These children also learn from their mistakes and develop a positive attitude towards life; they develop good self-esteem and are confident. This style of parenting pays rich dividends especially as it develops healthy communication between family members. Children are encouraged to speak their mind and at times the children can suggest changes at home to their parents. As a result, the children can relate better to their parents and treat them as their confidantes. Such a parenting style fosters not only a healthy bond between parents and children but also develops a sense of great trust.

PARENTS MUST PROVIDE INPUTS FOR A BALANCED GROWTH

One of the best examples of balanced growth is found in the life of Jesus:

> And Jesus grew in wisdom and stature, and in favor with God and man. (Luke 2:52)

There are seven areas of life that need to be developed so that our children grow up to be mature, godly, and productive people making a difference for the kingdom of God. We will deal with them one by one.

PHYSICAL

CREATED IN GOD'S IMAGE (Gen 1:27)

Our children need to understand that they are created in the image of God. This is vital to understanding the basic questions of life, like where do we come from? Why do we exist? Where are we heading? And finally, what is the purpose of life? Only as they begin to see that they are made in God's image, can they understand that they have been created by him for a specific purpose (see Eph 2:10).

EVERY CHILD IS SPECIAL (Ps 139:13–16)

> For you created my inmost being; you knit me together in my mother's womb. I praise you because I am fearfully and wonderfully made; your works are wonderful, I know that full well. My frame was not hidden from you when I was made in the secret place, when I was woven together in the depths of the earth. Your eyes saw my unformed body; all the days ordained for me were written in your book before one of them came to be.

Our children also need to understand that each of them is very special. God has planned him or her even before time began, even the minutest details including the length of our life and the specific physical features. Only after having conceived each one of us with great love, did He place us in our mother's womb after determining the era of our birth, with a clear plan to use us in that timeframe for His purposes. This is such an eye-opener, and we have seen children becoming wide eyed on having understood the awesomeness of their creation process. This becomes the benchmark on which their self-esteem develops which is not based on success or possessions, but on the foundational faith in a great God, who has fashioned them meticulously for His great purposes.

When we understand that every child is unique and perfect in his or her creation by a perfect God, we will begin to appreciate the fact that negatively comparing them to other children is to tell God that He has somewhere messed up. This not only shows our inadequate understanding of God's ways, but also discourages and demoralizes our children.

INTELLECTUAL

TEACH THEM THE FEAR OF THE LORD

> The fear of the Lord is the beginning of *knowledge*. (Prov 1:7)

> The fear of the Lord is the beginning of *wisdom*. (Prov 9:10)

Children should understand that everything in life starts with God, is sustained by God and ends with God. Fearing God is paramount, because it is the fear of God that gives us knowledge, makes us wise, keeps us away from evil, prolongs life and gives us confidence. All these and more can be found in the book of Proverbs and elsewhere in the Holy Scriptures. This fear is not a fear of punishment or fear of something dreadful, but this is a holy fear born out of the knowledge of who God is and who we are.

DO NOT PUSH THEM BEYOND THEIR CAPABILITY

It is very important to understand our children thoroughly, especially their limitations. Every individual has a particular personality and specific gifts given by God. Many times, we find parents forcing their children into submission so that they can achieve something that actually the parents themselves desire. For instance, a child may not be mathematically gifted and does not like mathematics. It would be meaningless to badger him or her to achieve top scores in this subject. This only demoralizes the child and makes him hate the subject. This also gives rise to much frustration in the child and the parents as well. Recognize the special abilities of your children and recognize to what limit they can be pushed without frustrating them. This will make both children and parents confident, content, and happy.

HELP THEM DO THEIR BEST FOR THE LORD

While pushing them beyond their capability can be counter-productive, parents also need to ensure that the maximum potential of the child is being utilized. The secret is to understand the threshold potential of your child and the limit beyond which it can become counter- productive. At the same time some children are lazy by nature and naturally averse to hard work. This needs to be rectified through counselling, discipline and the use of suitable rewards as well. The pivotal point is to help the child realize that no matter what he or she does, they have to do it to the best of their ability and as unto the Lord (Col 3:23).

BE AWARE OF WHAT IS BEING TAUGHT TO THEM

Parents need to be extra careful about what is being taught to our children in schools, colleges, and universities, because there are subtle philosophies and detrimental worldviews that are woven into their curriculum. Sometimes their teachers and professors can take liberties by pushing their own beliefs into the classrooms. Our impressionable children soak in such warped teachings which can thoroughly confuse their minds. So please make sure that you keep an eye on not only the official curriculum but also the bias of teachers/professors in the classrooms.

RELATIONAL

TEACH THEM TO HONOR THEIR PARENTS

> Honor your father and your mother, so that you may live long in the land the Lord your God is giving you. (Exod 20:12)

> Children, obey your parents in the Lord, for this is right. (Eph 6:1)

Right from the beginning, children should be taught to honor their parents. While treating them as equals when they are grown up is important, this relationship must still be rooted in honor. These days we hear constant complaints from parents that their children do not respect them. Honor does not develop overnight and you cannot demand honor. Honor must be inculcated from their infancy and must be embedded in their hearts and minds not only for the Lord, but for parents as well.

Honor is earned and built-in over a lifetime but can be shattered in an instant, especially if the child finds a dichotomy or duality in the parent's life. We see many small children trying to beat their parents when they are upset and the parents laugh over it finding it amusing. This reinforces the attitude in the child's mind that the parents find it recreational when they are subjected to the child's tantrum. This should be discouraged at all cost as it gives a wrong signal to the child. The child should also learn to relate to other people, take criticism, handle difficult people, and even handle bullies at times in the schools or colleges, as life is all about handling relationships. They should also learn to take defeats graciously and rejoice at the success of others. If parents fail to teach these important facets of relationships, children will become selfish, surly, and difficult to get along with.

SPEND TIME TOGETHER

Many parents do not understand the value of time spent with children. Children need a lot of parental time. The more the better. Parents need to prioritize their activities to make sure they allocate sufficient time to spend with their children, for academic, spiritual and emotional input.

It is not just the time spent at home, but time spent in fun activities as well. As a family we would always make time at least on some weekends and holidays to either head out towards a zoo or a park where we would spend a whole day lazing around, watching animals or birds, walking together, playing together and laughing together. We would take board games along like Ludo or Snakes & Ladders and have great fun kidding each other. Irwin would love to cheat occasionally and rest of the family would gang up against him. It was such great fun and at the end of the day, left us with a tremendous sense of satisfaction and improved relationships. Please make sure to understand that it is not just the family that prays together, but also plays and laughs together that stays together. And that means sacrificing something to make time for the family.

GET TO KNOW THEIR FRIENDS

Parents must make sure that their children are encouraged to bring their friends home and also to find out as much as possible about their friends at school or college. Proverbs 13:20 says, "Walk with the wise and become wise, for a companion of fools suffers harm." Someone has made a very pertinent observation, "Show me your friends and I will tell you who you are." Parents should understand that peer pressure is real and is instrumental in many ways in shaping our children. We do not have to be critical about our children's friends, but we can definitely guide them into good relationships and be adequately warned in advance of some undesirable elements that can befriend our children.

COMMUNICATION

SPEAK AND LISTEN TO THEM

Parents and children must understand the value of open communication at home. Make sure that you assign some time each day just to listen to them. Children have much to share, although parents might just think that it is unimportant and childish, yet these small and unimportant things are extremely important to children. So make sure you listen to them and respond suitably and sympathetically. Never use words like "shut up," "stupid," "I am not bothered," "you never understand," "I give up on you," "you will never succeed," "why can't you be like them?" "do not come back home unless you come first in class," "you are just plain lazy," "I am sick of you," "you cannot seem to do anything well," and so on and so forth. This kind of language never ever accomplishes anything except discouraging our children and making them dislike parents.

On the other hand, your speech must be encouraging, challenging and positive, having a pepping effect on the children. Please never give up on them. You never know what God can make of them when He is given the freedom to work on them and change them. This also means spending much time in prayer for them and with them.

SPIRITUAL

TEACH SCRIPTURE TO YOUR CHILDREN AT HOME

We have already dealt with this at length. Now it is sufficient to say that the home plays an important part in the teaching of Scripture to our children.

FAMILY DEVOTION

This aspect also has been exhaustively dealt with in our chapter on family devotions. Again, we want to reiterate, that this is essential if we want to embed a spiritual compass in the hearts of our children for a lifetime.

ATTEND SUNDAY SCHOOL

Make sure that your children attend a good and lively Sunday school. This is one place where you have systematic and concentrated teaching of God's Word. It also has a lively fellowship and worship time that develops healthy relationships with other Christian children. Sunday schools also have annual camps, Vacation Bible Schools etc. where basic theological education is imparted in a very simple and palatable fashion including studying about the missionary heroes of the church. They also have healthy competitions for singing, Scripture memory, etc. that spur our children to do better in their spiritual life. So make sure that Sunday school is an integral part of the spiritual upbringing of your children.

ATTENDING CHURCH

> And let us consider how we may spur one another on toward love and good deeds, not giving up meeting together, as some are in the habit of doing, but encouraging one another—and all the more as you see the Day approaching. (Heb 10:24–25)

Please make sure that your children understand the importance of the church in the plan of God for mankind. Many of us think that the church exists only for hatching, matching, and dispatching. Openly criticizing the church and pastor in front of the children should be avoided, rather speak well of them, no matter what. Ensure that you come to the church on time every Sunday. Children must understand that we go to church to worship, to honor God and to spend time with Him personally, for fellowship and to receive godly teaching.

DISCIPLINE

Proverbs 25:28 admonishes us, "Like a city whose walls are broken through is a person who lacks self-control." Discipline is essential to produce healthy and mature persons for the kingdom of God. The foundations of this are laid right in the early stages of the growth of our children.

Discipline is vital in areas like punctuality, healthy habits, tempered speech, staying away from excesses and the discipline of making sure that we keep our bodies and minds healthy. Discipline is more easily caught than taught. This means parents must lead from front and teach by example. Some time ago, a family came for counselling after the father and his teenage son had a severe argument. The father had simply asked the son to keep his room neat. The son just replied, "You do it first in your room and then come and tell me!" While the son cannot be justified in his response, we need to understand that we lose our authority to instruct our children when we ourselves do not adhere to it.

Children must also be taught the importance and value of having a quiet time every morning, or at least sometime during the day without fail. They must learn to quieten their hearts, and listen to the voice of God. This habit is invaluable and will stay with them all their lives.

We have had many arguments with our children about the amount of time that they spend watching television. We had made certain rules, such as the television will not be switched on at all in the morning. We also followed a rule that the TV would not be switched on while the children were studying. It is a sacrifice that parents must make to ensure the television does not become a stumbling block for our children. We also were very careful to ensure what our children could watch. There were some programs that we thought were unhealthy and we had to dialogue with our children explaining why they could not see these programs.

Displaying a dictatorial attitude will not help at home. The secret is to communicate and have a dialogue on thorny issues and if you have been setting an example to your children and your reasons are good enough, there is no way your children will disobey you or find fault with you. Some parents believe that keeping a television at home is detrimental. While we will not argue with this, one possibility is that kids end up watching television in their friend's homes where parents cannot exercise any control over what they see. We personally feel it is better to have a TV at home and make certain rules so that unhealthy programs are avoided. This enables us to limit the time our children spend watching television.

Parents must make sure that their children keep good personal hygiene and realize the value of cleanliness at home. Teach them not to litter, to pick up their toys and other things and put them back in their place. Children should also be taught to make their beds every morning after they wake up, folding clothes after using them and keeping bathrooms clean. Remember that this is a training ground for their future lives and this will go a long way in ensuring that your children's homes will also be always neat and clean in future.

Teaching table manners is also equally important. These days children are addicted to junk food. While we do understand that children love fast food, their intake should be limited explaining to them the dangers of obesity and the risk of heart disease and diabetes. Remember if you have maintained the coach/friend parenting style, your children will be more than willing to listen and obey. Children should also be taught to finish the food on their plate and not waste food by throwing it away.

LIFESTYLE

> Start children off on the way they should go, and even when they are old they will not turn from it. (Prov 22:6)

This verse is a firm reminder to parents to be consistent in the training of their children so that when they become adults they will live by it. It is the development of a lifestyle, from which our children will not depart lifelong.

Apart from the above seven aspects that go into making a lifestyle, there are four more areas that need to be included in this process of raising balanced children.

BE A ROLE MODEL

> Because we loved you so much, we were delighted to share with you not only the gospel of God but our lives as well. (1 Thess 2:8)

Paul is telling the church in Thessalonica that he was pleased not only to impart the gospel to them but his own life as well. As we begin to invest our lives in our precious children, they not only see us as role models but also learn to become role models themselves. It just means living out our message in actual life.

TEACH THEM TO HANDLE MONEY

Learning to handle money can be a great blessing later in the lives of our children. Firstly they must recognize that money is a resource that is given into our hands by God and as His stewards we are accountable to God for how we use it. The next thing is that while God is the master of everything, he has instructed us to honor Him with a tenth of all he has given us. It belongs to him! We show our gratitude when we give over and above the tenth that we are already instructed to give.

> Honor the Lord with your wealth, with the firstfruits of all your crops; then your barns will be filled to overflowing, and your vats will brim over with new wine. (Prov 3:9–10)

God should be first in everything; we use our gifts to bring Him glory. Both our children learned to tithe from their pocket money. They willingly gave away their first earnings completely to God; it gave them such a sense of joy and fulfillment. Children should also learn to ask God for their needs, and the fulfillment of their desires. Everything must point to their heavenly Father. Children should be taught elementary budgeting. Teach them not to indulge in impulsive spending and not to spend beyond what they have. They must also learn the value of saving and the importance of sharing, making them generous and unselfish.

BE CONTENT AND GRATEFUL TO THE LORD

This is one of the most important lessons in financial management to teach our children. Today's society is hung up on comparisons and one-upmanship, where self-image and self-respect becomes based on material possessions: the house we live in, the car we drive, or the company we keep. Our children must recognize this as hollow, and understand that "Better the little that the righteous have than the wealth of many wicked" (Ps 37:16). They should also understand the truth of 1 Tim 6:6, "godliness with contentment is great gain." They should also embrace the truth of Phil 4:19 "And my God will meet all your needs according to the riches of his glory in Christ Jesus." As we have already said, these things must be demonstrated to them through our own lives otherwise it will not make any sense to them.

ALLOW THEM TO MAKE DECISIONS

Decision-making is an integral and important aspect of our lives. Our children—if they are to grow up as confident adults, making good life-choices—need to be taught to make decisions early on in life. There is always a possibility that they will make mistakes. Instead of berating them, we can use their mistakes to teach them vital life lessons. Start when they are small, like allowing them to choose their own colors (even if you thoroughly disagree) in clothing, allowing them to buy small things with their pocket money without really demanding an account or supervising how they spend their pocket money. This helps them to understand that they are trusted, and that their opinion is valued by their parents, which also leads to accountability. Even in family matters, you will be surprised how often children show great sagacity in understanding complex issues. Allow them to participate in family discussions and allow them to give their opinions and if they are good, accept them, commending them for their wisdom.

When both our children were very small we asked our mentors Warren and Ruth Myers to give us some insight into parenting and we remember they gave us four simple instructions, saying that children need to be brought up by: MUCH prayer, MUCH patience, MUCH example, and MUCH love. These four instructions adequately sum up all that is said above.

THE ART OF DISCIPLINING CHILDREN

"True freedom is impossible without a mind made free by discipline." Mortimer J. Adler. *"If we don't shape our kids, they will be shaped by outside forces that don't care what shape our kids are in."* Dr. Louise Hart. *"An infallible way to make your child miserable is to satisfy all his demands."* Henry Home

> A rod and a reprimand impart wisdom, but a child left undisciplined disgraces its mother. (Prov 29:15)

LESSONS FROM THE TREE ON OUR HIGHWAY

We often travel on our local highway in India. Along the way, a large tree caught our attention which you can see in the picture. It had leant so far away from the perpendicular onto the highway that it was obstructing the traffic and had to be chopped down. God taught us some important lessons through observing this tree.

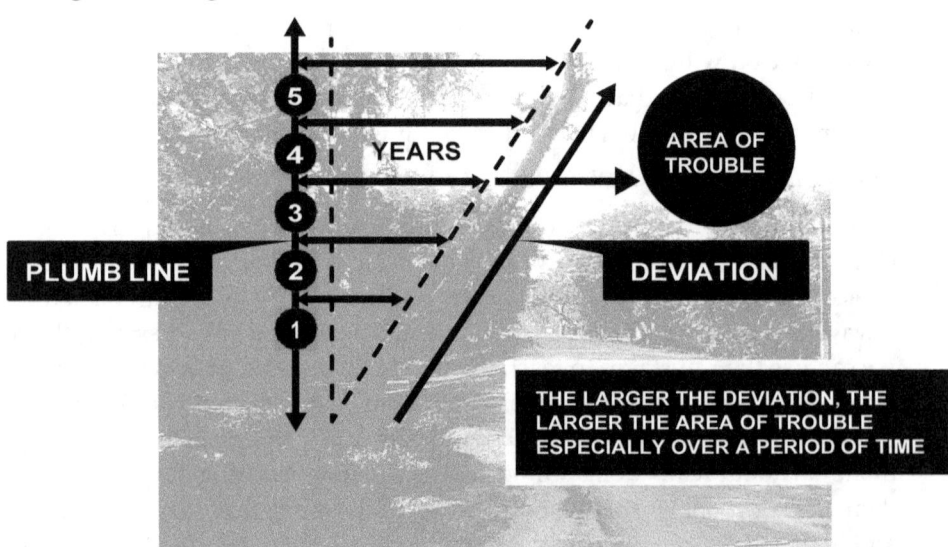

The deviation from the perpendicular would have taken about five years. Had a caretaker been there and observed it growing crooked when it was a small shoot, he would have stuck a perpendicular stick in the ground next to it and tied the young sapling to this stick. This would have helped the tree to grow straight. Since the support was not given and the shoot not straightened, it became completely crooked. We can draw lessons from this tree in bringing up our children:

A child left to itself (like the tree) will tend to deviate from the right way. If we fail to correct a child over a period, he/she will (like the tree) completely lean away from the vertical. Once a tree matures, it is impossible to bring it back to the vertical, and has to be cut down. We must not leave it too late to correct our children. Like trees, children are much easier to correct the tree in the initial stages of growth.

No wonder the Bible says in Proverbs 22:16, "Train up a child in the way he should go, and when he is old he will not depart from it." Training is not just teaching, but inculcating discipline and obedience. Such training demands and involves diligence, sacrifice, and consistency.

> Children are a heritage from the Lord, offspring a reward from him. Like arrows in the hands of a warrior are children born in one's youth. (Ps 127:3–4)

The verses in Psalm 127 tell us that children are a gift/reward. Children are God's gift and should be handled with great love, gratitude, and responsibility. Children are God's heritage. A heritage is something very precious passed down through generations. We are expected to treat children like a great honor that has been bestowed upon us by God. As a heritage: God expects us to cherish, guard and protect our children from all hazards and dangers.

Furthermore, God says children are like arrows given by God for us to fight life's battles. They are to be available and willing tools "in our hands" (guided and trained by us). They must be effective, as the outcome of the battle will depend on them. They have to be always in a state of readiness.

IF ARROWS ARE TO BE EFFECTIVE THEY MUST BE STRAIGHT

We had opportunity to visit some tribal areas of India, where they still hunt with their bows and arrows. It is very interesting to see the amount of time they spend on preparing every bow and arrow. Each arrow is examined meticulously and if necessary straightened over fire to make it pliable to remove any minor bends. A bent arrow cannot hit its designated target. If children are to be like arrows, effective, making a difference between victory and defeat, they must be straight, to be able to hit the bull's eye. We believe you can keep your children effective by the constant "straightening" of proper and regular discipline.

'STRAIGHT' THEN MEANS TO DISCIPLINE OUR CHILDREN TO REMOVE 'BENDS' & 'FLAWS'

> And have you completely forgotten this word of encouragement that addresses you as a father addresses his son? It says, "My son, do not make light of the Lord's discipline, and do not lose heart when he rebukes you, because the Lord disciplines the one he loves, and he chastens everyone he accepts as his son." Endure hardship as discipline; God is treating you as his children. For what children are not disciplined by their father? If you are not disciplined—and everyone undergoes discipline—then you are not legitimate, not true sons and daughters at all. Moreover, we have all had human fathers who disciplined us and we respected them for it. How much more should we submit to the Father of spirits and live! They disciplined us for a little while as they thought best; but God disciplines us for our good, in order that we may share in his holiness. No discipline seems pleasant at the time, but painful. Later on, however, it produces a harvest of righteousness and peace for those who have been trained by it. (Heb 12:5–11)

Discipline prepares children not only for life but for eternity too. But remember that discipline must always be fair (otherwise, it can be abusive). It must uphold the child's dignity and not be degrading. Discipline is meant to be shaping, not crushing. The amount or the kind of punishment we choose to impose must seem fair not only to us but also to the child. The child should not get a sense of being victimized. He or she should rather agree, although grudgingly, that the punishment was quite fair.

For instance, if the infringement is minor, like viewing the television over the allocated time, it would be extremely unfair to discipline severely. Discipline must always be balanced. Never let your personal frustration or anger get the better of you in this area. Discipline should be dispassionate, balanced, and prayerful. Although smacking is allowed in some countries, it is a last resort. The child can be controlled by just the tone of voice or curtailing his/her freedom in certain areas.

The freedom to discipline does not give us the freedom to degrade, berate, or insult the dignity of the child. At times, parents punish children publicly, shouting at them or running them down in front of their friends. This shames them; they lose the respect of their friends and their self-respect too.

Even a small child has his or her own personality and dignity. Degrading the child's dignity will mar their self-respect and scar them for a lifetime. That is definitely not the intention in disciplining the child. The objective is to train, improve and establish children on solid foundational principles that will help them lead effective and fruitful lives.

Parents should learn to distinguish between natural childishness and willful disobedience. Please remember children will be children, and we should not force them to become adults overnight. Respect their growing process which involves a little mischief as well. We should learn to tolerate some amount of harmless mischief. Please keep in mind that we are not bringing up fine-tuned robots but well-adjusted human beings.

We have heard of parents crushing their children by using belts to spank them violently. We even heard of a father who slapped his son so hard, that he lost his hearing in one ear. These are typical cases of child abuse! Such cases certainly merit the intervention of the authorities! Instead of following such awful examples, we will help you understand the practical dynamics of good discipline.

PRACTICAL DYNAMICS OF GOOD DISCIPLINE

START EARLY, BE FIRM, SAY "NO"

There are two views on this. Some parents think children can be disciplined only after they are three or four years old and their natural attitudes should not be curbed. Others teach their children much younger that "yes" means "yes" and "no" means "no." Psychologists say that by the time a child is three years old, his or her emotional patterns are almost set for a lifetime not counting the intervention and grace of God. Even a baby begins to understand basic permissible and non-permissible attitudes. The Bible tells us through Romans 2:15 that people show the work of the Law written in their hearts, their conscience bearing witness and their thoughts alternately accusing or else defending them. It also says that God has placed a moral compass called "conscience" within our hearts which accuses or defends us. Most psychologists agree that a small baby, from the time he or she starts to recognize people and things, can also recognize the word "no" reinforced by suitable supplementary actions. As the child begins to understand that this word is being used to stop him or her from doing something, the conscience gets sharpened to understand actions that are allowed or prohibited. So, we tell young couples to start the discipline of their child soon after the child can understand the meaning and value of the word "no."

Most of the time it is the parents who should be blamed for not instilling discipline, and thereby the right behavior in a baby. Every couple loves their baby and sometimes, as the baby indulges in repetitive tantrums they find it rather amusing, and not something that needs to be corrected. Please remember that childhood tantrums can lead to disobedience and sulking as they grow up. Small brats eventually become adult brats if their willful disobedience and penchant to have their own way is not curbed and addressed right from the beginning.

Parents should be firm. Children know how to manipulate their parents. Never change a "no" to a "yes," because of the manipulation of the child, either through tantrums or through constant cajoling. The child should know that once the parent says "no," it will always remain so (except in exceptional circumstances). The Scripture warns us that a child who has his way will bring shame on their parents.

STAY TOGETHER / STAY BALANCED

Yet another ploy of children is to manipulate parents and pit them against each other. For example, a child wanting to stay out late in the evening might approach the mother knowing that she is kindhearted, and take her permission. In the evening, the father does not find the child home, and questions the mother, to realize that permission has been granted to come late, even though he had already said "no." This not only angers him but drives a wedge between the parents. Please make sure that in discipline, both the parents are on the same page and that no decisions are taken by either of them without consulting the other. Please also make sure that if one parent has decided, the other spouse too stands by it.

Discipline is a consultative process and there must be a balance struck in every decision. It usually happens that one parent is a disciplinarian, whereas the other is easy-going. Each must balance the other. The secret is to avoid excesses in discipline that could frustrate the child, and at the same time reassure him/her that the parents are reasonable and caring and the only reason they could be saying "no" is because they are concerned about his/her safety and well-being.

BE CONSISTENT

We will illustrate this with an example. A school-going child misbehaves by answering back to his/her mother. When the father comes home in the evening, the mother tells him about it. The offence is minor, so it can be handled with a very simple session of counselling and warning. The father does just that, and the matter is settled. One week later, the same scenario is repeated. However, on that particular day the father comes very late from work and is extremely tired. On this occasion he just ignores the misdemeanor. Some weeks later it is repeated again, but on that particular day the father comes home after having a big argument with his boss and is irritable and touchy. When he comes home, and on being apprised of what had transpired, he shouts at the child or even smacks them.

Now, for the same identical misdemeanor, one day there was counselling and warning, yet on another day it was ignored, and yet on another day it was handled with anger! This just confuses the child, who wonders why for the same misdemeanor there have been three different responses from his or her father. Hence, being consistent is important. Rules have to be laid down beforehand. Before a child can be punished, he or she should be told about the rules of the home. Otherwise it would not be reasonable for us to mete out punishment.

Explain violation of rules and consequences. Children must know the reason for the rules, and the consequences when they break them. When the child knows this, punishment that follows would be understood by the child thereby removing the possibility of resentment. Also, explaining the consequences of violating the home rules can act as a deterrent for the children.

DISCIPLINE PRIVATELY

Children are very sensitive. As we have already said, they feel extremely bad if they are disciplined/told-off before their peers or even their own siblings. It also builds up resentment in the child against you for belittling them before others. You may not notice, but children can remember these little things for a long time and hold them against you. Much later in life you will find these little walls standing between you and your child preventing you from enjoying a great relationship.

CREATIVE WAYS OF DISCIPLINE

For parents who wish to avoid physical punishment (which, in any case, has limitations), there are other creative ways of disciplining children, especially as they are already on the road to maturity. We have used these three creative ways of discipline in our own home and found them to be very effective.

NATURAL AND LOGICAL CONSEQUENCES

Sometimes it is fine to let the child make a mistake (obviously not serious ones that can have tragic consequences) and then learn from the consequences that follow it. To give you an example: our younger daughter Preeti was very playful and despite being repeatedly reminded, she would forget her packed lunch while leaving for school. Vijaya would discover this after she left for school and you can understand a mother's heart! She would feel very sorry for Preeti. So on the way to work, she would take the lunch and ask the school office to give the lunch box to Preeti. This would happen quite often and because Preeti knew that somehow her mother would feel sorry for her and bring her lunch without fail, she would not take our instructions seriously. Finally, Vijaya realized that she was perhaps making Preeti careless. The next time Preeti forgot her lunch, we decided not to go to the school to hand it over, although this was a painful decision and we did realize that Preeti would have to stay hungry.

That evening Preeti came home very angry, and she said "do you know I forgot my lunch and had to stay hungry today? How come you did not bring it to the school?" Vijaya very calmly replied, "Yes of course, we did notice that you forgot to take your lunch, but we also realized that you have not been taking our repeated instructions seriously. So we purposely did not bring it, and hence-forward if you forget it again, you will have to stay hungry!" Preeti found it very difficult to believe that her mother was cruel enough to let her daughter stay hungry, but from that day onwards she never forgot her lunch! You see sometimes the learning that we get from our mistakes is more powerful than we learn from being warned about it. Nothing educates us as much as a shock!

WITHHOLDING PRIVILEGES

We had an ongoing battle with our teenage children to make sure that their room was kept neat and clean. Every time we admonished them sternly, the room would become spick and span, but within a few days the mess would return. We got sick of telling them and finally Vijaya told them something that stunned them! Both our daughters were very fond of attending the Methodist Youth Fellowship that would be held in our church every Saturday afternoon. They would miss anything but this fellowship. Vijaya made a rule that she would come and inspect their room at least every alternate day and if it was not found clean, they would lose the privilege of attending the fellowship on Saturday. You must have guessed, they took great care from that day onwards to make sure that their room was in order.

GIVE ADDITIONAL TASKS

Another way of disciplining them at home is to give them additional tasks. In our home, both Sruti and Preeti were assigned some jobs daily. For instance, the house had to be vacuumed once a week, the dog given a bath once a month, one of them had to make tea for us every day, and help in table-setting. In case we found them slipping up or cutting corners, Vijaya would give them extra tasks like cleaning the wash basins, dusting the grills etc. which was unpleasant to both of them. This encouraged them to become more diligent in the duties already allocated to them.

Although we have just listed three creative ways of discipline, we are sure you can find many more ways to encourage the children into changing their behavior and becoming diligent.

IF ARROWS ARE TO BE EFFECTIVE, THEY MUST BE SHARP

No matter how straight the arrows are, if they are blunt and dull they cannot accomplish the purpose for which they are created. In this context, "straight" means disciplined, and "sharp" means fully trained. Discipline without sharpening is an incomplete task in bringing a child to maturity.

WHY TRAIN? (Prov 22:6; 29:15)

A person is more malleable and teachable early in life. If that window of opportunity is grasped and the child is taught continuously at every stage of growth, it would ensure the strongest possible foundation, ensuring that the child reaching adulthood will never deviate from the teaching and training received.

WHAT IS TRAINING? (2 Tim 2:15, 3:16–17)

Training is to align oneself to God, His Word, and His Holy Spirit in moving a child towards maturity: spiritual, mental, emotional, and physical. This is to ensure that the child becomes adequately equipped for every good work and an effective tool in the hands of God.

HOW TO TRAIN? (Ps 139:13–16)

Teach them to know their uniqueness. Parents must recognize that every child is unique and is endowed with specific gifts from the Lord for His special purposes. So our job is to bring out and polish the gifts God has given our children. We must:

Teach them to obey God

> Keep this Book of the Law always on your lips; meditate on it day and night, so that you may be careful to do everything written in it. Then you will be prosperous and successful. (Josh 1:8)

Teach them to give themselves wholeheartedly to God

> Therefore, I urge you, brothers and sisters, in view of God's mercy, to offer your bodies as a living sacrifice, holy and pleasing to God — this is your true and proper worship. (Rom 12:1)

Our children must learn before anything else, to obey God and to understand the importance of laying themselves on the altar of God as a living sacrifice. That means they must be able to turn away from the world and towards the Lord.

Teach them to live for others

> In the midst of a very severe trial, their overflowing joy and their extreme poverty welled up in rich generosity. (2 Cor 8:2)

The Macedonian church is one of the finest examples of how they expressed the abundance of their joy, that although there was deep poverty in the church, they still gave liberally and sacrificially. In today's times the mantra of modern living is to be self-serving, and this can be contagious. Generosity is one of the most important Christian virtues that must be recognized and practiced by our children.

Teach them to tell others about Jesus

> Therefore go and make disciples of all nations, baptizing them in the name of the Father and of the Son and of the Holy Spirit, and teaching them to obey everything I have commanded you. And surely I am with you always, to the very end of the age. (Matt 28:19–20)

Our children must understand the mandate that Jesus gave each one of us to tell others about Him. This should be taught right from the beginning, by including our neighbors, colleagues, and friends in our daily prayers for their salvation. As we parents demonstrate evangelism in our everyday lives whether through preaching, or through friendships, it imprints the urgency and importance of reaching out to others. It must become an important part of our lifestyles which our children must learn to emulate.

IF ARROWS ARE TO BE EFFECTIVE, THEY MUST BE POINTED IN THE RIGHT DIRECTION AND AT THE RIGHT TARGET

Arrows have a purpose, and not designed to be in the quiver always. The purposeless life is a meaningless life. Life is all about purpose, priorities, and choices. Our children, right from the beginning, must learn the priorities of life and make their choices. Friends, what are the goals and value systems that your children will imbibe from you? Children learn from what they see and not hear. You might be teaching them the Scriptures regularly, but if you do not live by them yourselves, your teaching will be in vain. Please make sure that your own priorities are right so that they will be replicated in the lives of your children.

Arrows are meant to hit a designated target. It is all about the right goals. What are some of the goals that you could designate for your children? You can be certain that if you do not help them find the right goal, they will never hit the bull's eye!

ARROWS MUST BE 'PREPARED' WHEN THEY ARE THE CHILDREN OF OUR YOUTH (Ps 127:4)

God clearly tells us we must train our children from their infancy, when we parents are still young. This training continues each passing year. Our children will either be a cause for us to feel elated or ashamed later in life (Ps 127:5–6). Children become what we make them. Ultimately when we are old, they will either bring us joy or they will bring sorrow, either they can bring us shame or they can make us proud; they can either be a curse or a blessing. There is a window of opportunity which is wide open, but which starts to close as the child begins to grow up. It is in the child's first few years that we have this opportunity to impact him/her to become a godly person. If we miss this vital calling at the crucial time, we will lose our children, to our never-ending sorrow. If we recognize the importance of this stage and take every opportunity to shape our children into what God wants them to become, then we will reap the blessings later in life. It is our prayer that you would labour with the Lord to bring up your children in His fear, knowledge, obedience, and love.

HANDLING TEENAGERS AND THEIR RELATIONSHIP WITH THE OPPOSITE SEX

As our children reach adolescence, the way they relate to people and especially people of the opposite sex changes drastically. We need to prepare our children for adolescence. At this stage many of them develop inhibitions and fears, such as:

- I am not beautiful/handsome.
- I don't dress well.
- I sound stupid.
- What will people think of me?
- Will anybody love me? (and many more)

These are perfectly normal fears which they will need to resolve over time. But in the meanwhile, parents can do much to reassure them of the following truths:

- It is natural to find the opposite sex attractive.
- God has created sexuality and within God's laws, sex is holy and perfect.
- Satan has distorted sex and is using it to destroy mankind.
- God has wired us for sex, but he has placed traffic lights in his Scriptures to protect us.
- You are beautiful and unique, because you are made in God's image.

Parents, it is our duty to help our teenagers to develop a healthy relationship with the opposite sex and there are 12 aspects that need to be inculcated in our children during their teen years.

- Help them cultivate a brotherly/sisterly relationship.
- Don't keep looking for life partners, rather ask the Lord.
- Keep them acquainted in groups rather than pairing off with someone of the opposite sex.
- Neither let their friends bulldoze them into opposite sex relationships.
- Encourage them to invite their friends home.
- Discourage long and frequent phone calls and encourage them to limit their use of texting and social networking. Apprise them of the dangers of chat rooms on the internet.
- Discourage them from sharing personal problems with friends of the opposite sex.
- Encourage them to focus on life and career building.
- Encourage them to always keep you informed about their whereabouts.
- Reinforce the idea that parents always want the best for their children.
- Encourage them to dress modestly.
- If possible, help them concentrate on friendships with the same sex.

Open communication is vital especially when our children become teenagers. Many parents complain of teenage rebellion. While we do understand that every generation has its own challenges. The teenage years are when children/teenagers begin to think that they know almost everything there is to know and their parents are so old-fashioned that they can never relate to them. This is the age when the opposite sex begins to interest them quite a bit. Dreams begin to blossom. The world is their stage to experiment, and at this stage, their belief is that they are invincible.

SOME SIMPLE RULES TO HANDLE TEENAGERS

- Accept them as they are.
- Appreciate them, focus on strengths rather than weaknesses.
- Show affection—a hug never hurts!
- Do not be suspicious.
- Explain repercussions of wrong behavior.
- Be a good example.
- Spend time together.
- Give responsibility to them at home, involve them in family decisions.
- Make sure that you have an effective family altar.
- Encourage them to have a daily quiet time.
- Keep communication lines open; encourage them to talk their own lingo (but not swearing, etc.).
- Let them verbalize their anger; otherwise it could be expressed in undesirable behavior.
- Make every effort to know them better, and the issues they are facing.
- Be open to accept new ideas.
- Allow reasonable freedom and trust them.
- Pray with them and for them.
- Display a sense of humor that goes well with them (not outdated).
- Do not berate them or their friends.
- Give allowance for errors, and allow children to learn from them.

- Encourage church, Sunday school and youth fellowship attendance.
- Keep your eyes open and be sensitive to what is going on in their lives.
- As the common saying goes, "if you cannot beat them, join them." Befriend them!

RECOGNIZING THE DANGERS AND KEEPING OUR CHILDREN SAFE FROM SEXUAL PREDATORS

We live in extremely turbulent times. There are looming dangers from predators who may try to befriend our children to exploit them. This danger is very real and parents would do well to apprise and arm themselves. We will deal with this very briefly, yet trust that some parents will be helped by this and some children protected and saved. One of the most horrifying facts of sexual abuse is that the perpetrator is generally a close relative or a person who is well known to the family and is allowed free access to children.

Please read the following points carefully and file them away somewhere in your minds. You never know how this will either help you or someone else you know.

- Children of single parent homes, broken homes, or homes in distress are especially vulnerable.
- Beware if someone takes an unusual interest in your child or gives them gifts.
- Be wary if someone offers to spend time with your child. Babysitters must be 100% trustworthy.
- If your child receives calls from someone or makes calls to someone you do not know, you should be on your guard immediately.
- Is your child spending too much time on the computer or have you found pornography or inappropriate messages on the computer? Please make sure that you also check the history of the computer regularly to find out about this. This raises a red flag. Get to the bottom of the matter.
- Does your child quickly shut off the computer or blank the screen as you enter the room? This too raises a red flag and you should investigate.
- Is your child withdrawn from the family? Something is going on—please be on your guard.

- Children who are being abused sometimes try to deal with their problems by engaging in 'escape' behavior. This may involve running away, drug or alcohol use, daydreaming or totally becoming isolated.

SOME ESSENTIAL REMEDIAL STEPS TO BE INITIATED

Keep well informed. Do not feel that your child is safe from anyone! Statistics say that at least one out of every four children will be molested by the age of 18 (and boys are not exempt from this).

Don't expect your child to be able to protect themselves or assume that he or she will be able to tell you of the abuse.

Keep communication lines open at all times, and at any cost. Listen, believe and trust what your child tells you. Children rarely lie about sexual abuse.

Teach your adolescent children healthy values about sexuality. If you don't teach your child, someone else will. Younger children should be taught to recognize unhealthy touching and fondling.

Give your child specific information about which part of his or her body are not right for anyone to touch, no matter who.

Watch for any symptoms of sexual abuse the child might demonstrate: pain, bleeding, itching, stomach ache, physical complaints, sleep disturbances, bed wetting, unexplained fears, refusal to go to some places, clinginess, aggressiveness, secretiveness, emotional and physical withdrawal, cringing from being touched, crying and going into shock, among other things. One other symptom to be concerned about is when a child becomes overly interested in his or her body.

Some predators brainwash the child into something that is labeled as "secret touching." Remind your child that "secret touching," is never the child's fault. Talk honestly to your child about the ways someone might try to trick him or her into going along with the "secret touching."

Encourage your child to tell you immediately if something should happen, despite what anyone else may say. Reassure them that he or she will not land in trouble.

Get to know your child's friends and the homes in which your child plays. Watch for warning signs in that family.

Be wary of older children who want to play with your children on their own.

Trust your intuition. If you feel something is not right with your child, act on it.

Almost one quarter of children are exposed to unwanted pornography via the internet. Today with 3G and 4G mobiles becoming common, pornography can also be found on mobile phones. Use an ISP (Internet Security program) that offers screening for obscenity and pornography, like Net Nanny, Safe Eyes, and others.

In the event of child abuse, please do not hesitate to seek help of trained or qualified professionals or counselors, or the police. By doing so, you might probably be helping many other innocent children who would be at risk in the future at the hands of these criminals.

"An ounce of prevention is worth a pound of care"- Benjamin Franklin. Very well said indeed! We trust that you will be prepared to help your children stay safe.

The greatest safety would be to make sure that you do not neglect to pray with and for your children every day, and that you ensure the presence of God in your life, in the lives of your children and in your home. That is the best prescription we can suggest for the safety of your home.

ELEVEN: DYSFUNCTIONAL FAMILIES OF THE BIBLE

"Remember Lot's wife." Luke 17:32

"Those who cannot remember the past are condemned to repeat it." George Santayana

This side of heaven, there are no perfect families. Every family has its own set of struggles and debacles. No two families and their problems are alike. While every family grapples with some extent of dysfunctionality, in some families this dysfunctionality can be so crippling that it gets in the way of them achieving God's goals. It also can become so severe that it threatens to tear the family apart, and leaves behind scarred individuals who are unable to pull their lives together and achieve something for God's glory. Thankfully God does not gloss over the blemishes of His people, and in His divine wisdom, has incorporated their struggles, blemishes, moles, and warts in His Word, so that we can learn lessons from their failures.

Many Christians do not take the Old Testament seriously, yet God says in 1 Cor 10:11, "These things happened to them as examples and were written down as warnings for us, on whom the culmination of the ages has come." The Bible speaks about many dysfunctional families! Starting with Adam and Eve who ate their way out of God's will, or Abraham who ventured off into Egypt on his own, masquerading Sarah as a sister and was later chastised by Pharaoh, or Jacob who showed favoritism and thereby sowed enmity between his two sons, and many more. Yet we find that these apparently dysfunctional families made course corrections, kept in touch with God, got going despite their handicaps, and left their footprints on the sands of eternity. They made their dysfunctional families functional enough to accomplish God's purposes for them. And this is exactly what we must do. For turning dysfunctionality into functionality, we will have to learn from the Scriptures why some families failed and others succeeded. Sometimes we learn greater lessons from failure than from success.

LESSONS FROM LOT

The history of Lot and his family is found in the book of Genesis chapters 12–19. The Bible tells us that Lot was married and when the story begins, he had two young daughters who were yet to be married. In Genesis 12, God specifically instructed Abraham to come out from among his relatives. Surprisingly, Abraham allowed Lot, his nephew, to tag along. Lot ultimately separated from Abraham and settled down in the land of Sodom. God appeared to Abraham revealing His intention to punish the lands of Sodom and Gomorrah for their abject wickedness; but God in His mercy and loving-kindness to His friend Abraham, sends two angels to warn Lot of the impending destruction of Sodom. God told Lot through the angels that He would rescue anyone else Lot wanted to rescue from the destruction of Sodom. Lot went out to warn his future sons-in-law who were to marry his daughters, but tragically his future sons-in-law thought he was jesting (Gen 19:12).

Genesis 19:26 tells us that Lot's wife, as they were escaping from Sodom, looked back, contrary to the clear instructions of the angels. She paid the price for her disobedience, as she turned into a pillar of salt. After Lot escaped from Sodom, he took refuge in a cave along with his two daughters. Both his daughters concluded that since the whole of Sodom was wiped out, marriage was now out of question and in their fallen human understanding, made their father drunk and committed incest with him to preserve the family line. Although they did not have a written law available to them, God's compass—the human conscience—was embedded within them. They failed to give heed to this compass and this led to disastrous results. The elder daughter gave birth to Moab, the father of Moabites, and the younger one to Ammon, the father of Ammonites and their descendants were a thorn in the flesh for the children of Israel. Vance Havner says, "When you go against God's laws, you do not break them - you break yourselves."[xvi]

If we had to summarize Lot's life through a balance sheet of assets and liabilities, they would be:

- His possessions were all gone.
- His future sons-in-law laughed at him and were destroyed.
- His wife disobeyed the instructions of the angels and turned into a pillar of salt.
- His daughters committed incest with him.
- His descendants were a nuisance to the chosen people of God.
- He left behind no legacy, except a warning. Jesus aptly says, "remember Lot's wife."

We find only liabilities in Lot's life. What went wrong with his family.

LOT'S LIFE: AN ANALYSIS!

Character never collapses suddenly. It happens over a period. First, the cracks begin to show, and when these are neglected, eventually comes the final collapse. Another word for this phenomenon is "erosion." How did this "erosion" occur in Lot's life?

As Abraham and Lot continued their journey, God not only blessed Abraham but also Lot, immensely. As their flocks began to multiply, it led to a shortage of fodder for the livestock and caused strife between the herdsmen of Abraham and Lot (see Genesis 13). Abraham suggested that they separate and go their own individual ways. Abraham being older and large hearted, asked Lot to make the first choice in selecting the area where he would like to settle down with his family and livestock. Abraham would choose the opposite direction, so that there would be no chance of their flocks getting together again, leading to a skirmish.

In Genesis 13:10, we find that when Abraham suggested this, Lot promptly looked around and chose to travel eastward and settle down in the proximity of Sodom which was around the Valley of the Jordan (even though in the social customs of the East, it was customary for the older person to be given first choice). This brings us to the first character flaw of Lot.

LOT WAS SELFISH

What was true during the time of Lot is true today! Even within God's chosen people, many are so self-oriented and selfish. All they can think about is themselves, and they will do anything to achieve happiness and prosperity, sometimes even at the cost of others.

Genesis 13:10 tells us that Sodom had a good supply of water to make it lush green to support livestock, a means of prosperity. It is no wonder that Lot did not think twice and made a beeline towards Sodom. It is a great tragedy that Lot never realized the value of having the Lord on his side rather than material comforts. This brings us to the second character flaw of Lot.

LOT WAS MATERIALISTIC

This is adequately displayed in the following three verses.

> Lot looked around and saw that the whole plain of the Jordan toward Zoar was well watered, like the garden of the Lord, like the land of Egypt. (This was before the Lord destroyed Sodom and Gomorrah.) (Gen 13:10)

> Abram lived in the land of Canaan, while Lot lived among the cities of the plain and pitched his tents near Sodom. (Gen 13:12)

> They also carried off Abram's nephew Lot and his possessions, since he was living in Sodom. (Gen 14:12)

Initially, Lot looked at Sodom, found it attractive, and pitched his tents close to Sodom. Thereafter we learn that he began to live inside Sodom. The motive was very clear. Sodom was promising and had an interesting and successful financial and social life. We believe that his wife probably influenced Lot into moving and settling down in Sodom.

Today, one does not have to go outside the church to find the materialistic world. There are many church members who are trying to juggle between the sacred and the sinful, the holy and the hypocritical, the meaningful and the mundane!

To those who have tasted the goodness of God and His grace, this song penned by Rhea F. Miller is so refreshingly real and challenging that we cannot but be touched by the simplicity and the spirit of commitment communicated in this song. We would do well to live by its soul-touching sentiments. We wish that Lot had heard this song in his time.

> I'd rather have Jesus than silver or gold;
> I'd rather be His than have riches untold;
> I'd rather have Jesus than houses or lands;
> I'd rather be led by His nail-pierced hands.
>
> *Refrain:* Than to be the king of a vast domain
> Or be held in sin's dread sway;
> I'd rather have Jesus than anything
> This world affords today.
>
> I'd rather have Jesus than men's applause;
> I'd rather be faithful to His dear cause;
> I'd rather have Jesus than worldwide fame;
> I'd rather be true to His holy name.

In Genesis 13:13, we read, "Now the people of Sodom were wicked and were sinning greatly against the Lord." Lot and his family had moved their tents close to Sodom. In the mid-Eastern customs of the Bible lands prevailing then, we understand that wealthy livestock owners hired shepherds to graze their livestock. These shepherds would get together, eat together and pick up some juicy gossip from one another. Through them Lot would have got a warning about the wickedness of Sodom even before he had moved to live inside Sodom. Yet, despite this clear warning signal, Lot went ahead and became a prominent citizen of Sodom. That brings us to the next character flaw of Lot.

LOT REFUSED TO LISTEN TO WARNINGS

Lot's refusal to listen to warnings and wisdom cost him dearly! The Bible says in Proverbs 6:27, "Can a man scoop fire into his lap without his clothes being burned?" If one plays with fire, one should be ready to pay the price of this dalliance with the devil.

As we travel further in the narrative, we come across in Genesis 19, the visit of two angels that God sends to warn Lot of the impending destruction of Sodom. The Bible tells us that many of the inhabitants of Sodom were homosexuals, who on seeing these two angels in the form of two men come to the house of Lot, demand that they be brought out, so that they could indulge in their carnal desires with them. While we do appreciate Lot's generous hospitality towards these two angels, his response to the demand of the Sodomites is shocking. He is prepared to deliver his two virgin daughters into the hands of the Sodomites to be ravished by them rather than have his guests violated. Lot would definitely go down in history for two things: firstly, as a protective and caring host, but secondly and more importantly, as a horrible father who was willing to sacrifice his daughters for the sake of his guests. As parents of two precious daughters, we are shocked by Lot's despicable response, which was also watched and heard by his own daughters. This brings us to the fourth character flaw of Lot.

LOT COMPROMISED ON VITAL ISSUES OF LIFE

A preacher once remarked, "The collapse of character often begins at compromise corner!" Compromise begins small, but ends up giant size. It could innocuously start in the form of failing to have a personal time with the Lord, or perhaps be willing to pay a bribe to get planning permissions, etc. The list can be endless, and each action might appear justifiable. Proverbs 14:12 tells us that there can be a way that appears right but ruin awaits us at the other end. This is exactly what happened with Lot.

Genesis 19:1 tells us that the two angels came to Lot's house in Sodom in the evening and he took them home. Surprisingly, Genesis 19:15 inform us that, when the morning dawned, the angels urged Lot to flee Sodom immediately. The word "urged" amply demonstrates the fact that Lot needed a great deal of persuasion from the angels and was unwilling to leave without adequately salvaging his possessions. Verse 16 gives an insight into his utter unwillingness: "but he hesitated, so the men (angels) seized his hand, and the hand of his wife and the hands of his daughters and brought them out. They just had to be forced out of Sodom. It is abundantly clear that Sodom had deeply embedded itself into the very fabric of their lives that to wrench it out was to wrench out a part of their own life, which was very painful indeed. This is also seen from the fact that despite being severely warned by the angels not to look back, Lot's wife had to sneak a final lingering look at all that she was leaving behind. She was running away from Sodom, but Sodom was alive and running inside her heart and she paid the price of disobedience by turning into a pillar of salt. This brings us to yet another character flaw in the life of Lot.

LOT HESITATED IN TAKING VITAL DECISIONS

This whole episode of escaping from Sodom is bathed with a sense of attachment to material benefits, doubting God and hesitating in obeying Him. This tendency to hesitate is so well embodied in the sinking of the Titanic. On 15th April 1912, RMS Titanic sailed from Southampton to New York City with around 1300 passengers besides crew. As it was labelled unsinkable and capable of being able to sail through any mishap, Captain Smith ignored warnings of icebergs that were drifting in its path. It is said that he hesitated in altering the course in time for the Titanic to avoid a direct collision with the iceberg that sank it. This delay in altering the course proved costly and the iceberg ripped a jagged tear along the starboard side, ultimately causing it to sink, with the loss of nearly 1500 lives! Hesitation in the face of warning of impending danger can lead to disastrous results.

While both Abraham and Lot moved out of Ur and travelled together for some distance, it is quite an education to see how both differed in their lifestyles. In Genesis 12:7, 12:8, 13:4, 13:18, 20:17 it is found that Abraham was in direct communication with God, while the Bible does not have a single instance informing us of any communication between Lot and God. There was a very interesting survey done in New England prisons where 600 teenagers were interviewed to find out the reason for their being incarcerated there. Some interesting facts that emerged were:

> 60% had fathers who drank excessively.
>
> 75% had no parental control.
>
> 70% had no family activity, like playing or spending time together.
>
> 100% had no family prayer or Sunday school participation.

There are no guarantees in life except God. Not having Him on board in our family is a recipe for disaster which brings us to Lot's next character flaw.

LOT NEVER BOTHERED ABOUT GOD

In Genesis 19:30, we find that Lot began to stay in a cave with his daughters and it ended in an incestuous relationship. It is quite mysterious that after

Lot had lost everything except his two daughters, and there was nothing to look forward to except dangers and hardships, he did not think of going back to his uncle Abraham whom he knew was large hearted, caring and loving. Had Lot used his wisdom and quickly made his way back to his uncle Abraham, perhaps his life would have taken a different turn. But alas! He just continued in his folly and made a mess of his family, bringing us to the next character flaw in his life.

LOT NEVER LEARNED FROM HIS MISTAKES

In our counselling experience we come across many families who make a mess and never stop to learn from their mistakes. They continue repeating them over and over, thereby amplifying their problems. In concluding the study of Lot's life, 2 Peter 2:7-8 is a seemingly contradictory passage:

> and if he rescued Lot, a righteous man, who was distressed by the depraved conduct of the lawless [8](for that righteous man, living among them day after day, was tormented in his righteous soul by the lawless deeds he saw and heard).

Many are unable to reconcile this passage with the apparent mistakes that Lot committed in managing his life and his family. While the apostle Peter addresses him as 'righteous Lot', it does not imply that he was without sin. David mentions in Psalm 51, that even our conception in our mother's womb is in sin, since every human being inherits the Adamic nature. Isaiah 53 tells us that everyone, with no exception, has turned astray into doing our own thing, and Jesus had to bear the iniquity of each one of us on Himself on the cross. Jesus was the only sinless person ever born or would be born in the entire history of mankind.

Hence Lot was not sinless and like all of us, had inherited the Adamic nature. The apostle Peter tells us that Lot was righteous in the sense of not participating in the lawless and godless deeds of the people of Sodom, and his soul was tormented day after day. In the context of not participating in the debauchery and sinful living of the people of Sodom, Lot appears righteous. Now if Lot was tormented day after day relentlessly, the most obvious question that one can ask is what prevented him from leaving Sodom and its sinful environment. Strange is it not? Again, when the angels came to Sodom, they found Lot sitting at the city gate of Sodom. In the ancient customs, it was the prominent people of the city who would sit at the gate of any city. It means that he was not only continuing to live in Sodom despite his soul being tormented day after day, he had somehow risen in social stature to be a prominent citizen of Sodom.

In the light of what is mentioned above, the most logical explanation of Lot's continued existence in Sodom was the influence of his wife over his decisions. Had she been a godly woman, the history of Lot and his posterity would have been different. She was so worldly that even Jesus talks about her in Luke 17:32 saying, "remember Lot's wife." He was speaking about the end times in the passage and how some people love their lives so much, it results in ultimately losing out on eternal life. This brings us to the last character flaw of Lot.

LOT NEVER EXERCISED GODLY LEADERSHIP AT HOME

It is so tragic to note that right from the beginning, almost every decision taken by Lot was detrimental to the family. It stems from the fact that he, unlike his uncle Abraham, was not in touch with God. The other reason is that he let his wife influence him rather than the other way around. We find this so true in families where husbands fail to take the reins of leadership and this naturally results in their wives taking over the leadership. This can sometimes work if the wife is a godly person, but if she is not, it leads the family on the path of distress and ultimately ruin. Yet another fallout of this is that our actions negatively impact our children and the generations to come.

We trust that Lot, although dead, has spoken God's wisdom into your lives and that you would desist from going the way of Lot!

DISASTERS FROM DAVID

We know of Lot because of his uncle Abraham, yet he did not play an important part in the history of God's people. Moreover, at that point of time, the written law of God was not available for knowing the mind of God. One had to walk with God personally each day, and seek His mind on life's issues. But the scenario had totally changed by the time of David. The written law of God was available. There were operational offices of the priests and the prophets who could reliably disclose God's mind and will from the clearly and meticulously defined personal, social, and spiritual laws found in the Pentateuch. And yet we find David, falling far short of the standards expected of a godly father and husband.

King David was one of the greatest kings ever in the history of Israel. He:

- was a man after God's own heart.
- slew a lion, a bear and a giant named Goliath.
- was a giant among men in his passion for God.

- was a hero of the faith mentioned in Hebrews 11.
- firmly established and expanded the kingdom of Israel.
- wrote many of the Psalms that still edify and encourage us even today.

What impressive qualifications! Yet, his posterity relates a sad story of murder, rape, rebellion, coups, apostasy, disobedience, and much more. He was a fearless king yet a foolish philanderer, a brave warrior yet a bad husband, insightful theologian and yet an insensitive father. He had great passion for God yet blatant disregard for his people at one point of time. Very sad indeed!

Let us delve into the Scriptures and examine David's life to identify some character flaws, weak spots, and blemishes of David as a husband, father and leader. In fact, David's decisions and actions had an almost immediate effect on the lives of his family, bringing in consequences that were not only immediate but also long-term, impacting eternity! So we will examine each of his character flaws in two stages: actions and consequences. Please remember we are examining David's life only to the extent of his dealing with his family, and beyond this. While examining David's flaws, we do it with much apprehension, being fully aware of our own inadequacies to even delve into the life of a man like David.

HE HAD A STREAK OF INDISCIPLINE

God specifically says in Deut 7:3, "Furthermore, you shall not intermarry with them; you shall not give your daughters to their sons, nor shall you take their daughters for your sons." Furthermore, God also says in Deut 17:17, that kings, "He must not take many wives, or his heart will be led astray. He must not accumulate large amounts of silver and gold." Yet 2 Sam 3:2–5 gives us some of the names of the wives of David, among whom we find the name of Maacah, the daughter of Talmai, King of Geshur. David had failed to obey.

The offshoot of this marriage with Maacah is the birth of her son whose name was Absalom. The Bible tells us that while Absalom was a very handsome man and was loved dearly by his father David, he tried to stage a coup and throw David out of Jerusalem (see 2 Sam 15).

David marrying Maacah from Geshur sent out a wrong message to his own children, who felt this was an acceptable and approved practice. The Bible recounts in 1 Kings 3, that King Solomon, David's son formed a marriage alliance with Pharaoh, the King of Egypt, by taking his daughter to be his wife. 1 Kings 11 also tells us that Solomon loved many foreign women and that his many wives turned his heart away towards other gods, thus angering the Lord, the God of Israel. This resulted in the Lord wrenching his kingdom away from his hand and giving it to his servant as said in verse 11. The Kingdom of Judah that was to remain with Solomon's posterity and the remaining tribes which would be called the kingdom of Israel, were given to be ruled by other kings. Also out of David's marriage with Maacah came his daughter Tamar, whose tragic story we will deal with later.

HE HAD A STREAK OF IMMORALITY

One of the saddest chapters ever written about this great servant of God, David, is 2 Samuel 11. We are grateful to God, for not glossing over the tragic flaws of His people, rather getting out their history as it happened, so that we could learn from the mistakes of His chosen servants.

This chapter opens with a restless David pacing his rooftop, while his army was fighting with the sons of Ammon. From the vantage point of the roof he sees Bathsheba, who happens to be bathing. In verse 2, it says "the woman was very beautiful." Many theologians argue over this and come to different conclusions. But the fact remains that whether Bathsheba engineered this, or it was an inadvertent act, David was smitten by her beauty and wanted her at any cost. He sent and enquired about her and in verse 3 a servant came back and promptly informed David that the woman was Bathsheba, the daughter of Eliam, the wife of Uriah the Hittite. Unspoken words hung heavy in the air communicating to the King that she was the daughter of one of his subjects and the wife of one of his valiant warriors who was fighting for the King at that moment. David's lust was beyond reason and control. He sent messengers and took her and lay with her. What follows is too horrendous for words. But the fact of the matter is that David had an eye for beauty.

1 Samuel 25 carries the story of Nabal and his wife Abigail and how after Nabal's death, David sent his servants with a marriage proposal to Abigail, who becomes his wife. The Bible although very casually tells us in verse 3 that Abigail was intelligent and beautiful in appearance, reiterates the fact that beauty attracted David, and this was his Achilles' heel; his weakness would cause him many troubles.

1 Kings chapter 1 deals with the history of King David when he had advanced in age and become so infirm that he could not even keep warm although covered with a heap of blankets. So his servants looked for a young girl who could lie with the aged monarch to keep him warm. Although any young woman could have been chosen, the Scripture tells us in verse 3, that

they looked for a beautiful girl, and found Abishag the Shunnamite. It is painfully obvious that even his servants knew his weakness for beautiful women and looked for one who would fit the bill.

It comes as no surprise, that Solomon, after he had his fill of licentious living, acquired enough wisdom to say in Proverbs 31 that charm is deceitful and beauty is vain but a woman who fears the Lord is the one who is honoured.

THE CONSEQUENCES

David's son, Amnon born to him through Ahinoam, the Jezreelitess, obviously had an eye for beauty too. He begins to lust after his own half-sister Tamar born to David through Maacah from Geshur. He was frustrated because he could not satisfy his lust. Listening to his shrewd and wicked cousin Jonadab who happens to be his friend, philosopher, and guide, he feigns sickness and requests David to send Tamar to make food in his sight and feed him personally with her own hands. It is quite surprising that David fails to see through this charade and succumbs to this request. Sadly, Amnon rapes his own half- sister and throws her out after satisfying his lust. Tamar runs home in great distress and is hushed by her brother Absalom. The Bible records in 2 Samuel 13:22, that Absalom hated Amnon for this violation of his sister and waited to exact revenge, which he does after a period of two years.

David's daughter is raped by his own son, her half-brother. Mortal enmity is sown between two brothers leading to the death of one and the expulsion of the other from the kingdom. This also paves the way for a coup to be staged against David and his eventual escape from Jerusalem. David as a father had to suffer tremendously, because he had set the stage by stealing somebody else's wife, and having her husband murdered. His moral compass was askew, and his conscience blunted.

After David escapes from Jerusalem following the rebellion of Absalom, Ahithophel, David's wise counsellor, deserts him and joins forces with Absalom. He advises Absalom to prove his complete control over David's kingdom by defiling David's concubines. This would symbolize his absolute takeover of power. So a tent is pitched on the roof of the palace, where Absalom goes into his father's concubines in the sight of all Israel. One cannot begin to imagine the public shame and revulsion that David had to endure over this act at the hands of his own son. However, this should not come as a surprise to us as this was prophesied by the Lord, through Nathan the prophet in 2 Sam 12:11 as a punishment for stealing Bathsheba from Uriah his servant and murdering him. We are sure of this one thing, that all this must have haunted David, and he would have definitely wished from the bottom of his heart that he had never gone to the roof of his palace and looked upon Bathsheba.

The following are the four lessons that the Lord has helped us glean from this very tragic story of David and Bathsheba.

- Beware of the unoccupied mind.
- Beware of unguarded eyes.
- Beware of unchecked thoughts.
- Beware of unbridled freedom.

HE HAD A STREAK OF INACTION

David was a man of action but when it came to his family, he appeared strangely bereft of the willpower to act in the area of disciplining his children. Amnon rapes his half-sister Tamar, leading to her being disgraced. This resulted in the rage of Absalom and his decision to punish Amnon. Later on, Absalom manages to lure away Amnon and murders him. Absalom fearing a backlash of this action, flees to the land of his mother, Geshur, where he stayed for three years.

When King David heard of the defilement of his own daughter by her half-brother, he was very angry (2 Sam 13:21). Thereafter on hearing about the murder of Amnon at the hands of Absalom, he tears off his clothes and lies on the ground mourning. The Bible nowhere records that he ever called either Amnon or Absalom to deal with their wrongful acts. On the contrary, the Bible says that he longed to go out to Absalom, making us believe that Absalom was his favourite, and hence enjoyed the lenience of his father. Otherwise through the Mosaic law, Absalom should have been punished for Amnon's murder by the death penalty. David's singular disinclination to set an example of justice starting with his own house, was the result of two facts:

- How could he call Amnon and confront him with this ghastly act of defiling his sister, when he had Uriah killed to obtain Bathsheba?
- Likewise, he could not confront Absalom for murdering his brother because the "Bathsheba episode" where he had murdered Uriah.

David, the wife-stealer could not take the role of child-corrector, and David the husband-killer could not condemn the act of the brother-killer.

THE CONSEQUENCES

David, the one who killed the giant Goliath, the brave warrior and the man who translated faith into action was ready for anything except dealing with his own family. This was one of his greatest weaknesses. And it is no wonder his sons capitalized on this weakness of David.

1 Kings 1:5–6 speaks about the rebellion of his son Adonijah and how he prepares to grab the kingdom for himself. Verse 6 tells us that his father David had never crossed him at any time by asking, "Why have you done so?" As mentioned earlier, his family knew fully well that David loved his children and would never confront them.

Likewise, 2 Samuel 15 gives details about the rebellion of Absalom. Royal conspiracies generally have a way of leaking out, and it is more than possible that warning about the brewing rebellion could have been brought to the ears of David. But David never felt it necessary to give credence to this rebellion, discover the plot, confront Absalom, and stop it.

Finally when a messenger warns David in 2 Samuel 15 that Absalom was certain to grab the power and expose David to mortal danger, he decides to leave Jerusalem. This must have been very painful for David, as he had to leave his beloved Jerusalem and the seat of his power. After defeating the armies of Absalom and his subsequent death, David could come back to Jerusalem but life had changed much and David grew old perhaps regretting the way he dealt with his family.

HE HAD A STREAK OF INSENSITIVITY

2 Samuel 13 gives us many insights into the family life of David. Verse 1 mentions Tamar as the beautiful sister of Absalom. The fact that the narrative omits to mention Tamar as the daughter of King David probably indicates that Absalom, as a male offspring, was his favorite. One fact that clearly stands out is that David played favorites with his children. Verse 2 speaks of Amnon's frustration at not being able to sexually exploit his half-sister Tamar. In the subsequent verses, we find Jonadab was sensitive enough to discover the lustful frustration of his cousin and friend, whereas David as a father, neither discovered the frustration of his son nor sensed something amiss in the request of Amnon to have Tamar come and minister to him. We believe David probably had weightier kingdom issues on his mind that occupied so much of his time and blinded him to the immediate realities of his family, leading to catastrophic results. In his blind love for his sons, especially Amnon, he ignored social and royal customs by ordering Tamar to wait on her half-brother, a task which could have been done by any of the servants of the King's household.

After the episode where Amnon exploits Tamar, King David gets very angry, but does nothing, and remains silent. Again, his hands were tied not only to save the family from shame, but also to avoid a confrontational showdown with Amnon which he did not want. It is so tragic that David, while executing justice for the people at large, failed to deliver justice to his own daughter wronged so greatly.

THE CONSEQUENCES

David forgot that when parents play favorites they divide their children and sow enmity between them, as was the case of Esau and Jacob. Likewise, we find that there is no love between the siblings and many of the sons were solely interested to grab the throne and rule in the place of their father.

This streak of insensitivity continues in the posterity of David. His grandson Rehoboam refused to be sensitive and listen to the wise counsel of elders, and eventually treated the people harshly and became arrogant, which culminated in the division of the united empire that was established by David (1 Kings 12).

HE HAD A STREAK OF INDIFFERENCE

We come to the inevitable confrontation between the armies of David and Absalom (2 Samuel 18). Even as the army of David is ready to depart for battle, David gives an important instruction quietly to his trusted commander Joab as found in verse 5. He wants his armies to show mercy to Absalom and spare his life.

The Bible records that the fierce battle, won by David's army, resulted in the death of 20,000 men. Obviously around 20,000 homes had lost their breadwinners, wives their husbands and children their fathers. This tragedy is epic, as Israel was fighting one another. In the meanwhile, Absalom's head gets caught in the thick branches of an oak tree and as he is hanging there, Joab spears and kills him. Joab was a very practical man and he fully understood that had Absalom escaped, he would be a potential threat to the throne and life of David as long as he lived. Joab fully understood that if David was to reign, Absalom had to die.

As the armies of David return and messengers approach David who is waiting to hear of the outcome, it is shocking that he is not as anxious to hear about the battle as he is to hear about the well-being of his son Absalom. On hearing of his son's death, David was so deeply moved that he went up to his chamber and wept saying, "O my son Absalom, my son Absalom! Would I had died instead of you, O Absalom, my son, my son!"

Following the strange behavior of the King, his jubilant victorious army returns by stealth, as people who are humiliated when they flee in battle. The King is indifferent to the suffering in the homes of 20,000 people who have lost their lives on both the sides. He is blinded by his love for his son and can see no further than his dead body.

THE CONSEQUENCES

This insensitivity and duality of David does not escape the attention of Joab. Joab's response to David's insensitivity comes as a slap in the face:

> Then Joab went into the house to the king and said, "Today you have humiliated all your men, who have just saved your life and the lives of your sons and daughters and the lives of your wives and concubines. You love those who hate you and hate those who love you. You have made it clear today that the commanders and their men mean nothing to you. I see that you would be pleased if Absalom were alive today and all of us were dead. Now go out and encourage your men. I swear by the Lord that if you don't go out, not a man will be left with you by nightfall. This will be worse for you than all the calamities that have come on you from your youth till now." So the king got up and took his seat in the gateway. When the men were told, "The king is sitting in the gateway," they all came before him. Meanwhile, the Israelites had fled to their homest." (2 Sam 19:5–8)

The valiant hero of Israel, the fearless victor of many battles and the gifted writer and singer of many Psalms, the man after God's own heart, is now being chided and being instructed by his own general! What a tragedy! This happened because David had become insensitive to people.

We trust that the Lord has spoken to us as husbands and wives, parents and children through the lives of Lot and of David. It is good to apply the lessons learnt, to our own situations and prayerfully accept the correction of the Lord in our families, if we have fallen into the same trap which led to the ruin of the families of Lot and David. Be warned! Whatsoever a man sows, that he shall reap!

TWELVE: HANDLING IN-LAWS & LIVE-IN PARENTS

"Cutting the cord between mother and son is a process that has to be relived from time to time." Norman Wright

"A diplomat is a person who handles his mother and wife at the same time without hurting any of them." Lity Munshi

One problem that keeps cropping up in families, causing much heartache, is the relationship with in-laws. This issue is universal, in varying degrees. It is most pronounced in our home country of India because of its joint family system (which still prevails in some places), where parents live with their married children. Often in joint families, the problems are usually confined to those between the mother-in-law and daughter-in-law.

At some point in time some "in-laws," either the husband's parents or the wife's, could be staying with you. It is also possible that both sets of parents could end up staying with you, especially if you happen to be an only child.

Before we get deeper into the subject let us first clearly define what God meant by, "man leaves his father and mother" (Gen 2:24).

After marriage, the new relationship between husband and wife takes precedence over all other relationships except that with God. This is the closest and the strongest bond in all earthly relationships. The spouse's opinion is to be valued in all major decisions and considered more important than the opinion of others. The allegiance of the husband or wife shifts from their parents to their spouse. It does not mean that the new couple has to stop loving or helping their parents (as 1 Tim 5:8 makes clear).

IMPACT OF CHILDREN'S MARRIAGE ON PARENTS

In the euphoria of marriage and the bustle post marriage—the new couple sometimes fail to grasp the impact of their marriage on their parents. They see life through rose-tinted glasses and the dark side is missed out. It is advisable for couples to understand the changes their marriage brings in the life of their parents. There is no doubt that parents experience great happiness. No one ever expects any trouble, and look forward with happiness to new adjustments that might be required.

When a bride leaves her parents to make a home at her husband's house, the bride's parents experience a sense of void. Their daughter who was the apple of their eyes is sorely missed at home. Though they are happy, there is a great underlying sense of loss and they can feel the palpable vacuum.

Adding to this, many new husbands feel that, to settle into the new life, their wife should not visit her parents too often, which only adds to the parents' sorrow.

The bride's parents also feel a sense of unfairness for having to give away their daughter, whom they have lovingly nurtured and brought up, to a man who whisks her away. On top of this, they are not supposed to expect anything from their daughter who now practically "owned" by the bridegroom and his family.

By the time children get married, their parents have either retired or are on the verge of retiring. Added to this, with the expenses of marriage etc., you find parents (especially of the bride) getting into financial difficulties. Many husbands do not even allow their working wives to help her parents. Before marriage, the daughter's earnings would bring in some financial relief to her family, which after her marriage suddenly dries up bringing in a financial crunch on her parents. Many parents of brides undergo severe psychological stress after their daughter's marriage.

The parents of the bride also face a loss of self-respect. Till yesterday, their opinions, ideas, and inputs mattered, which now are more or less overlooked while those of the bridegroom become more important.

Both sets of parents, of the groom and bride, go through a lack of emotional support. This is natural, as the newly married couple gets busy with establishing their own home. Parents face the loss of their decision-making authority as the new couple starts to make their own decisions, and a sense of loneliness descends on the parents, which although it is to be expected, is always difficult to deal with.

In the bridegroom's family, his mother on finding her son's wife suddenly taking on the most important role in his life begins to feel threatened. Before marriage, her opinion was paramount in her son's life. Suddenly, a new woman has stolen the affections and allegiance of her son. No wonder she begins to view the daughter-in-law as a threat. Sometimes the mother tries to re-assert her supremacy over her son, which is apt to develop resentment in the daughter-in-law.

The bridegroom's father always relished the role of the leader in his house till the marriage of his son. He does not take kindly to the fact that he must relinquish this role once his son gets married. Many fathers fail to recognize this fact and continue to try to control their sons after marriage, causing a lot of friction in the family.

ROLE PLAYED BY IN-LAWS

CRISIS-MANAGERS

By the time we got married, Irwin's mother had already gone to be with the Lord. When our first child Sruti was born, we ran into many unexpected challenges. Vijaya was working and had to find someplace to leave Sruti while Vijaya was at work. As Sruti's immunity began to develop with the onset of many common infections, we had to find someone who could not only give us sound child-rearing advice but also help us through these infections. Here is when the crisis managers came in, in the form of Vijaya's parents who graciously stepped in to help us. No matter what the crisis, they were more than willing to help us through it. Soon after Sruti was born and Vijaya was recuperating at her mother's, Irwin became ill. Once again, Vijaya's parents stepped in to help look after Irwin with Vijaya and the baby. Although the strain must have been enormous on them (as they were getting older) they stepped in to ease our difficulties. We are grateful to their loving and sacrificial service. Friends, it would be good to understand the role in-laws play and make sure that we nourish this relationship which repeatedly yields great dividends. Remember, our in-laws love us and mean well. When minor misunderstandings crop in, we need to handle them appropriately so that this relationship does not become thorny.

CHILD-MINDERS

Vijaya, till the Lord convicted her to quit her job, used to work for a bank. This meant that we had to leave our children with someone during the day. Enter the crisis managers again, this time in the role of child-minders. Although Vijaya's mother was in her 60s and not keeping too well health wise, she graciously invited us to leave our child with her during the day. We were not only assured of proper care, but they lavished tons of love on Sruti and taught her the basics of Christian faith, melodious choruses, and pleasing manners. Their contribution in bringing up Sruti cannot be repaid in any way and we will always be grateful to them for this tremendous assistance. At times, when we had to attend church programs in the evenings, we left our children with the in-laws. Later on, as Vijaya's mother became afflicted by severe arthritis, Irwin's father stepped in to help us in looking after both his grandchildren on their return from school.

FINANCIAL SUPPORTERS (AT TIMES)

In the early years of our marriage when Sruti was just one year old, Vijaya had to undergo a surgery. Those were financially challenging years where making ends meet was always an act of juggling. While Vijaya was admitted to the hospital, her father came down to the hospital and offered to pay for the surgery (we had no NHS or health insurance in India). Although Irwin appreciated his father-in-law's thoughtful generosity, he gently refused to accept any financial help. But the fact remains that in-laws, on many occasions, become our financial supporters without any thought of seeking return favors. We have come across many families that are being assisted by their in-laws. If this is done voluntarily, it is truly appreciable. But there are many families who treat their in-laws as a goose that lays golden eggs and are perennially demanding that the wife get financial and material help from her parents, even if they are financially not well off. This is a very bad practice and cannot be accepted.

DOMESTIC SUPPORT

Whether they are live-in parents or in-laws living separately, they are always willing to lend their support in domestic matters. When we would invite guests to dine with us, Vijaya's mother not only supplied great recipes, but also came home to help Vijaya turn these recipes into delicious dishes. Whether it was helping in the kitchen, buying the groceries, making pickles during summer or making Christmas dinner, we could always count upon Vijaya's mother. In those days when bills (for electricity etc.) had to be paid in person at their office counters, Irwin's father would personally go to all these departments, stand in a queue, and make the payments. This saved a lot of time and effort and our precious leave, which we could use later on when needed.

While parents and in-laws are more or less always at the giving end, we forget that they have some needs of their own too. Let us look at some of them.

WHAT PARENTS/IN-LAWS NEED FROM THEIR MARRIED CHILDREN

There are a couple of things we should keep in mind while taking care of ageing parents and in-laws.

ACKNOWLEDGING THEIR SIGNIFICANCE

> Stand up in the presence of the aged, show respect for the elderly and revere your God. I am the Lord. (Lev 19:32)

God clearly wants us to honor not only our father and mother (Exod 20:12) but also every person who is aged, with no strings attached. By doing this we demonstrate our fear of the Lord and obedience to His Word. This not only pleases God but also pleases our parents and in-laws.

Jesus says in Matthew 7:12 "So in everything, do to others what you would have them do to you, for this sums up the Law and the Prophets." The onus of doing it first lies with us. Friends, try it and see! It works! Irwin can tell you from personal experience that his relationship with his in-laws was so good that Vijaya once remarked that she felt Irwin was her parents' son and she was their daughter-in-law. Praise God! Let your in-laws know that they are as important and significant as your own parents, and hence never treat them as if they did not matter. Personally, we always demonstrated that we had two sets of parents and not in-laws. This made both sets of parents immensely happy resulting in a very loving and cordial relationship.

ASSURANCE OF THEIR NEEDS BEING MET

In many countries, old parents and in-laws do not have any social security net or adequate financial means to look after themselves in their sunset years. So, they have no other choice but to completely depend on their children to meet their needs. Even in more affluent Western countries, elderly parents may struggle to make ends meet. We have come across many instances where parents have felt humiliated when their children refused them financial assistance. We are not talking of luxurious demands but rather of necessities. You can imagine their embarrassment, alarm and discouragement when they find themselves neglected, bereft of emotional and financial support. Apart from this, with advancing years, medical problems multiply, necessitating additional expense. Being taken care of is their just due, and should not be considered as a matter of charity. Remember, everyone will grow old one day or the other, and what goes up comes down. History repeats itself. If we are not generous and caring, not only will our past come back to haunt us, but our children may treat us the way we treated our in-laws and parents. Paul tells Timothy, "Anyone who does not provide for their relatives, and especially for their own household, has denied the faith and is worse than an unbeliever." (1 Tim 5:8). Please remember, our parents deserve the dignity to live well in their sunset years and be gathered to their forefathers in peace and contentment.

TREATING THEM WITH LOVE

Merely providing financial assistance in itself would be meaningless unless it is done with love. Our in- laws and parents, as they grow older, can at times become demanding and critical. Some of them also become nitpicking and are not easily pleased. They may also interfere in the functioning of the home. As people grow older their ideas and attitudes become inflexible which can be a source of irritation. We need to love them despite this. Please remember, at that age, it is impossible to expect a change in them. The best we can do is to adapt and sometimes ignore certain things that cannot be helped. But remember to communicate with them with gentleness, understanding and forbearance. The best way to demonstrate love towards them is to set apart a little time each day to talk to them. Please also make sure that they are able to attend church, as much as their health permits.

TREATING THEM WITH SYMPATHY AND UNDERSTANDING

There is a famous Native American saying, "Don't judge a man until you have walked two moons in his moccasins." For young married children, it is impossible to understand their ageing parents and in-laws. Old-age brings in a host of problems. Loneliness (especially after the loss of their spouse), boredom, insecurity, health issues like diminishing eyesight and hearing, aches and pains, insomnia, loss of limb coordination, incontinence, elevated blood pressure and so on. While it may be bothersome to us, most of the time these issues are real. Showing sympathy and understanding serves to soothe our parents and give them much needed confidence. Many of their issues can disappear or lessen with a little sympathy and understanding. And in case of any continuing medical issue, please make sure that you attend to it immediately. Make sure they get the right medical attention. If you delay, the problem can get compounded and can further raise their anxiety levels.

VISITING THEM REGULARLY

If you have in-laws and parents who live far away from you, you can be sure that they are longing to see you and spend time with you. Please make sure you visit them as often as possible and spend quality time with them. This will go a long way to make them happy. If at times when you cannot go, plan for at least your children to visit and spend time with them. Some husbands have double standards. While he makes sure that his family visits his parents often, he shows great reluctance to have the family visit his wife's parents (at times this can be the other way around). This is unfair and will surely cause a rift in his relationship with his wife. As said earlier, in marriage, we acquire two sets of parents and we should not treat them differently. Try this and see how it helps to make your relationships satisfying not only with your in-laws and parents, but your spouse as well.

BEING FINANCIALLY INDEPENDENT FROM IN-LAWS

Many couples, even after several years of being married, still depend on their parents for financial assistance. If your parents and in-laws are financially stable and can chip in willingly, it might be acceptable to some extent. However, it is ideal not to depend on your aged in-laws and parents for financial help. Please remember, whatever assets are owned by in-laws and parents will eventually be passed down to their children. So we must let our in-laws and parents make their own financial decisions and do what pleases them. While on one hand there are couples who seek such assistance, on the other hand there are also those who love to do something for their in-laws and parents. We have seen couples who have sent their in-laws and parents on foreign trips, bought them a car, house, etc. Just imagine the delight and joy of these in-laws and parents when they experience the generosity of their children. By doing this, you are setting down some great memories both for them and your children as well so that they can emulate you.

AMICABLE DIVISION OF PROPERTY

Division of property is a very thorny issue, which ends up in bitter fights and destroys relationships. Often seemingly healthy and happy families end up in bitter wrangling over division of their parents' property. Brothers and sisters become enemies. While this is happening, just imagine the mental anguish and suffering of the parents who have worked hard, sacrificed a lot of their needs to acquire some property so as to pass it on to their children. Some guidelines on how to handle this very important issue (for parents and in- laws):

It is ideal to execute a last will and testament and register it as early as possible. Make sure that a lawyer drafts this, suitably witnessed by independent witnesses and registered with the appropriate authorities. This will avoid any lawsuits later and protect the rights of all the beneficiaries.

The contents of the will should not be divulged to anyone except the executors of the will, who will carry out your instructions. This will come into operation only on the demise of the person making the will. The will should clearly mention what should be done with all the movable properties, like gold, jewelry and cash on hand, bank balances-savings account and fixed deposits, other investments like shares, debentures, policies, other monies receivable etc.

Be just in the division of the property, because playing favorites will divide your children and pitch them against one other. In the event where an immovable property cannot be equitably divided, it is advisable to sell it and the proceeds divided among all the children.

If there are some outstanding loans payable, they should be clearly mentioned, also clarifying the specific resources to be utilized in their repayment. Try to never leave behind any uncleared loans for your children to repay on your behalf from their personal resources after you have gone.

The executor should be carefully selected and preferably could be a lawyer himself who will take his fees in advance or it could be a trusted friend/relative who has no personal gain/stake in this matter.

GOOD AND FRIENDLY COUNSEL FROM THEIR PEERS

In their advanced years, in-laws and parents can at times become cranky and unreasonable. They may not be willing to listen to the advice of their children. We remember a time when Irwin's father was going through a time of depression. He became demanding and unreasonable. He had a stroke and was only able to move with a Zimmer-frame within the confines of the home. Both of us were working, and it was difficult for us to stay back to be with him. We hired a carer to look after him round the clock. In spite of all this, he expected us never to go out in the evenings. This was not practical, and could not be helped. We tried to reason it out with him which made no headway. Ultimately, we realized the only person who could probably speak logically and make him see reason would be one of his contemporaries. We requested one of his church friends, who was ailing himself but still mobile, to come and spend some time with him. This worked and we found it made sense to Irwin's dad who became more settled in his mind and less demanding from then on.

PROVIDING SPIRITUAL INPUTS

Our parents and in-laws need good spiritual nourishment. Make sure that they are able to attend church regularly, and if possible visit friends or relatives. Encourage some friends of theirs to visit as well, which can ensure continuing fellowship with like-minded people. Make sure that they are involved in family devotions. You will realize that this can go a long way to keep them happy and keep many troubles away from the family.

OUR ATTITUDE TOWARDS IN-LAWS & LIVE-IN PARENTS

DO NOT EXPECT TROUBLE

Many of us have heard so many tales about trouble with the in-laws, that we enter marriage with a pre-conceived notion that they are troublemakers. Please do not harbor this attitude. On the other hand, we could become the troublemakers by anticipating imaginary trouble and reacting to tiny issues with a negative emotion. Please keep your minds open and your attitudes positive.

INTEGRATE GOOD TRADITIONS OF BOTH FAMILIES INTO YOUR OWN

You and your spouse have grown up in different families from different backgrounds, perhaps from different cultures or geographical locations. Every family and culture has their own typical traditions, customs, and habits. There is no centralized authority that can stand in judgment to pronounce whether these are good or bad. Remember these are all neutral, and how you view them will ultimately determine whether you see them as friends or foes. We have come across many couples where one of them looks down upon the other's background/family or culture like eating habits or cultural traditions. As long as they do not go against Scriptural laws or hurt anyone, they cannot be discriminated against. On the other hand, these can be looked at with interest and if possible, the good ones can be integrated in your own family. Let our children have the best of both the sides and get to understand that both families are equally important. This fosters healthy relationships with each branch of the family.

VALUE YOUR SPOUSE'S FAMILY: TREAT THEM AS YOUR OWN PARENTS

Sadly, we live in a male dominated world, and it is no wonder that the husband's family is given more importance than the family of the wife. It is time to do away with these gender related attitudes. In the new dispensation of grace, God clearly states something important in Galatians 3:28, "There is neither Jew nor Gentile, neither slave nor free, nor is there male and female, for you are all one in Christ Jesus." If we are one in Christ, then we are to be viewed on the same level, and so are our families.

We have already mentioned that Vijaya's parents were so fond of Irwin, that sometimes Vijaya would feel that she is the daughter-in-law rather than the daughter in her own house, of course to her own delight. Irwin had the gift of carpentry, repairing gadgets, and would love to take on small projects around the house and in the house of his in-laws, to the delight of Vijaya's parents. Irwin was handy, always available for crisis management and willing to lend a hand no matter what. This endeared him to Vijaya's parents and they began to see him as a son, and not a son- in-law. You would do well to value your spouse's family as that can be a cementing factor between you and your spouse apart from generating great happiness and contentment.

DO NOT BURDEN THEM WITH MORE THAN THEY CAN TAKE

As your parents and in-laws become older, whether physically, emotionally, or financially, there is only so much that they can handle. Putting burdens on them beyond what they can take can unsettle them, cause them to become anxious and trigger medical or psychological issues. Please recognize their limitations and boundaries and avoid straining them beyond these. Many working couples, to avoid employing child-minders to take care of their small children, just mercilessly dump them on their old and infirm parents. If your parents are happy to take on daycare work, it is fine, but if they have health issues that can prevent them from looking after the children, please do not force them. However, if they are still willing to take care of the children with some additional help, then you can definitely think on those lines. Do not burden them with financial matters also, unless they themselves willingly, happily, and voluntarily come forward to help you without dipping in to their precious little resources.

SEEK THEIR WISDOM

We often forget that our in-laws and parents once walked the way that we are walking now. They have a fund of wisdom that can be beneficial to us if we are willing to tap into it. Do not hesitate to seek their advice and wisdom when needed, of course with a clear understanding that the final decision to act should be taken between you and your spouse. You will be surprised that often they can give you sound advice, and it costs you nothing except a big smile, a hug, and a big thank you.

FINALLY

There are some categories of in-laws and parents who are forever a source of irritation and strife in our homes and we are listing them for your better understanding:

- The case of the meddling matriarch.
- The case of the lonesome widow/widower.
- The case of the bulldozing patriarch.
- The case of the controlling superiors.
- The case of the critical/never-too-happy parents.
- The case of the nitpicking mother-in-law.
- The case of the sticking-too-close parents.
- The case of the martyr matriarch.
- The case of the attention seekers.
- The case of the manipulating mothers (and fathers too!).

If we allow them to have their way, they can cause misunderstandings and drive wedges between couples. Here are some ways to effectively handle them without hurting them:

THROUGH HUMILITY

They are our parents and no matter what, they deserve our respect. God loves humility and as we demonstrate this in our dealing with our in-laws and parents, we not only find favor with God but also with our in-laws and parents.

THROUGH ACCEPTANCE

Remember, it is too late to expect behavioral changes in them. Their mental attitudes are all set and the sooner we accept it, the better for us. Sometimes it is best to ignore some negative attitudes in our in-laws and parents.

THROUGH STAYING UNITED

We are speaking about you as a couple. No matter what, you must stay united, communicate effectively and jointly agree on the course of action to handle in-laws and parents.

THROUGH CLEARLY DEFINED BOUNDARIES

As a couple, you need to discuss and chalk out certain boundaries which can be enforced at home with your in-laws and parents. You can gently convey to them that this is where their liberty ends and trespassing commences, that can lead to strained relationships. Each home will have to define their own boundaries depending on the attitudes observed in the in-laws and parents.

THROUGH HOPE

God never gives up on us! Our God is a God of hope and as His people, we need to demonstrate hope in our relationships and in our dealings with our in-laws and parents. Hope keeps us positive and balanced.

THROUGH PRAYER

Prayer changes things. Never give up praying for your in-laws and parents. Prayer made in faith and in accordance with God's will achieves the impossible.

We trust that this little chapter on in-laws will go a long way in bringing understanding, clarity, and peaceful relationships in your dealings with your in-laws and parents. God bless you as you strive to live amicably with your in-laws and live-in parents.

THIRTEEN: HANDLING FINANCES

"God is not against money, He is against the money being used outside His purposes." Sunday Adelaja

"Every time you borrow money, you are robbing your future self." Nathan W. Morris

We live in a time where the focus is largely on affluence and materialism. We are galloping towards a cashless society. Paper money is being replaced with plastic money, which in plain language spells credit cards and debit cards. Spending patterns are changing rapidly, customers are being wooed with gusto and small shops are being replaced by massive glitzy malls. Children are being driven to excel, not for the sake of excellence but because parents are frightened that their children will miss the affluence bandwagon.

Sadly, materialism has also invaded the hallowed portals of our churches. Couples come in with alarming regularity to be counselled on financial matters, having made a mess of their lives through mismanagement of their finances. The buzzword today is "buy one-get one free," and "buy now-pay later." We buy glitzy dreams only to wake up from them, short-changed, in terrible debt and with no logical or practical plan for getting out of it. It is a vicious cycle. It is also very addictive. There are so many families who are at their wits end about paying their monthly bills and hence end up quarrelling with each other. So it is important that we talk about family finances and how to deal with them so that God may be glorified through our finances.

By the way, some of us might think that the Bible does not have much to speak about finances. The fact is, Jesus spoke more on the matter of money than about heaven and hell put together.

SOME TRUTHS ABOUT MONEY

- Money reveals a lot about the character of a person.
- Jesus talked about convenient giving and costly giving.
- Amount is secondary to attitude and motive.
- God never wanted a person to be satisfied with things. True treasure is in heaven.

We are stewards of all the resources that God has given us. A steward does not own what is given to him; he is responsible to dispense the same according to the instructions of its owner. Simply put, a steward is just a manager. John H. Reumann describes stewardship as "the practice of systematic and proportionate giving of time, talents, material possessions and all God's gifts to us, based on the conviction that they are a trust from God, to be used in His service for the benefit of all mankind in grateful acknowledgement."[xvii]

Let us look at some Scriptural principles relating to finances.

TRUST IN GOD AND NOT MAN

> But seek first his kingdom and his righteousness, and all these things will be given to you as well. (Matt 6:33)

This verse literally covers every basic human need. Jesus commands us not to be worried about our lives, food, drink, our bodies, or our clothes. To reinforce this, He gives examples of the birds of the air and the flowers of the field and how God watches over them, feeds them and clothes them Himself.

In the same passage (Matt 6:25–33) He also tells us that worrying is unprofitable, since our Heavenly Father knows our needs beforehand. So he commands that we do not fret and worry about tomorrow, because all our needs for the day are assured, provided we keep our focus right—which is to seek God's kingdom and His righteousness at all times.

Many of us have put our faith and trust in wrong places, as Psalms 20:7 tells us, "Some boast in chariots and some in horses." God again reiterates in Isaiah 31:1 "Woe to those who go down to Egypt for help, who rely on horses,
who trust in the multitude of their chariots and in the great strength of their horsemen, but do not look to the Holy One of Israel, or seek help from the Lord." The horses and the chariots of yester years can be compared to other material comforts or financial investments of our present day. As long as we trust in them, we will only continuously discover the truth of Genesis 47:15 (KJV):

> And when money failed in the land of Egypt, and in the land of Canaan, all the Egyptians came unto Joseph, and said, "give us bread: for why should we die in thy presence? For the money faileth."

There can always come a time when money, status, wealth, health, human wisdom fail. How important then it is to take God for His word and trust Him alone for all our needs, so that we will never be disappointed, no matter what.

STEWARDSHIP vs OWNERSHIP

Everything we have belongs to God. Job says it so well in chapter 1:21, "Naked I came from my mother's womb, and naked I will depart. The Lord gave and the Lord has taken away; may the name of the Lord be praised."

As uncontrollable events unfolded around Job, he realized that nothing was under his control and eventually he had to look up and acknowledge God's sovereignty over the affairs of mankind. In this profound verse, Job concludes that God was the giver of everything and hence He is qualified to take it back. If we apply it in our own lives, we recognize that we are only stewards of the wealth God has given us. Once we recognize this truth, we will become extremely careful in managing His wealth and use it for His glory alone. While the world around us focuses on earning more and more money, the Bible clearly teaches that our focus should not be in that direction. Here are some disadvantages of having excess money.

IT CAN HARDEN OUR HEARTS

> When you have eaten and are satisfied, praise the Lord your God for the good land he has given you. [11] Be careful that you do not forget the Lord your God, failing to observe his commands, his laws and his decrees that I am giving you this day. [12] Otherwise, when you eat and are satisfied, when you build fine houses and settle down, [13] and when your herds and flocks grow large and your silver and gold increase and all you have is multiplied, [14] then your heart will become proud and you will forget the Lord your God, who brought you out of Egypt, out of the land of slavery. (Deut 8:10–14)

This does not only apply to the people of Israel, but to our lives as well. When our wealth multiplies, our pride multiplies, leading to a diminishing dependence on God. Jesus says to His disciples, "Then Jesus said to his disciples, "Truly I tell you, it is hard for someone who is rich to enter the kingdom of heaven. Again I tell you, it is easier for a camel to go through the eye of a needle than for someone who is rich to enter the kingdom of God." (Matt 19:23–24).

WE CAN GET ATTACHED TO THE WORLD

> Do not love the world or anything in the world. If anyone loves the world, love for the Father is not in them. For everything in the world—the lust of the flesh, the lust of the eyes, and the pride of life—comes not from the Father but from the world. The world and its desires pass away, but whoever does the will of God lives forever. (1 John 2:15–17)

God knows that material things have tremendous power and can sway us. He bluntly exhorts us not to fall in love with three things:

- Lust of the flesh: trying to satisfy our sexual/sensuous urges.
- Lust of the eyes: trying to satisfy our material urges.
- Pride of life: post-gratification gloating over our acquisitions with pride.

God clearly says these cannot be from Him, but are worldly. People who obey God and keep away from these three strong temptations will have the joy of living together with God forever, enjoying all the heavenly blessings that He has prepared for us.

Since many of us are not financially astute and have no training in financial management, we end up making some major financial blunders. Let us now look at seven major mistakes that families make, that end up in a financial mess.

SEVEN MAJOR FINANCIAL MISTAKES

GETTING INTO DEBT

> The rich rules over the poor, and the borrower is slave to the lender. (Prov 22:7)

> You were bought at a price; do not become slaves of human beings. (1 Cor 7:23)

> Let no debt remain outstanding, except the continuing debt to love one another, for whoever loves others has fulfilled the law. (Rom 13:8)

If we combine the three passages together, we find some basic principles on handling debt. Firstly, the borrower is always at a disadvantage and beholden to the lender; secondly being under the control of another man is not a happy state of affairs; and thirdly, we are asked to make sure that we owe nothing to anyone whatsoever, except love. So basically, we are to keep away from any kind of debt. However, we will talk little more about permissible and non-permissible debt later.

IRRESPONSIBLE USE OF RESOURCES

In the parable of the ten minas (read Matt 25:14–30; Luke 19:11–26), there are some vital insights on handling finances.

- God trusts us with His resources.
- God expects us to make profitable use of His resources.

- If for some reason we are unable to profitably deploy His resources, we are expected to involve others (such as a bank) in using them profitably.
- There is a day of reckoning at the end, where we will have to give an account of all the resources entrusted into our care.
- Depending on our use of resources, we will either reap commendation and rewards or denouncement and punishment.

Many of us live on the earth as if we are going to spend all eternity here with never a care for anybody else except ourselves. Jesus denounces this kind of attitude and if we are not careful with our attitude towards our finances, harsh punishment awaits us.

A MONEY CENTERED LIFE

> Then he said to them, "Watch out! Be on your guard against all kinds of greed; life does not consist in an abundance of possessions." (Luke 12:15)

Jesus warns us against greed and running after possessions because in God's sight, life is not about acquiring possessions. The Scripture tells us to be content with what God gives us (1 Tim 6:6). Therein lies the secret of a happy life. As long as we run after possessions, they will always be a step ahead of us. It is like the proverbial carrot before a donkey. The moment we realize this folly and turn around, and begin to run after God, the same possessions that eluded us begin to run after us. A life that is not centered on money is a liberated life. It frees us to worship God and allows Him to change us into what He wants us to become.

TRYING TO GET RICH QUICK

> The stingy are eager to get rich and are unaware that poverty awaits them. (Prov 28:22)

Today, children are being driven hard to excel: not for the glory of God, but to have an affluent lifestyle. The objective is to reach the top within the shortest possible time. This apart, it is also hilarious to see how many Christians are dreaming of and participating in get-rich-quick games like, "Who Wants to Be a Millionaire." The dreams and aspirations of the common man are being fueled by palatial mansions, snazzy cars and a high-flying lifestyle. God is not against riches, but He is concerned about how we acquire them, what price we pay for them, and how we utilize them. He is also concerned about our worldly attitudes and aspirations to become affluent, as that would dethrone Him from His rightful place in our lives.

WITHHOLDING BENEVOLENCE

> One person gives freely, yet gains even more; another withholds unduly, but comes to poverty. A generous person will prosper; whoever refreshes others will be refreshed. (Prov 11:24–25)

God encourages us not only to be generous, but be over-flowingly generous. The Gospel of John chapter 6 recounts the incident of the five loaves and the two fishes. There were about 5000 men alone (theologians say there could have been between 15,000 and 25,000 individuals) on that day when Jesus fed them with the loaves and the fish given to Him by that generous lad. Logically, there could have been many more who would have brought something to eat that day, but when the disciples wanted to know if someone had brought food, the foremost thought in these people's minds was, "If I give away my food, what about my needs?" Obviously, these people had not understood the truth of Proverbs 11:24, that it is in giving bountifully, we receive bountifully. God is no man's debtor, and He multiplies and blesses us many fold of what we give to Him. In Luke 21 we find Jesus commending a poor widow for putting two copper coins, which is all she had, unlike the Pharisees who were giving large amounts out of their abundance. Withholding something that is legitimately due to someone can result in our blessings being blocked. Some principles we learn from this passage are:

- We cannot hold back legitimate dues.
- We are to be generous in giving, and our giving should be bountiful.
- It is in giving that we are blessed and receive many fold.
- Withholding dues and benevolence can result in poverty and want.

So let us learn to be generous and not withhold benevolence from anyone that the Lord instructs us to help.

CHEATING

> The wicked accept bribes in secret to pervert the course of justice. (Prov 17:23)

> He said to them, "Then give back to Caesar what is Caesar's, and to God what is God's." (Luke 20:25)

The above passages coupled with Isaiah 33:15 clearly tell us that we cheat people and God, when we pervert justice for monetary gain, or fail to pay our taxes. We come across many believers who meticulously pay their tithes but fudge their income tax returns to pay less tax to the government. God does not approve of this and wants us to be on the right side of the law always!

A BUSINESS/JOB ORIENTED LIFE

> No one serving as a soldier gets entangled in civilian affairs, but rather tries to please his commanding officer. (2 Tim 2:4)

Every child of God is an enlisted soldier for His kingdom and entangling himself with things that detract him or take precedence over His kingdom must be avoided at all cost. Many of us become busy in earning money that we lose sight of the real purpose of our existence. We are so busy running around, giving ourselves and our family a good life that it takes up most of our time, energy, and resources. That leaves us with nothing to give God or just let Him have some leftovers. This must never happen to us. God deserves and must get our best.

FOUR STEPS TO ACHIEVE FINANCIAL INDEPENDENCE

Many couples come to us for counselling after having messed up their finances and their whole focus is on how to get out of their debt. While there are certain steps of practical wisdom that we can initiate (which work), but there are no quick fixes. Here are four helpful steps to gain financial freedom from crippling debt.

RECOGNIZE THAT WEALTH-CREATION COMES FROM THE LORD FOR A PURPOSE

> But remember the Lord your God, for it is he who gives you the ability to produce wealth, and so confirms his covenant, which he swore to your ancestors, as it is today. (Deut 8:18)

Concerning finances, we must come to clear understanding of the following points:

> The power that allows us to make wealth and achieve success in financial matters is the prerogative of God. (Deut 8:18)

> The riches of the whole universe belong to God. (Hag 2:8)

> The inhabitants of the earth belong to God. (Ps 24:1)

> Jesus promises us that when we ask something in faith it shall be given to us. (Matt 21:22)

> We do not receive from God when our motives and goals are wrong. (Jas 4:3)

If He holds all the riches and all the people in His hands, and has the power to help us make wealth, it would be a pity if we do not start with Him, seek Him, and ask Him to get us out of debt by generating adequate finances. So, our request for freedom from debt should not be to free us from the clutches of our creditors but to give us a new lease in our financial life to glorify Him, and to use our resources for His kingdom.

We need to understand that God blesses us so that we might seek godly goals in our lives and achieve them. All the resources God has given to us must become ministering resources. One of the examples of only receiving and never giving is that of the Dead Sea. The Dead Sea only receives inflows, being at the lowest point below sea level; hence there is no way for its water to flow out. Therefore, it cannot support any life, hence its name. Remember it only receives and never gives. Some of us get into this mindset, jeopardizing our spiritual lives to the extent of becoming like the Dead Sea.

We once saw a beautiful poster somewhere which had the picture of the five loaves and two fish and the caption read: "Love is ... never enough until you start to give it away."

GIVE GOD TIME TO WORK

> "For my thoughts are not your thoughts, neither are your ways my ways," declares the LORD. (Isa 55:8)

The trouble with us is, we have already worked out the minute details of every event of our life and want God to work alongside us. God does not operate like that. You will have to give the reins of your lives, especially your financial lives, into His hands and trust Him to work out all the solutions. That can only happen when you have confidence in God and his ways and are willing to wait. In the meanwhile, you also have to identify the areas where you have been doing things wrong and avoid repeating the same mistakes. Also remember to steer clear away from any fresh debt.

TITHE YOUR INCOME – GIVE WITH GRACE AND NOT A GRIMACE

> And Melchizedek king of Salem brought out bread and wine. He was priest of God Most High, and he blessed Abram, saying, "Blessed be Abram by God Most High, Creator of heaven and earth. And praise be to God Most High, who delivered your enemies into your hand." Then Abram gave him a tenth of everything. (Gen 14:18–20)

> Honor the Lord with your wealth, with the firstfruits of all your crops; then your barns will be filled to overflowing, and your vats will brim over with new wine. (Prov 3:9–10)

These passages highlight the act of giving to God, starting from a tenth of all our earning, and giving it cheerfully. Giving is a very touchy subject and raises a lot of questions and heartaches. Many families are divided over this issue, where either the husband or the wife finds it very difficult to separate a tenth of their income for God's work or house.

Before we go further, we would like to give our personal example. At the beginning of our marriage, in the late 70s and the early 80s, while we were both working in different banks and earning reasonably well, we still could not make ends meet. Even before half the month was over, money would run out, and we would start hunting for small change and forgotten notes kept here and there. Vijaya would lament because she was managing the finances and paying the bills. Every month was a new financial challenge and the situation seemed impossible. One day, God hit us with a passage of Scripture that jolted us. It appeared that this passage was tailor made for us:

> You have planted much, but harvested little. You eat, but never have enough. You drink, but never have your fill. You put on clothes, but are not warm. You earn wages, only to put them in a purse with holes in it." This is what the Lord Almighty says: "Give careful thought to your ways. ... "You expected much, but see, it turned out to be little. What you brought home, I blew away. Why?" declares the Lord Almighty. "Because of my house, which remains a ruin, while each of you is busy with your own house. (Hag 1:6–7, 9)

This passage jolted us, caused acute consternation, but illuminated our thinking. It was as if it was our life that was being analyzed. Twice in the first chapter, God says, "consider your ways"! Through this passage, God caused us to examine ourselves. It looked next to impossible, and scary, but both of us made a commitment with God. We decided to separate a tenth of all our earning on the day we received our salaries and put it in a different account which was labeled as "God's Account." God also convicted us that this tenth was from our gross earnings and not our net earnings. Net earnings can shrink due to our various commitments, but remember it is the gross earning that matters—it is what we actually earn every month. This was a huge financial shock for us but God convicted us and we separated the tenth of our gross earnings.

While all this was going on, God also brought another Scripture passage to our attention from Malachi 3:10, "Bring the whole tithe into the storehouse, that there may be food in my house. Test me in this," says the LORD Almighty, "and see if I will not throw open the floodgates of heaven, and pour out so much blessing that there will not be room enough to store it."

We felt God was challenging our faith by asking us to test Him in the matter of giving. We took God seriously and accepted this challenge, knowing that God would open the heavens and pour out a blessing.

Although with a sense of trepidation, we separated the tenth for the first time, and experienced the unbelievable. God began to relieve our financial pressures, added to our income, reduced our expenditure and in the first month we could sail through financially with some money left over! We were so excited that we had taken a great leap of faith and put our burden on God and found Him sufficient to carry us through. Since then we have never looked back. In fact, we believe that giving the tenth is only returning what actually is owned by God, but our actual giving starts with the amount that is over and above the tenth of our gross income. Elsewhere in this book you will find our personal testimony which is going to challenge you, but we will put this down here as well, for the glory of God. After both of us had quit our jobs to serve the Lord full-time, we discovered in 2001 that Vijaya had a slight renal malfunction. This eventually developed into complete renal failure necessitating dialysis for nearly 4 years. Many of you must be aware that treating renal failure and getting dialysis (in India) is a very costly affair. We had to spend an enormous amount of money, and amazingly God provided. We did not have to spend anything from our own resources in this prolonged battle with renal failure! This is how faithful God is, and His provision is endless! The trouble with us is that we are unable to cross the bridge of faith, take the plunge and put our weight on the promises of God. No wonder we are unable to discover His wondrous provision! We challenge you to try Him and see how He can leave you speechless by His care, provision, and faithfulness.

Further, our giving should be from a joyful heart and not as a matter of mere obedience to the letter of the law. We give out of our love and not compulsion. God loves this (2 Cor 9:7). God greatly appreciates sacrificial giving as can be seen by his commendation of the widow who gave the two copper coins, which is all she had (Luke 21:2).

PRACTICE PRACTICAL MONEY MANAGEMENT SKILLS

There are three areas we will have to look into to understand the art of practical money management.

BUDGETING

Effective money management begins with budgeting. Budgeting is nothing but knowledge of what you are earning, how you are spending it, and how to balance these two so that you do not get into debt. Budgeting has two components: firstly, a plan for spending and secondly a record of spending.

This involves a little extra work but pays rich dividends. We suggest you take a lined book, and on one page, list every income that comes for any given month, and on the opposite page list all the expenses which will have to be paid that month. The difference between these two tabular forms will show you whether your income is adequate to cover your expenses, or your expenses exceed your income. Please remember that the income you mention here will be the income after deducting your tithe money.

In case your expenses exceed your income, you will have to devise ways and means to cut back on your expenditure. We have all heard the very astute saying, "cut your coat according to your cloth." On the expenditure side, there are non-negotiable items, over which you have no control like groceries, doctor's bills, medicines, school fees, utility bills like electricity and water etc. However, if your outflow on utility bills is high, you will have to find ways to prune them suitably. Some of items that can be worked on thereby freeing up extra resources are:

- Cut down on expenditure for commuting to work. Take a cheaper mode of transport (perhaps public transport).
- Stop making impulsive purchases. Keep a list of items to buy, and do not buy beyond the list.
- Do not gift expensive items to anyone.
- Do not spend money on non-essentials: clothes, holidays, entertainment. Make do with what you have till finances ease off.
- If you live in a rented house, consider moving to a house where you will have lesser rent.

The whole idea is to lessen expenditure to the extent that it can come much below the level of income generation. Thereafter, you need to meticulously record your spending. This serves two purposes. Firstly, you will be able to relate every item of expenditure to the budgeted amount. Secondly it is only when you keep a record of income and spending you can tweak your budgeting and control your finances.

SAVING

Many Christians believe that saving is not for God's children who have the promises of God to meet all their needs. So why save? Let us look at two Scriptural passages for greater clarity on the matter:

> Go to the ant, you sluggard; consider its ways and be wise! It has no commander, no overseer or ruler, yet it stores its provisions in summer and gathers its food at harvest. (Prov 6:6–8)

> Four things on earth are small, yet they are extremely wise: Ants are creatures of little strength, yet they store up their food in the summer; (Prov 30:24–25)

God speaking through the wisest king Solomon, draws our attention to the little ant, who gathers her food during summer when it is freely and abundantly available to prepare for the harsh winter months when gathering food becomes difficult. God wants us to learn from the ant and become wise.

In Genesis 41, Joseph advised Pharaoh to store up grain during the first seven years of great abundance, thereby piling up a buffer stock that would see them through during the following seven years of the great famine. This godly wisdom not only saved the land of Egypt but also saved many hungry people across the world. God has given us wisdom, and wisdom dictates that we should not waste, but save God's resources when they are abundant, so that in days to come, not only us, but other people too may benefit from this wisdom and provision.

Here are four rules on saving:

AMOUNT OF SAVINGS

Financial experts say that our saving levels should be to the tune of 20 to 25% of the gross income per month. Savings below 10% of the gross income is not advisable. When we say savings here, it includes every kind of saving including pensions directly deducted by the employer, life insurance policies, and savings accounts. Sometimes we are tempted by the high returns offered by certain investment companies, but there is a question about the safety of your funds, as investments can go down as well as up.

SAVING TO SPEND

It makes sense to divide your savings into two or three parts. One part is to be kept aside as a reserve for spending on holidays, or buying household articles, etc. A word of caution: we generally do not recommend buying anything on installments. This can encourage impulsive buying at times. Only purchase when you have saved enough to buy.

SAVING NEVER TO SPEND

We have used the term "never" very loosely. We do not mean that this money can never be spent. We are referring here to saving for later long-term expenses like paying fees for professional college for your children, marriage or buying a house etc. You must never touch this money to meet your short-term expenses, no matter how tempting it may be.

AVOID HOARDING

There is a fine line between saving and hoarding. Some people are compulsive hoarders. They like to accumulate money and possessions just for the love of it. You feel elated to see fat amounts in your bank deposits and lovely possessions that you cherish at home. You need godly wisdom to avoid this. Regarding possessions like furniture, books etc. at home, we prescribe a golden rule to de-clutter your life. If you have not used something for over a year, give it away! It obviously means that you can make do without it and will not be any poorer without it. Remember, our resources must be sanctified, ministering resources.

In conclusion we would like to discuss a very important topic in financial management which is handling of debt.

DEBT

Although we are personally against incurring any kind of debt, we do realize that some debts are permissible. Debt can be divided into two categories:

PERMISSIBLE DEBT

The only permissible debt we do accept is a mortgage. This is because for most of us, no matter how much we save towards buying a house, we would never have saved enough to buy the house! Buying a property saves on the house rent that you would have had to pay for a rented property. However, remember that it is a fully secured loan, which means if you fail to keep up repayments that your home can be repossessed. It is generally repayable over a long-term usually 15 to 25 years and low and fixed interest rates are available.

NON-PERMISSIBLE DEBT

These debts should be avoided at all cost. To give you a few examples: borrowing to buy consumer durables like furniture, gadgets, television sets, music systems, clothes, borrowing money to go on holidays, celebration of festivals, etc. The outlay on all these expenses must come from the saving mentioned above under the category of "saving to spend."

SIMPLE STEPS TO GET OUT OF DEBT

If you are in debt and find it difficult to wriggle out, let us give you simple steps to get out of debt:

Pray. In 2 Kings 4:1–7 we find God used the vessels and the little oil that the widow already had to multiply it to get her out of debt. Often God has the power to multiply the little we have.

Have a written budget. We have already seen how a written budget can be a tool for financial analysis and positive, beneficial financial decision-making.

List out all your debts and start paying the one with the highest interest first, and stay away from new debt.

Be content with what you have, never compare yourself with others.

Do not let the craze of credit cards blind you to the harsh realities of debt and charges hiding behind these little plastic cards that magically pay your bills.

A little wisdom about the use of credit cards would be greatly beneficial. Read the fine print about the charges levied on the use of credit cards. You would be shocked to know that many banks charge as much as 36 to 45% per annum over delayed payments. We know many people who ended up in this vicious cycle and spent precious resources just paying the interest and could not extricate themselves from the vice-like grip of the credit card banks.

Use a credit card only as a means of convenience to save time and effort in paying your utility bills or travel bills. You can get the booking of your air, rail tickets done on the internet from the comfort of your home. This is where your credit card and debit card can come to your rescue.

Please ensure you have adequate cash balance in your account to cover all these purchases. So in practical reality you will use credit or debit cards as cash cards.

Make sure that you always pay the total monthly outstanding on the credit card at one stroke every month.

At no time, draw cash on credit cards unless in an emergency, in the event of which, make sure that this cash withdrawal is covered by cash deposits in your accounts which pay out the credit card expenses every month.

Initially, buying with a credit card seemingly does not hurt our pocket, but please remember that the bills will have to be paid at the end of the month. Accordingly, never use your credit cards for impulsive buying, but only for budgeted items for which adequate cash levels are maintained in your savings accounts. We recommend using debit cards over credit cards.

As far as possible and unless you regularly travel overseas, please do not have more than one credit card at any point of time. It becomes a great temptation to use in times of financial stress. But please remember that no matter what, all expenses paid through the credit card must be backed up by cash balances in your savings.

In conclusion we would like to suggest to you four questions you should always ask yourself before buying anything. If the answer to the first question is "yes," you can go to the next question and so on. If the answer is "no," do not go to the next question because you should not proceed with your purchase.

- Do we need it?
- Can we do without it?
- If we do not buy it, can we use the money more profitably elsewhere? (for kingdom purposes)
- Will God approve of it?

If you are serious about asking these questions, being accountable to God for your spending habits, you will never get into trouble. We trust that this chapter has touched your hearts to bring about a financial revolution in your family that will touch others, gladden God's heart, and bring great blessing in your families. May God bless your finances to make you a good financial witness always!

FOURTEEN: HANDLING FAMILY AND MINISTRY

"I am only one person, I cannot do everything; but what I can do, and should do, I will do for the glory of God." Unknown

Henrik Ibsen tells the story of a rural pastor serving in a church in Norway. He was passionate about evangelizing Norway. Norway is a cold country with severe snow bound winters. He had a small son who fell sick and was advised by a doctor to be taken to a place with a warmer climate. But this pastor was so passionate about his work in Norway that he ignored the doctor's advice which led to the death of his son, and later his wife.[xviii]

Soon his wife began to fall sick frequently, and doctors suggested that she too move to a warmer climate as the climate in Norway was unsuitable for her. Again, the pastor refused to budge and ultimately his wife succumbed to the sickness. After this incident the board of the church which he served in, summoned him for a meeting. In the meeting he was informed of the board's decision to dismiss him from service as he was found to be insensitive to the needs of his own family, and as such could not be trusted with the larger family of God's people. This tragic story tells us that this pastor, although passionate about his call, was so insensitive to the people closest to him that it clouded his judgment. Perhaps he also failed to see and understand what God was trying to communicate to him through his family.

What a revelation! We can be passionate, alive to the task, but insensitive to people. Time and again we come across many families in our own country who have been experiencing similar tragic circumstances although not exactly on the same level. While serving God is great and a specific call, God always keeps the larger picture in mind and continuously makes course corrections throughout our lives. If we are married, God does not take us alone into consideration, he also takes our families into His plan.

Many wives of full-time ministers have complained (as also have the wives of secular workers engaged in the ministry in their spare time) that their husbands have become insensitive to their families under the pretext of serving God. And if they are badgered, they blame their wives and families to be the tools of the devil in trying to prevent them from serving God. This is far from the truth, and we hope to help these ministers reorient their ministry, in consultation with God and their families.

To begin with, here are some signs of disturbance generally noticed in families (to be precise, in wives and children), when husbands are unable to strike a healthy balance between the ministry and their families.

- Frequent quarrels.
- General disinterest and unresponsiveness in their behavior (sometimes plain rebellion).
- Vocalized feelings of neglect.
- Frequent complaints (about husband, children, and circumstances).
- Frequent sickness (sometimes stress and anxiety can manifest through physical sickness).
- Demands (often unreasonable – like purchase of non-essentials or constantly wanting to stay at in-law's house).
- Dwindling sex life.
- Reduced interest in spiritual matters (Ministry is viewed as a competitor).
- A demand to shift the base (seen as something that will shift the attention of the husband and father towards the family).
- General critical attitude.
- Not easily pleased (even if you try hard).
- A sudden shift of interest (either in general matters, hobbies or habits).
- General indifference towards life (a fatalistic attitude).
- Silence (withdrawal).

While some of the above indicators could be pointers of something else, by and large these indicate that all is not well in the family. They also speak volumes of the silent messages being sent by the family to you, crying to be heard and addressed. You would do well to take a break from a busy routine, take some time off to spend time alone with God in silence, and we are sure God will reveal the truth behind all these indicators and give you fresh directions to handle your situation, your family and the ministry. Please also note that the above is also applicable to people totally immersed in their secular jobs. Most of us think that ministry means either to preach or to be involved in some activity directly or indirectly that could contribute to evangelism or build up the body of Christ. While this is true, let us look at the larger understanding of ministry. The word "ministry" is taken from the Greek word *diakoneo*, meaning "to serve" or *douleuo*, meaning "to serve as a slave." In the New Testament, ministry is perceived as service to God and to other people in His name, including your own household!

Ministry basically is to serve God and His people as a slave. It implies that both sides of the spectrum are equally important and need to be appropriately balanced. Remember the story by Henrik Ibsen – if you are not sensitive, you are in danger of losing both your family and your ministry.

1 John 4:20–21 is incisively clear:

> Whoever claims to love God yet hates a brother or sister is a liar. For whoever does not love their brother and sister, whom they have seen, cannot love God, whom they have not seen. And he has given us this command: Anyone who loves God must also love their brother and sister.

The elder must be a man who serves God is sensitive towards people around him and manages his own household well, keeping his children under control, children who believe, and prove to be examples (Tit 1:6–7; 1 Pet 5:3).

So God is telling us that our love for Him is known by our love for people around us. If you carefully study all the above passages, you will realize that these are directly speaking of our ministry to those around us, especially our families and to be more specific, our wives and children. (See especially Eph 5:25–29; 6:5–7; Col 3:19; 1 Pet 3:7–8 and 1 Tim 5:8).

A friend of ours, also a preacher, told us a very amusing incident of a pastor and his family. The pastor had a small son who was very fond of him. Every time the father would sit with the Bible either to have his quiet time or to prepare a sermon, his son would come running, sit in his lap and start turning the pages of the Bible, making it difficult to concentrate on his sermon preparation. To avoid this, the pastor got up very early one morning, and quietly went into his study to prepare a sermon for the coming Sunday. Somehow his son realized his father was missing, quickly got down from the bed, went in search of him and on finding him, promptly sat on his lap. The preacher got so vexed that he shouted at his son and roughly pushed him from his lap. The little boy was shocked at his father's treatment and went crying to his mother who was in the kitchen. The mother, taking the child in her arms, said to him loudly so that the father could hear too, "don't cry son, don't you know your father is busy preparing a sermon to preach to the children of the church." Her husband heard her, including the unspoken words behind the retort, which pierced his heart. He quickly got up, went into the kitchen and took his son in his arms, comforting him.

We can get so busy with ministering to other people that we forget to minister to our own family! Both of us, from our own personal and ministerial experience have listed out priorities that contribute to a happy family and a great ministry:

- GOD (your personal walk and relationship with Him);
- FAMILY (especially spouse and children);
- MINISTRY. Whatever you do, you represent God to those around you. If you are a doctor, you are a doctor for God, if you are a banker you are a banker for God, if you are a teacher you are a teacher for God, if you are a homemaker you are a homemaker for God. You do everything as unto the Lord, who is your real master.
- SOCIETY "In the same way, let your light shine before others, that they may see your good deeds and glorify your Father in heaven." (Matt 5:16)

Your office can find another employee, but your wife and children cannot find another husband and father. At the workplace, it is usually seen that extra work is dumped on people who are willing to take on more. Both of us have worked for over two decades in different banks. We worked diligently and were considered indispensable by our superiors, yet there was a fine line which we would not cross in working beyond the office hours. While we obliged our organizations in emergencies, we would not go beyond office hours on regular days. Even our superiors knew that our family was very important to us and we were never expected to come on holidays and Sundays or go beyond the working hours as a rule. And by the way, we were respected for our convictions, and at times this formed a platform for others to come and seek our guidance and counsel about their own families.

While you work as unto the Lord (Col 3:23–24), and do your best for your organizations, know for sure that your family is a higher priority. View everything through the grid of eternity, as you have limited time, and you are asked to redeem your time. Ask yourselves, what difference will it make for me and my loved ones in terms of eternity? The answer to this question will help you get your priorities right.

SEVEN STEPS TO RESTORE BALANCE BETWEEN FAMILY AND THE MINISTRY

STAY TUNED

Many of us have forgotten the art of being "in tune," and we need to inculcate this discipline. When we are tuned to God completely, it also leads us to be in tune with our family. This simply means that as we listen to God we will listen to our family as well. This also means making sure that our daily altar—both personal and that of the family—is in good shape. This will get us back on target.

STAY ALERT

We need to be observant, to open our eyes and see what is happening all around us. Many times we rush through life in blissful ignorance, which is the surest way of missing the truth and destroying our relationships. Please watch your family carefully and you will find many silent indicators in the way your wife responds, the way your children answer back. As you discover these indicators, you also need to persist in finding the underlying cause of things. For instance, a casual question, "is something wrong?" Will get a very nonchalant answer, "not at all, what gives you the idea?" You might be satisfied with this but don't be. If your conscience is telling you otherwise, persist until you know the truth and you will be able to address it.

STAY CONCERNED

We need to be concerned not just for the family unit, but also about every individual in the family. While the family is a complete entity, every individual is an essential part and unless every part is happy, the family will never be healthy and functional.

There is a common saying, "the squeakiest axle gets the grease." It is so true about the family as well. We have those members who are loud and outgoing; we generally know them as extroverts. We tend to notice them since these personalities are quick to vocalize their feelings and we are always trying to address their issues and minister to them. On the other hand, we tend to praise those who are silent saying, "Oh, they are so sweet, they never give us any trouble!" You need to be extra cautious about these people as they might be hurting inside, although appearing normal on the outside; we know them as introverts. Be observant! Stay concerned! Spend time and energy to know them better, understand and address their concerns as well.

BE OPEN

Openness to four aspects is vital to restoring the right balance. Firstly, be open to God's promptings. God speaks all the time, in different ways. It is sad that we have not inculcated the art of hearing God by tuning our hearts to Him. But if we do so, God will speak to us through His Word, His Spirit, His people (godly people who can see what is going wrong), our conscience, circumstances, and our family too.

Secondly, be open to God's people. As some wise man has remarked, "no man can see his back, but everybody else can!" Our blind side is visible not only to our family, but also to godly people around us who are prompted by God to take up the issue with us. Most of us might term it as interference. But if we tune ourselves to hear God and His promptings, we will also open ourselves to God's people when they point out our deficiencies. Be open to them! Do not resent them! On the other hand, be grateful to God for sending them to speak to you.

Thirdly, be open to reality. Sometimes we develop the "ostrich mentality," a refusal to see or face the truth. It just shows that we are scared to know the truth. When the truth hits us through the reactions of our loved ones, it devastates us. We should be open to realities around us that people could be hurting and might be forced into hurtful behaviors just because we were unwilling to face the truth and find remedies. So be open to what you see, analyze it thoroughly and act upon it. Do not be scared, as you and God can handle anything!

Finally, be open to change. Every relational difficulty demands attitudinal changes in everyone, starting with us first. Change is not only difficult, but painful as well. If you're not open to change—and people can sense this—they will never be open about their own feelings, convinced that no matter what happens, you will not change. So unless you demonstrate to your family that you are willing to change, you cannot expect them to open up and share the hurts they have been facing.

BE AWARE

We need to understand that failure to take suitable action in restoring our families can lead to serious consequences. The first thing that we will lose is our peace of mind. This will make life difficult and can colour every area of our life, sapping happiness and strength from our existence. The second thing is a loss of respect among family members. This does not happen overnight! It is the result of our obtuseness and our indifference. The third thing is a loss of inner peace and outer vitality. Life will seem to drag, and progress whether in the ministry or in the family will be elusive and ultimately lead to what is known as a 'burn-out.' The fourth and the final consequence will be the loss of ministry that is Spirit-filled, power-backed and effective. We will somehow plod on with a lack-lustre and ineffective ministry.

BE SURE

Be sure that God loves you as much as He loves your family. They are as precious to Him as we are. Jesus loves them so much that He died for them.

As we begin to see them as how God sees them, we will begin to live by the truth of Matthew 7:12, "Therefore whatever you want others to do for you, do so for them; for this is the Law and the Prophets."

Be certain to get your family behind you in the ministry enthusiastically. Having them on your side can be joyful, productive, and fruitful. You might get some interesting inputs from them that you are not aware of. As mentioned earlier, many men think that God has called them alone to serve Him, forgetting the truth of Genesis 2:18. Our wives are given to us as helpmeets and not impediments, they are likened to a fruitful vine in Psalm 128:3, and our children, given as a reward (Ps 127), are to be around our table as olive plants (Ps 128). These truths do not apply to domestic areas alone, but to every area of our lives. When you get your family on board and enlist their help, your ministry can blossom and be very fruitful, with lasting impact.

BE RESPONSIBLE

We are responsible for our families as our primary mission fields. We may preach elsewhere around the world, but if it has not touched our family (especially if we have unbelieving wives and children), we have hardly achieved anything! We remember a very interesting anecdote, where a mother of 12 children approached a servant of God with a complaint, "Brother, I have a missionary call, but what can I do with 12 children to care for?" The man of God replied, "Madam, I am so glad that God has not only given you a missionary call, but a missionary field as well!" You see! Our family is our primary missionary field! This is where everything starts and everything must conclude.

With due respect to the holy Scriptures and with much prayer and faith we want to rephrase a famous verse of the Bible found in Matthew 16:26 to illustrate what this chapter is all about: "For what will it profit a man if he gains the whole world and forfeits his family? Or what will a man give in exchange for his family?" Nothing, we repeat, nothing can ever take the place of the family (of course not counting God) and we should make sure that we strike a healthy balance between our family and ministry.

In exceptional circumstances and for a short duration, God could ask you to give prominence to ministry over the family, but this will happen only when God speaks to your wife and children as well, and they are convinced that this is God's short term will for you, happily releasing you for this task. On completion of this task, you must revert to your original priorities. May God bless you and may you keep God first, and family next, all the time.

FIFTEEN: HANDLING ABUSE AND DIVORCE

"If we are to fight discrimination and injustice against women we must start from the home, for if a woman cannot be safe in her own house, then she cannot be expected to feel safe anywhere." Aysha Taryam

"It takes two to destroy a marriage." Margaret Trudeau

We will in this chapter deal with a very difficult subject, rampant yet rarely discussed and remedied. In our twenty plus years of counselling we have come across girlfriends, wives, mothers and daughters who have experienced horrifying abuse, both mental and physical, at the hands of men who thought the only way to control a woman is through violence. Abuse, whether physical or verbal, leaves women helpless, trapped in loveless marriages at the receiving end of bullying husbands. And they are unable either to help themselves or find a way out.

Violence against the fairer sex is a problem worldwide. Even in civilized and highly advanced nations, this is quite a common problem, with about 6% of adults in England and Wales experiencing abuse between 2013–2016.[xix] Yet this figure may actually be much higher; many crimes go unnoticed and unreported, because women are unwilling to report them to the police, fearing social stigma. Added to this is the fear of the repercussions this reporting might bring, not only on them but also on their immediate family members.

Many self-help groups and NGOs are bringing much comfort and succor to these battered women. Tragically, churches either turn a blind eye, or are unequipped to handle such cases. It is high time that people of God woke up to the fact that we serve a God of justice, and "to one who knows the right thing to do and does not do it, to him it is sin" (James 4:17).

It is also important to become proactive in our counselling in cases of domestic abuse, in terms of identifying and confronting bullies. For instance, take the case of Mary (name changed) who would frequently come for counselling with a black eye, swollen cheeks, or bruises on the body. Of course, we involved the authorities, who came to arrest the man. Being warned that he could face jail, and so lose his job and perhaps not find another one owing to his police record, brought about a willingness to get help and rehabilitation. Although the verbal abuse continued for some time, the physical violence completely stopped. Sometimes it is only a threat of serious action that brings in results.

POSSIBLE SIGNS OF AN ABUSIVE MAN
- He is jealous and extremely possessive.
- He likes to be in control always and in every situation (whether in actions, relationships, or finances).
- He feels superior to his wife.
- He manipulates through emotional blackmail.
- He has trouble controlling his anger and is easily provoked.
- His actions and words do not match.
- He is unwilling to seek help, as he believes that his behavior is above reproach.
- He disrespects women.
- He most likely has a history of abusing women, or was abused himself.
- He pressurizes his wife sexually and demands sexual activities she is not comfortable with.
- He tries to isolate his wife by cutting off her social contacts and friendships.
- Those around him frequently worry about his actions and reactions.
- He loves belittling people and making "jokes" that shame, humiliate, demean or embarrass his wife and children whether privately or when around family and friends.

FALLOUT OF ABUSIVE RELATIONSHIPS

The victim may leave and then return to the abuser repeatedly, against the advice of friends, family, and loved ones. Children in the family go through tremendous pain and distress; and since children watch and learn, an abuser's son is more likely to become an abuser himself in his adult life. There is a complete breakdown in the family system—there may only be negative communication; conflicts are never resolved, as decision making is one-sided.

HOW TO HANDLE ABUSIVE RELATIONSHIPS

Perpetrators and victims of emotional or physical abuse need prolonged therapy, and monitoring by law agencies; perhaps by a restraining order and a rehabilitation order from a court of law.

Here are some pointers on how to deal with an abusive partner.

- If you are physically hurt, go directly to your doctor or hospital for treatment.

- In the presence of reliable witnesses, mention directly to the person abusing you that you do not want to see him, in order that he may not be able to get in touch with you. Avoid contact with them as far as possible.

- Do not feel ashamed or guilty to share your situation with someone you trust.

- Keep a record, for the authorities, of dates and details when abuse happens. With the modern cell phones making it possible to take "selfies," please take pictures of yourself, showing bruises or lacerations. If you have a close friend or relative, it would also be good to intimate them and have them look at your bruises.

- Do not hesitate to go to the police and seek protection.

- Always carry your cell phone, credit cards, debit cards and money. If you have a passport, either keep it in a bank locker along with your jewelry or keep it with your parents, some trusted relatives or friends.

- Do not walk alone outside the house, try and make sure that there is someone with you always. In case the person is following you, call for help immediately—do not wait for it to resolve by itself.

- Always have domestic violence help numbers handy, like the local police department and self-help groups.

SOME ADDITIONAL WARNINGS ABOUT ABUSIVE RELATIONSHIPS

Abusive people try to run you down or tear you apart at every level. They may call you names like stupid, fat, ugly etc. Believe in your heart that you are none of those things and rather you are smart, healthy, and beautiful and ignore his remarks. This will keep your self- image intact and give you the staying power to handle the abuse positively. Reading Psalm 139 helps to restore your self-image.

Physical abuse perpetrators generally know who will let them have their way. Consequently, the more you tolerate, the more abuse is heaped. So, do not stand for it. Stand up for yourself, even if it becomes very uncomfortable, and tell your partner plainly that you will not tolerate verbal or physical abuse, and will to go to any length to make sure it stops.

Do not hesitate to file a police complaint and follow it up with the authorities to initiate suitable action.

Get out. Nothing is worth an abusive relationship. Leave with your children, and any material possessions you can carry, because you cannot fathom what might happen next. Many women in these situations have been hospitalized or killed. These are not imaginary scenarios, you can find them being regularly mentioned in our newspapers. Find a safe haven, gather the kids and get out when the abuser is not around.

Seek therapy and help for yourself from your network of friends. There are quite a few NGOs that are helping women who are physically abused. Find one such NGO in your own city and enlist their help. This will also help bolster your self-sufficiency. An honest assessment of your abusive relationship will help you see that it is not worth putting up with.

At times the abuser, finding you want to get rid of him, is likely to come back to you, appearing very penitent and willing to make amends. He will cajole you to get back, or emotionally blackmail you. Do not give in. He must first agree to seek professional and psychological help and only after he is certified free from his anger outbursts, mood swings and lack of control, can he be trusted.

Do not let this abuse get you down. Trust God and walk with Him consistently. God is sufficient for all your needs, be it emotional, financial, physical, mental, or spiritual. He is all you need. Seek God consistently, His will and His plans for your life and be ready to obey Him at all times.

Get a grip on your life, and get back to your normal routine as quickly as possible. You can choose to forgive, as the Bible teaches, but *do not go back* unless there is a complete turn-around in behavior and attitude.

Do your best to be self-sufficient financially, both for yourself and your children. If you are not working, think of getting a job to support yourself till God shows you a way to handle the situation. Otherwise you will land back either at his doorstep, or with your parents, relatives and friends who can only look after you temporarily.

Also remember that we serve a great God for whom nothing is impossible, and when we trust Him and give Him the control of our lives, He has all the answers and all the solutions. He is in-charge of the department of change in the lives of His people. We have seen the worst-case scenarios turn around completely. It pays to be prayerful, godly, forgiving and optimistic. You will be surprised by what God can do!

DIVORCE AND REMARRIAGE

Divorce and remarriage is the thorniest and the most difficult topic found in the area of marriage relationships. Whether we like it or not, divorce has become an integral part of our lives in some sense or the other. It is happening everywhere! Thank God if our marriage is strong and vibrant, but chances are someone dear or near to us has gone through the sticky mess of handling divorce, and is picking up the shattered pieces of their lives. Divorce is a costly business financially, emotionally, and spiritually. It shatters the couple, children, parents and others close to them. It seems that everywhere, divorce is on the rise, and the price-tag attached is enormous.

In our own counselling experience, we have come across many cases that came with a wide spectrum of problems, finally concluding that the only way out was divorce. Some are clear-cut cases, while some are extremely complicated to understand and handle. Take the case of Jayne, whose husband was working overseas and would visit her either once a year or once every two years. Jayne was lonely and was finding this responsibility of being a single mother difficult to handle. She was working in an office where she met another man who began to show interest in her and help her in small everyday issues. Before long they found themselves in a sexual relationship. It doesn't take long for these matters to go around and soon her husband found out about this and initiated divorce proceedings.

Men, when they find out their wives have been unfaithful, cannot bring themselves to forgive them. However, if it is a man who is at fault he fully expects his wife to "understand," forgive, and go on as if nothing has ever happened. This duality in standards is so obvious across the world, but especially in India.

Val, a school teacher, had endured abuse from her alcoholic husband almost every night for years. Added to this, he would not give her enough money for everyday expenses. She was expected to run the house with her earnings. Any request for financial assistance from her husband would result in severe verbal and physical abuse. She had great difficulty staying in this loveless marriage, but she had to think of two teenage children who were at a critical stage of their academic lives. She shielded them from abuse. Her life was one long story of being pushed around, and she silently suffered. Well-meaning friends counselled her to "pray" and continue in the marriage as "divorce was not in the will of God." With repeated abuse being heaped day after day, there was no ray of hope in sight. After nearly two decades of abusive marriage, and many sessions with pastors and counsellors, she finally decided to seek divorce to save her life and those of her children.

Many Pastors and counselors had bluntly said that divorce was unacceptable and not permissible except for adultery and asked her to just have faith and patience and wait for God to solve the issue. They however, had no comfort or solutions to offer for the immediate problem of violence or the fact that the children were growing up with a tremendous amount of fear and lack of self-confidence and self-respect.

We can go on and on with countless such cases where workable solutions are elusive, ultimately ending in divorce. We would like you to briefly examine the Scriptures to enumerate guidelines on the issue of divorce, to find comfort and answers for troubled marriages: Exod 20:17; Deut 22:13–22; 24:1–4; Ezra 10:10–17; Mal 2:16; Matt 18:15–18; 19:3–11; Rom 7:1–6; 1 Cor 7:8–17, 24–28.

Please read these passages carefully. We will trust the wisdom of the Scripture and the anointing of God the Holy Spirit to lead you to your own conclusions that will be in consonance with His will and bring glory to His name.

God did not intend, in His divine and original plan, for husbands and wives to separate, or divorce each other for any reason whatsoever as long as they lived. The Scripture dissolves the bond of marriage only on the death of a spouse, after which the surviving partner is free to remarry.

However, owing to the fallen nature of mankind and the subsequent hardness of some of the husbands in leaving their wives for trivial reasons, the Scripture permits divorce, although it does not approve or give a blanket permission. It is always God's desire that husbands and wives work out their differences and allow Him to work in their domestic and marital tangles to bring about His perfect solutions that are lasting.

The Bible is also very clear about the fact that God hates divorce and it was not in His original plan for mankind, yet certain pressures necessitated Moses to allow it. In the Old Testament (during the time of Moses), the children of Israel picked up some of the pagan customs of Egypt, and were practicing putting away their wives for reasons labelled as indecency, acts that were other than adultery. Adultery was of course punishable by stoning to death. While the old rabbinic schools did differ widely on the issue of "indecency," one thing they agreed upon was that it was something that did not amount to adultery, thereby meriting the punishment of being stoned.

Deuteronomy 24:3 mentions the fact that owing to certain undesirable traits of the wives, their husbands began to detest them. Some versions use the word "hate" in describing the attitude of the husbands towards their wives, some versions say "does not love her," and hence throws more clarity on the fact that these wives were no longer welcome in their own homes, and that their husbands wanted to be free from this relationship. As Jesus mentions in Matthew 19, these husbands had become so hardhearted and unfeeling that it became next to impossible to sustain such marriages. And that is one of the reasons that Moses allowed the permission for divorce.

However, there were some built-in safeguards that had to be observed, lest husbands begin to divorce their wives on extremely trivial issues. They had to give their wives a legal certificate of divorce. This meant that they had to go through a legal procedure in obtaining a certificate and divorce. This also implied that there would be some reasonable delay in obtaining this certificate. It meant that during the period of such delay, the husbands had ample time to rethink on this issue and only go forward if they were certain that they wanted to leave their wives. The second built-in safeguard was that once the man divorced his wife and she remarried, she could never get back to her first husband, in the case of the death of the second husband or obtaining divorce from him. This was a kind of punishment for the first husband, if he had sent his wife away on some trivial issue and later began to regret it and desired that she came back to him.

Therefore, the first valid legal reason to seek a divorce mentioned in the Old Testament is where one's spouse had committed adultery. In such cases, it was implied by the rabbinical schools, that the innocent spouse was free to remarry after the divorce. This reasoning stands valid even today.

Subsequently, post exile, Ezra made it clear to the Israelites who returned with pagan wives from exile, to separate from them. This was another valid reason for divorce. While Ezra was speaking to the children of Israel who were under the old covenant and bound by laws given by God through Moses, Paul had to deal with the rapid growth of the church especially in the non-Jewish countries of the world. He had to deal with wives and husbands from a non-Christian background, who had come into Christian faith and had to live with unbelieving husbands or wives. At times the unbelieving spouses of those who had now become Christians found it difficult to adjust with them. In such cases, if the unbelieving spouse wanted to be released from the bond of marriage, they could be. But if these unbelieving spouses wanted to stay in their marriages, their believing spouses were to stay in the marriage because their children were sanctified because of the partner who had become a believer. Paul adds that in cases where the unbelieving spouse seeks release from the marriage, the believing spouse is under no bondage after such a divorce to stay single, and is free to re-marry a believer. However, Paul recommends people in these mixed marriages to remain married to their unbelieving spouse, but in case they are forced into divorce by their unbelieving spouse, to preferably remain single. For in doing so, their whole undivided focus would be to please the Lord.

What about spouses who are victims of severe physical abuse? What we mention here is our personal opinion, born out of years of counselling experience. While we write this, we will also urge readers who are themselves victims or some who have known such victims, to prayerfully consider Scripture and come to a conclusion that fits their situation.

If you read Mal 2:13–16; Eph 5:25–29; Col 3:19; 1 Tim 3:1–6 and Jas 1:19–20, you will find that the Scripture exhorts husbands to love, care, nurture and honor their wives as their own bodies, just as Christ did for the church. They were exhorted to be even willing, if necessary, to put their lives at risk or die, for the sake of their wives. There is no way husbands are permitted to use any sort of violence against their wives. Anyone doing so is going against a very basic teaching of the Bible, directly amounting to sin. Jesus talks about handling a church member who is found in sin in Matt 18. Applying the same principle, when a counsellor confronts a violent or abusive husband, and he refuses to listen, the clear course of action as Jesus pointed out through Matthew 18 would hold good here too. That is, in addition to any police action, he is to be warned before two or three believers. If he refuses to their listen to wisdom and counsel, he must be taken before the whole church and warned, and if he is still unwilling to mend his ways, he must be removed from the church and treated like an unbeliever. We have clearly outlined in our chapter on domestic violence, the path the abused spouse needs to initiate. The course of action must culminate through the instructions of Jesus found explicitly in Matthew 18. Obviously, if he is to be finally treated as an unbeliever, separation would very much be in order. It remains possible, after a reasonable time-frame of waiting, counseling and supervising, if the husband is genuinely changed, he may be restored to the church first and later into the family, after a time of observation.

On the other hand, if he shows no remorse, stalks his wife, continues to threaten her and the children, and vows harm and vengeance, divorce is a valid solution. It is the course of action needed to save the wife and children from an unrepentant husband and father. However, we need to mention that no case is beyond God's ability to change and transform. Much prayer coupled with patience and a winning behavior can transform even extremely hardened and difficult husbands.

SIXTEEN: MARRIAGE MAKERS AND BREAKERS

"Our lives begin to end the day we become silent about things that matter." Dr. Martin Luther King Jr

A chain is as strong as its weakest link. In marriage too, there are many forces that affect the strength of the bond to weaken and break the marriage. Here, we have elaborated on some "marriage breakers."

DOUBT/SUSPICION

It takes years to build up trust, and it takes only suspicion, not proof, to destroy it. C. S. Lewis, the profound Christian thinker and writer says, "suspicion often creates what it suspects."[xx] Suspicion is so dangerous that it can lead to total obsession, and subsequently prevent healthy and sustainable relationships. It amplifies misunderstandings and makes a person possessive of his or her spouse, thereby preventing them from having a meaningful and satisfying relationship. Suspicion can be compared to termites, which cause damage to our house, without being visible.

In our counselling experience we have met many husbands and wives who made certain assumptions about their spouses based on observations alone, without verifying the facts, resulting in ruining their peace of mind and their marriage. For example, a wife may find a red spot on her husband's shirt, and without even verifying, jump to the conclusion that it is a lipstick smear from some woman with whom her husband is having an affair. One thought can lead to another dangerous one and end up with the wife believing that the husband is cheating. She begins watching him constantly and covertly, and if she finds him speaking to a lady, her doubts are further amplified. This begins to strain the relationship, and she begins to badger her husband. The husband who is unaware of the reasons for her suspicion, begins to get weary and angry. Arguments start, leading to constant bickering. We have come across some wives who go to the extent of hiring private detectives to keep an eye on their supposedly erring husbands.

Simple instructions to husbands and wives on handling doubt and suspicion:

- Always clarify when in doubt.
- Never be afraid to confront, but be gentle in your dealings.
- When a reasonable explanation is given, accept it in faith.
- Continue to trust your spouse. You cannot be a policeman or policewoman and monitor your spouse. Please remember, if a

spouse wants to cheat and does it, he or she will ultimately be found out and must face the inevitable. But remember God is the best "policeman" you can ever have and nothing, no matter how small, escapes His attention.

- If the matter becomes serious, seek the help of a godly counsellor.
- If the matter is cleared, forget about it and do not keep bringing it up.
- In the meanwhile, do not nag and neglect to meet each other's needs, especially in the area of sex.
- Do not neglect to pray individually and together all the while. Such battles are often won through prayer.
- Do not discuss this with your friends or family to gain their sympathy and support, as this would tarnish the image of your spouse, and eventually harm your family in society.
- Please keep in mind 1 Peter 3:1–9, where in Peter makes it clear that often husbands can be won over by the good/gentle and godly behavior of their wives. The same principle holds good for husbands as well.

INDIFFERENCE

There are many humorous stories about "the seven-year itch" in marriages. It is said that the sheen of marriage gets dulled over a period, and if you have survived seven years of your marriage, you have supposedly put the worst behind you. This is partly true and if you are not careful to keep the fires of your marriage burning bright, it slowly becomes dull. In a humorous vein, someone said that if a man is opening the door of his car for the wife to get in, either the car or the wife is new. The first few years of life generally set the tone for the marriage in the long term. It is important to make sure that our spouse continues to be the most important person in our life, after God.

Good marriages are cultivated, while poor marriages are caused! It takes much work to build good marriages. It is when we take each other for granted that indifference sets in. Indifference at home can be compared to dampness caused by water seepage. When you notice a small patch of dampness and do not take immediate steps to stop the leakage of water seeping in, you will find the patch growing larger and larger over a period, ultimately endangering the house. Here are some symptoms and their remedies for tackling indifference in a marriage:

Symptom: Ceasing to appreciate your spouse.

Remedy: Appreciate your spouse often. Compliments go a long way in building good marriages.

Symptom: Ceasing to anticipate the likes and dislikes of your spouse.

Remedy: Anticipating and doing something that your spouse wants done, before being asked. This shows how deeply you care for your spouse.

Symptom: Ceasing to meet the needs of your spouse and only doing it when told.

Remedy: Jesus gives a beautiful insight on relationships in Matt 7:12: "So in everything, do to others what you would have them do to you, for this sums up the Law and the Prophets." If you want your spouse to respect, love and care for you, set an example. Do it yourself first. Everything begins with you, and Scripture says, that what so ever a man sows, that he shall reap. If you wish to be treated as someone special, start treating your spouse as someone special first and we challenge you to see what happens thereafter!

Gentlemen, be chivalrous! Vijaya always said, "Irwin treats me like a queen; he still does after nearly 35 years of marriage." And in return, he gets treated like a king by her! Make sure your wife is comfortable at all times and she is not overburdened. Be quick to anticipate and meet her needs. We promise you, by doing this, you will fan even dying embers of your marriage into a blazing fire. The magic of a gentle touch cannot be underestimated, neither can that of a big hug and a kiss. Remember to take your wife on a fresh "honeymoon" trip now and then. Wives love gifts! May we quickly clarify that cost does not matter to them. A rose given with love is as precious as a diamond—and most wives love chocolates too. Give them a surprise and cook them a meal if possible. Even if it is not delicious, your wife will just love it! Lead your wife by example, and demonstrate what the love of Christ is to her. Your marriage is certain to be rekindled!

ANGER

Leon Brown says, "A moment of anger can destroy a lifetime of work, whereas a moment of love can break barriers that took a lifetime to build."[xxi] Very insightful indeed! Many marriages get into hot water and head for a split, often because of the misuse of emotions and tongues. Someone once wrote, "Speak when you are angry and you will make the best speech you'll ever regret."[xxii] Anger has three primary components: emotions, speech and actions. Anger can be both negative and positive. Anger directed towards sin, injustice and undesirable behavior is understandable, but how we handle anger makes it wrong or right. Anger can also be the outcome of feelings of rejection, not being able to have our own way, envy, seeming injustice meted out to us, and bruised egos. This can lead to un-tempered speech and dysfunctional behavior. Many marriages have either disintegrated or become joyless because of uncontrolled anger. Solomon admonishing us in Ecclesiastes 7:9 says, "Do not be eager in your heart to be angry, for anger resides in the bosom of fools." Proverbs 14:29 says, "He who is slow to anger has greater understanding, but he who is quick-tempered exalts folly." James 1:20 says the anger of man does not accomplish the purpose of God. Paul writing to the church at Ephesians 4:26, exhorts us not to let the sun go down on our anger.

How to manage anger:

- Start by being humble; humility is a great antidote to inflated egos.
- Walk with the Lord consistently, with a daily intake of His Word and a renewed submission to the Lordship of the Holy Spirit. A Spirit-controlled temperament will control egos and anger. Being able to pray at all times will help you tide over anger (1 Thess 5:16–18).
- Never vent your anger through wrong words and actions. Always wait till you have cooled down.
- Do not keep company with angry people as you will learn their ways (Prov 22:24).
- Learn to accept and tolerate the mistakes and errors of people around you. Forgive easily without keeping grudges and scores. Remember we are imperfect ourselves, and we deal with imperfect people. Our dealing with them can change the course of their lives, affecting even eternity.
- Learn the art of de-stressing – this could be through deep breathing exercises, indulging in pleasant activities, or turning your mind to dwell on good memories.
- Memorize Scripture and when you are angry or tempted to give vent to your anger, recollect those memory verses.
- Go for a walk in a pleasant place and if possible listen to soothing music.

- Learn to look on the funnier side of life. Being able to laugh and inculcate a sense of humor can work wonders in calming you down.
- Remember getting angry is a choice and you can choose to reject anger.
- Look for solutions rather than getting stuck with problems.
- Never seek vengeance, let the Lord handle it His way.

POOR MAINTENANCE

Behind every accident, whether in aviation, or rail, or construction, there is some slip-up in the maintenance of the machinery, systems, or buildings. Although the cracks begin to appear, we tend to ignore them thinking that they pose no serious threat until the actual mishap takes place. These can be prevented with careful and regular maintenance. The same is true of marriages. Failure to properly maintain relationships or marriages can result in disasters. Building a healthy marriage and happy families is a time-consuming task.

There are four areas that we will have to consider if we have to carry out proper maintenance of our marriages:

- Being sensitive and observant of our spouse and children.
- Giving adequate time to build, develop and repair relationships.
- Being open to correction and lifestyle modifications.
- Ensuring a regular time of devotion with the entire family and a time of relaxation too!

Susanna Wesley (better known as the mother of John and Charles Wesley), is often referred to as the mother of Methodism. She had 19 children, nine of whom died in infancy. She brought up the remaining 10 children in the fear and love of God and the rest is history. It is said that she would spend time individually with each of her children, talking and listening to them.

We live in a time-consuming world, where time comes at a premium. But remember, there is nothing more important than your own family, except God! Developing and helping them become what God wants them to become should be one of the greatest passions of our lives. Paul tells the church in Ephesus to redeem the time (5:16) "making the most of your time, because the days are evil." We can either redeem the time and put it to use in making our family better, or regret our insensitivity later. Time management is the key to improved and better relationships.

Some simple tips on time management to build our families:
- List all activities for the next day on the previous night.
- Prioritize these activities.
- Put off those that are not essential.
- Identify time-wasting activities (magazines, TV, social media).

Make sure you give quality time to your spouse, listening, reflecting and responding to their inputs. Every child individually deserves at least some portion of your time daily when they can feel free to share. Make sure that as far as possible you eat at least one meal, breakfast, or dinner together because that is a great time to bond over food and build up healthy communication between family members.

FAILURE TO PARTICIPATE IN HOME-BUILDING

Many husbands think the task of homemaking is the responsibility of the wife which is a wrong notion. Genesis chapters 1 and 2 adequately throw light on this. Proverbs 29:18 says, "Where there is no vision, the people perish." A shared vision of where the family needs to be in the times to come is essential to achieve the goals that God sets before us. It need not just be a grand spiritual vision, but a vision that manifests in everyday tasks at home such as cooking, cleaning, gardening, marketing, keeping the house, etc. along with your spouse. Get involved even in taking care of your young children, changing diapers, getting their milk ready, feeding them and keeping watch at night while your wife sleeps. This helps deepening the bonds between family members and ironing out relationship kinks because you are in touch in real-time with the whole family. Remember you are building memories that will last a lifetime, and are setting an example for your generations to come.

Our daughter Preeti, when she was an infant, had the habit of sleeping during the day and would keep awake literally the whole night. Vijaya's nerves would be frayed by the evening and she would look apprehensively at the prospect of minding her again during the night, losing her own sleep. Irwin saw her predicament, and took on the job of minding Preeti, letting Vijaya sleep throughout the night peacefully, so that she could be ready for Preeti during the day. Irwin had to sacrifice much of his sleep during the night, and would be drowsy in the office the next day, but somehow saw through this difficult phase, earning the love and gratitude of Vijaya. It helped build and deepen his relationship with Vijaya.

PROCRASTINATION - UNRESOLVED ISSUES

Like unchecked rust and corrosion that eats up metal, unresolved family issues eat away and corrode the fabric of marriage and family one bit at a time leading to its weakening and eventual collapse. Sometimes we are not willing to face up to our issues. We think they are unimportant and can be left to be discussed at some other convenient time, which of course may never happen. At times we are scared to tackle them for fear of the consequences that might emerge. It is a mistake to avoid confrontations, or think that time as a great healer, will anyway take care of the issue. But rather than face a problem, we are willing to compromise and somehow live with it.

It is like sweeping dust under the carpet or letting rust grow on metal. It never works, as it ferments beneath the surface and explodes much later when least expected. And by then it would have become larger, more painful and difficult to handle. No wonder Paul advises us through his Epistle to the Ephesians, asking us not to let the sun go down on our wrath. The idiom, "a stitch in time saves nine," is so true, and following it will benefit us. Some additional pointers to tackle this issue are given below:

- Never put off anything that needs correcting or mending for longer than a day or two. If possible, resolve it before the night is over.

- Handle issues amicably and not with an attitude of complaining or blaming. Tackle issues rather than tackling people.

- Discuss solutions with an open mind. Try to understand the other person and the issue as a small part of the big picture.

- Be open to criticism and change.

- Seek the Lord's mind and if necessary, enlist the intervention of godly people if the solution evades you.

- Continue with family devotions without fail, despite temporary irritations.

- Initiate accountability goals with periodical monitoring of the issue.

ADULTERY

This is something that can be compared to an earthquake that practically demolishes a house. It is the most dangerous family destroyer in which the guilty and the innocent both suffer and eventually the name of the Lord is tarnished.

SOME WISDOM AND ADVICE

Adultery does not happen suddenly, it takes time to develop in the mind and finally erupts. While we do sympathize with the innocent spouse, it is possible that he/she may have contributed to this eventuality in some way or the other. This of course in no way, justifies the "guilty spouse."

Do not fear to confront the guilty party, although with gentle firmness and courage. Do not fear the consequences; instead identify causative factors and also solutions. The "guilty partner" must demonstrate genuine remorse, repentance and a willingness to turn away from sin and seek forgiveness from the wronged spouse (Prov 28:13). The "wronged spouse" must understand that choosing to forgive can be a genuine remedy for the situation, in the Lord.

The "guilty partner" must immediately break away from the adulterous relationship and never even try to get in touch with the other man/woman, whether personally, through the phone, or through the internet. He or she must ruthlessly discourage all efforts from the other person to contact him or her.

The family altar must be restored.

The couple must undergo counselling from a godly counsellor and meet regularly for follow-up.

They must also try and enroll in a good Bible-study group for regular study of the Scripture, fellowship and mentoring.

The incident must not be referred to repeatedly, to prevent subsequent irritations in the marriage.

These home-breaking threats are like a wedge that is hammered into a small crack. The devil is an expert in continuously hammering it in, so that the crack widens. The wedge gets deeper and deeper, ultimately destroying the family.

Please remember that marriages need to be worked on, cared for, and protected from every destabilizing act. Marriage is like a ship carrying the husband, the wife, and the children. If the ship springs a leak, we do not make it bigger, rather we plug the leak. Remember, either we sail together or sink together!

It is our prayer that your marriage and family will progressively reflect the perfect relationship between God the Father, God the Son, and God the Holy Spirit.

EPILOGUE: OUR PERSONAL STORY

Irwin Lall

"And I will bless them that bless thee, and curse him that curseth thee: and in thee shall all families of the earth be blessed." Gen 12:3 (KJV)

"The woods are lovely, dark and deep, But I have promises to keep, And miles to go before I sleep, And miles to go before I sleep." Robert Frost[xxiii]

"Through many dangers, toils and snares, I have already come; 'Tis grace hath brought me safe thus far, and grace will lead me home." John Newton in Amazing Grace

This chapter may appear to be the fitting finale of this book, but in many ways, it is the gateway for the readers to get to know us better, feel with our failures but celebrate our successes and blessings as well. We want to let you know that just because we have been teaching on the family for almost thirty years, and are now penning this book, we can by no stretch of imagination be labelled as either a perfect couple or as perfect parents. Often, we have made messes larger than we could handle and but for the awesome grace of God and the repairing work of God the Holy Spirit, we would have faded off into eternity without a trace.

Sadly, this chapter is written by me (Irwin) even as Vijaya has obeyed her home-call to be with her Saviour. She left us on the 18th November 2013. This chapter is a celebration of her life and this book is a testimony, that hers was an existence that was larger than life. To do justice to a life like hers that was extremely well lived by His standards, is next to impossible. Yet woven in the strands of our personal story is this brilliant strand, Vijaya. The perfect wife and faithful partner in the adventure of life and ministry; the doting and caring mother and mentor of many; an individual of the highest standards of integrity and the star that shone brightest for her Master, despite enormous clouds that threatened to engulf her.

This chapter will not only deal with our personal struggles and successes, but with issues of having to release our children into the world, thereafter grappling with an empty nest and ultimately with the inevitable—dealing with a life-threatening disease of one's spouse, and thereafter releasing your spouse into the hands of God for safekeeping till the time we join them in the heavenly realms. This is also about a simple truth, that despite losing a spouse who has not only been a friend, philosopher and guide but also a partner in the ministry, a prayer warrior and the anchor of one's life, how God moves in with greater grace, greater love and greater power to fill the void. This is also about how despite this life shattering experience, one can still find meaning and happiness in Him and serve Him effectively!

It is my prayer, that as I write about our life, more of this great God would be apparent in us and His intervention in our lives at every stage, despite meriting the worst. So then, this book is about bringing God the glory at every turn of our lives and to encourage you to be able to see His big picture for your life as well, in conjunction with His kingdom and eternal workings in history.

Very often people ask us about how two people from such different backgrounds could find a level of compatibility that could make our marriage so beautiful. Many couples would also come up to us and tell us how we were "made for each other," while others would call us a perfect couple. Well, we gently disagree with all these friends and as you continue to read our story, you will find that it is not us, but a great God behind us who helped us become who we were, and we believe He is willing to do the same and more for any family who would submit to His Lordship and give Him freedom to work in their lives. Many were curious about what language we would speak at home and Vijaya's gentle answer with a twinkle in her eye would be, "we speak the language of love."

Let me start at the very beginning. I was brought up in a loving home yet not without its problems. My father had a transferable job and he had to move often, and my mother realized its danger in adversely impacting my education. So she decided to settle down in Hyderabad, India, to make sure that I would be able to study well. I saw her struggle alone to bring me up and as my parents were managing two separate establishments, financial struggles were a way of life. The first lesson I learnt in family life was by watching my mother struggling to bring me up alone, despite a serious heart condition. I would always think, that when the time came for me to get married and have a family of my own, I would make sure that I would not leave my wife alone to fend for herself.

My mother answered her heavenly call when I was just 19, and it was a devastating loss. Yet God stepped in and changed the course of my life. From being a "mamma's boy," I suddenly grew up to be an independent youngster working for a bank. In 1976, two things happened that were life changing. Firstly on 8th January at a convention, I accepted Jesus as my personal Savior. Secondly, God brought a very godly mentor into my life, Warren Myers, who was the South East Asia director for a ministry called The Navigators, based at Singapore. Both Vijaya and I owe much to Warren and his wife Ruth Myers, who mentored, counselled, and prayed for us relentlessly. In fact, we call them our spiritual parents. I strongly suspect that the Myers prayed much, not only for my life partner, but also for my marriage to be ordained by God for a very special purpose.

Eventually as time passed, pressures mounted on me to get married. By then I was worshipping in the Methodist Church at Secunderabad and was also active in its choir and the youth fellowship. It is there I saw Vijaya for the first time and no sooner had I set my eyes on her, than something within me (obviously God) just confirmed to me that this was the girl I would be spending the rest of my life with. I was absolutely certain! Not to mention that she was very beautiful, articulate, well read, highly spoken of by everybody and yes, a believer. Of course, I discovered this much later. Deep down, I am very old-fashioned and I never gave Vijaya an inkling of what was transpiring in my mind. I sought the help of Dr. Vimla Samuel from Warangal who had taken on my responsibility as a surrogate mother. When God works, it becomes very obvious. It transpired that Mr. Samuel and Vijaya's mother had been colleagues at some point of time. It made things easy and before long, our wedding was fixed! Amazingly, my father who would always hint on getting a North Indian daughter-in-law for his son, showed absolute openness in accepting a Telugu girl and also heartily approved of Vijaya. God's wheels were turning to accomplish His purposes not only in our life but to prepare His instruments who would be used by Him much later!

We got married on the 7th of June 1978. Vijaya arrived home and we began the task of building our marriage and a family. I must confess that I did not have the foggiest of notions of how to go about doing this. I had a beautiful wife I had dreamt of, and I had enormous confidence that we could live and manage on love and sweet dreams. We were on cloud nine and could not see anything else for the stars that filled our eyes.

As I had lived alone with my mother most of the time, who had pampered me despite financial challenges, I had grown up to be a spoilt brat. With her going away in my 19th year and till my wedding in 1978, that is, my 25th year, I had gotten used to being absolutely independent in taking decisions and leading my own life. Even after Vijaya came into my life, I called the shots at home and generally had my way. Added to this, I was very short tempered, a spendthrift, very impulsive and reluctant to receive correction. What a deadly combination! But praise God for Vijaya, who rose up to the challenge of polishing my rough edges and being God's instrument of change in my life!

Although I was working for a bank and earning fairly well, owing to my spending habits I did not inculcate the habit of saving, especially for my wedding. I spent what I earned! Sadly, my father never taught or counselled me and strongly felt that as I was a grown-up now, I was a responsible person and should manage my own affairs. How I wished he had given me some financial wisdom. I later realized that as he himself was a spendthrift, he did not find my spending habits strange. As such I had to take loans for my wedding and when my new bride came home, she was surprised to find out that my take-home salary was drastically reduced because of the servicing of these loans. So we began our newly married life, although with great happiness and excitement, yet on a difficult financial note. It greatly helped that Vijaya was also working for a bank. We now counsel young people not to get married till they have attained financial stability to support a family on their own without any help from their spouse, if possible.

Meanwhile, I was not consistently walking with the Lord, neither were we as a new family honoring the Lord with our tithes. Our financial woes were seemingly unending and became worse by Vijaya's two miscarriages and two surgical procedures in the first two years of our marriage. Her second pregnancy had to be terminated after five months as the child in the womb had ceased to live, owing to certain complications. We were unaware of the fact that Vijaya was carrying a dead fetus all the while, as diagnostic facilities were limited in the late 70s. We discovered this fact just in time to prevent Vijaya from going into septicemia. This baby, which was carried by Vijaya for almost 5 months, was a male child, and had to be surgically removed from her womb in bits and pieces. This shattered both of us and we were depressed as we had no answers that could satisfy us. We came home from the hospital and the next day we opened the Bible randomly, to find that we had opened Habakkuk 3, from where verses 17 to 19 jumped out:

> Although the fig tree shall not blossom, neither shall fruit be in the vines; the labour of the olive shall fail, and the fields shall yield no meat; the flock shall be cut off from the fold, and there shall be no herd in the stalls: Yet I will exult in the LORD, I will rejoice in the God of my salvation. The LORD God is my strength, and he will make my feet like hinds' feet, and he will make me to walk upon mine high places. (KJV)

God ministered to us through this passage and it dawned on us, that our happiness or contentment was independent of what happened to us. It did not stem from advantageous circumstances, but on the firm conviction, that no matter what, we always had the greatest treasure which could never be taken away from us and that was the presence of the eternal God—every day, all the way! This understanding of God was the beginning of a great adventure that would eventually test our faith to the ultimate, and we are grateful that our faith and God's faithfulness carried us through!

The next test was the test of financial commitment to the kingdom of God. As mentioned earlier, we were not tithing our money and persistently having monetary problems. There came a time when we would, by the month end, look around for even some loose change that would be lying around to see us through the last days of the month. God knows how to get our attention. Again, He brought the book of Haggai and Malachi into focus, and as He had admonished Israel in the time of the prophets, He brought our attention to the chastisement through the Prophet Haggai, "Consider your ways" (1:7). It was one of the most painful decisions we had to initiate in our lives. We had not enough to see us through the month and now had to separate ten percent at least for Him. Impossible as it seemed, we prayerfully decided to separate ten percent on the date we would get our salaries, and then trust God. Difficult though it was, it was yet one of the best decisions of our lives and we have never had one moment to regret it. God began to stretch our money, lessened our wants and our spending, but with great contentment. In the months we needed more, money would come from unexpected sources. We also began to understand that our giving began after we had already given God the ten percent that belonged to Him.

I remember one occasion, when we ran out of money, we were left wondering how we would see the month through. I went to the office and my manager called me and asked me if I had drawn my diem/travel allowance for my posting to Warangal, a city about 140 kms from Hyderabad, our home town. You see, I was transferred to Warangal, and within 15 days of working there, had to be brought back on a temporary transfer to Hyderabad owing to a road accident that caused multiple injuries to my father. Although, in the fitness of things, I thought I was not entitled to draw this allowance, my boss was generous enough to sanction it officially, and I remember I came home that evening with over Rs.1000/- in my pocket. In the year 1981 that was a large amount. God did open the windows of heaven and we rejoiced over His faithfulness again.

God opened Vijaya's womb and gave us our first daughter, Sruti, who was a breech baby and was born despite many odds, in 1981. God opened Vijaya's womb a second time and in 1984, our second daughter, Preeti was born. These two daughters have brought great joy to our lives and I will talk more about them a little later.

Within one year of Sruti's birth, Vijaya developed a troublesome and tenacious infection called pilonidal sinus, which developed multiple tracts. After almost one year of suffering and going through two surgical procedures, it turned worse. She had to be admitted in a hospital for a major surgery. The surgery was successful, but she had to be on a high dose of painkillers. Before this she had another surgery for the removal of an abscess, and added to this was the fact that she had miscarriages twice, involving D&Cs with intake of a large amount of painkillers. She also had a history of seizures and migraines. Obviously, she had to be on painkillers on and off, which eventually damaged her kidneys, in the long term. We were in and out of hospitals continuously.

This was within the first few years of our marriage. We were also trying to adapt and adjust to our relationship, during that period. My rigidity in accepting to change was frustrating. Vijaya was undergoing severe stress battling with her own sickness and with a one-year-old toddler to manage.

No wonder it took a toll on our relationship, in that it was strained and we had no one we could turn to for counsel and help. It is around that time, that I became emotionally distant from Vijaya and almost broke my promise of faithfulness to her! In hindsight, I realized perhaps I was seeking to find comfort in my own stressful situation. Of course, this in no way justified my behavior. I cannot imagine how hurt Vijaya must have been! But God was watching and working. He brought me to repentance, severely warning me through Amos 4:12 "Prepare to meet your God." I humbled myself before God and my wife, and sought their forgiveness, both of whom gave it unconditionally and without any reservations. To Vijaya's credit, she completely closed this chapter and never referred to it again all her life. That is true forgiveness! And she stands tall as an example of what it is to forgive and forget and rebuild on the scars of life!

This was the next major turning point in our lives. Not only was our relationship restored but it became much better and became more so with each passing year. Our love deepened and matured and our appreciation for each other strengthened. It was during that time of recovery and recommitment that God gave us a new promise from Gen 12:3. He affirmed to us that He was going to greatly bless us and use us as instruments of His blessing to the nations and peoples, even to the ends of the earth. Honestly, we could not understand this promise as we were ourselves struggling to rebuild our relationship. But more than thirty years later, we know what God meant then! It is very mysterious why God chose us! We still do not have the answer, except to say that He is the Master and we are the clay. He is especially fond of weak, cracked, and broken vessels and uses them to bless others and bring glory to Himself.

Vijaya later confessed that she had a major issue in submitting to my leadership at home. Before marriage, she was a very independent woman, self-willed and a strong supporter of woman's emancipation. She in fact did consider staying single at one point of time, till she met me! However, God worked on her too and she began to slowly accept me as the leader of the home. These changes in both of us and our willingness to own up to our mistakes and allow God to work on us and change us brought in God's healing and peace, besides His cascading blessings. It also opened a new vista of ministry that we were unaware of till then.

It was in the mid-80s that we began to get involved in the Methodist Church, where at God's call, I started to teach in the Sunday School, and God greatly blessed this effort. I discovered that He had given me the gifts of preaching, teaching, and evangelism. Doors began to open, invitations began to multiply, and I found myself getting busier with each passing year, not only in Hyderabad but in other cities as well. However, I was also aware of the needs of the family and the necessity of my deep involvement in their lives. I refused many promotions at the bank as they involved transfers taking me away from the family. Vijaya was content to work in the bank, and also in bringing up our two lovely daughters.

It was around this time, somewhere in the mid-80s that the Child Evangelism wing of the Evangelical Fellowship of India invited me to teach in a one-day seminar organized by them on the Christian family. I promptly turned the invitation down as I had no idea of what it meant to teach on the family, except that family meant a team of husband, wife and children. Thank God, they persisted and badgered me and I took the first few classes on the Christian family with much trembling and despair. By the way, there were only three participants—all women—who turned up that day. This is not counting the hosts and Vijaya, who had come with me to encourage and strengthen me, convinced that I might even faint with anxiety that day. I came back fully convinced that I had done an extremely bad job and I do not remember what I taught except that I seemed to grope for words and repeated myself ever so often. To my utter surprise, one of the ladies who had attended the seminar called me up the next day saying that she was richly blessed by the seminar and how the seminar had helped her to change her mind on seeking a divorce from her husband. Whew! God was continuing to work and He had just started a new phase!

There was no looking back from then on. God was using me and confirming His will over and over, that I, and later both of us, were indeed chosen by Him to teach on the Christian family. In 1991, I attended the Haggai Institute International Seminar for advanced leadership at Singapore, after which I was invited to teach in their National and regional seminars on the Christian Family, and much later in their international seminars as well. I had a strong desire to have Vijaya teach in the seminars alongside as my partner, but she somehow did not sense God's call in this matter. In the meanwhile, as my sphere of ministry began to grow and I began to travel on ministry, Vijaya finding more time on her hands as the children were growing up, heard God's call to minister in the Sunday school. She began to teach the seniors class in the Sunday school at the Methodist Church, which she continued to teach till her home call. Noticing her gifts in teaching & preaching, other churches began sending her invitations to preach on Women's Sundays, Sunday-school Sundays, etc. Eventually, she too began to teach and preach on some of the issues related to the Christian home. She was an intellectual, and considered to be a gifted teacher and preacher.

Around 1996, some of our close friends in the church requested us to conduct a seminar on the family for a few select families that were close to us in our own church. We zeroed in on a retreat center at a hill-station named Khandala, where we held a seminar for them for the first time, where both Vijaya and I and some of our close friends who had been teaching on the family already, ministered. It turned out to be a great blessing and the starting point for our own seminars. We never imagined that God was leading us in a very specific direction and wanted us to continue with these seminars at Khandala, which we did! That is how Family Foundations came by and the Family Seminar at Khandala became an annual event attracting families from all over India. Added to this, God opened up the area of counselling to us and numerous couples began to come to us for help for their marital problems. Yet another offshoot of our ministry was the Bible studies for couples, where we enrolled half a dozen couples each year and discipled them through Bible studies, getting them into the Navigators Topical Memory System and encouraging them to love the Lord.

In the meantime, on the home-front, both our daughters were reaching their high-school levels and doing well academically. I do confess that I was less than a good father—overprotective and high on discipline. I was what you would label as a "perfectionist." Of course, I loved them to a fault and if I was strict, it was only to shield them from mistakes that would ruin their future. But nevertheless, Vijaya had to step in often and act as a buffer between them and me and often negotiated peace between us. We taught them to love the Lord and become people of integrity. We also taught them to stand up for the truth even if it meant to suffer. We also taught them to be independent decision-makers, and choose wisely. Vijaya had the larger role in this area.

As a result, even though we wanted Sruti to take up medicine, she refused to get into medicine and preferred psychology instead. We wanted Preeti to get into engineering, but she chose architecture over engineering. This apart they also chose their own husbands, and we have two outstanding sons-in-law, Daniel and Tunde, who are more sons than sons-in-law to us. We have never regretted the decisions of our daughters and are delighted over their choices and the way their life has shaped up. Before I forget, our daughters grew up with two lovely Labrador retrievers, Pongo the first one, and Max who stepped in after Pongo. Both these dogs grew up like our own children and the unconditional love they gave us was unimaginable and Sruti and Preeti enjoyed growing up with these two dogs who enriched our lives. Max was with us when both Sruti and Preeti got married in December 2009 and January 2011 respectively. Both the daughters, after their marriages, left behind a huge void that God's presence helped fill, and being busy in the ministry was an additional blessing. Max turned out to be a great blessing, and it was as if we still had one child remaining at home. He jealously watched over Vijaya. Yet the underlying reason for our sustaining through the void of our daughters leaving home was the fact that both Vijaya and I had developed an unshakeable and unbreakable bond of love, trust and dependence on each other and God. We have noticed some couples who fail to develop this bond, and when their children leave home, they are faced with the prospect of not just an empty home, empty time schedules, but empty hearts as well.

Our ministry was becoming busier, wider and deeper. Our family life seminars in Khandala were now an annual affair and because of this, I began to sense deeply in my spirit that God was calling me out from the bank to get into full-time service. This feeling got stronger and stronger and by the mid-90s, I was certain that the time was ripe for me to quit the bank job. However, by then there was an active talk of banks offering a voluntary retirement scheme with a golden handshake. This meant that I would get a decent amount of money over and above my retirement benefits. This was quite tempting, and I decided that no sooner the VRS with the golden handshake was offered, I would immediately quit. It is quite amazing how I was willing to trust the bank to meet our needs post-retirement, than to trust God. God was keeping an eye on me and decided to teach me a lesson on trusting him. In 1999, I went in for a small and routine surgery and was expected to rejoin the bank just the next day. Shockingly, the surgery failed and I began to bleed to death. My condition became so precarious that they had to stabilize me through blood transfusions and redo the surgery. This resulted in my hospitalization for nearly 16 days.

I had hardly any strength even to sit up and had to be fed lying down, and all I could do was to look at the white ceiling of the hospital and ask God to have mercy on me. God spoke very powerfully to me and gave me an option (humorously), to either choose my life and serve him or to serve the bank and obviously lose my life. There was hardly any option and God had me exactly where He wanted me to be. Waiting for VRS with a golden handshake disappeared from my horizon and I decided to seek premature retirement without any extra benefit. I instructed my assistant at the bank to bring in all the necessary papers for me to apply for premature retirement. By the way, I had just been promoted again and was expected to join a new office at Vijayawada, a city about 400 km away from Hyderabad, soon after recovering from my surgery.

The next morning, my assistant from the bank who was to bring me all the papers for premature retirement came to the hospital beaming from ear to ear. He blurted, "Mr. Lall, congratulations! Our bank has announced the immediate implementation of the VRS scheme with the golden handshake!" You see, when God saw that I was willing to trust Him for my family's future, He not only healed me, but He also got my bank to announce the VRS scheme with a golden handshake, to prove that He was in control not only of my situation but also of my bank and my future! I signed all my papers from my hospital bed and have never looked back. The whole family rejoiced over this and released me for full-time service of the Lord. Soon after I came out of the bank, I strongly felt that the ministry would greatly benefit if Vijaya joined me in serving the Lord. I began to pray for Vijaya to leave her job and join me in the ministry. I did not tell her about this as I did not want to influence her mind. God did an amazingly quick job and within fifteen days, Vijaya woke me up early one morning to tell me that God had spoken to her to quit her bank job as well, and join me in serving the Lord full-time. This was yet another crucial turning point in our lives!

Later on she confided in me that this was one of the best decisions she had taken, as this not only allowed her to serve the Lord more efficiently but also allowed her to spend a great deal of time with both our daughters who were in their teens now. This worked out extremely well, from every angle. Both our daughters of course did ask us about how we would make the ends meet. But they had by now seen God's generosity and provision in our lives and were content to learn from us that we would trust Him with all our future needs. And praise God, He has never let us down. I left my bank in December 2000, and Vijaya left hers in March 2001. We were both deeply impacted by the life of George Muller of Bristol who lived entirely by faith. When we left our banks, we made a commitment to the Lord, telling Him that we would never stretch our hands out to ask anyone except Him! We told Him, "wherever you take us, we will go, whatever you feed us, we will eat, and wherever you keep us, we will stay!" And He has always given us the best! That is the kind of God we serve, the absolute owner of everything – and generous beyond compare!

In September 2001, Vijaya developed severe back pain owing to spondylitis. In the process of getting some blood tests done, we stumbled upon the fact that her kidneys were slightly malfunctioning. We had to see a nephrologist and get a battery of tests done, and we were finally told that one of her kidneys was functioning at 50% and the other at 60% of their capacity. Over the next couple of months, we discovered little by little that there was every chance that she could eventually go into renal failure. This was very worrisome and quite scary initially. We had now left our banks behind just a few months ago. Our banks had hospitalization schemes which could hopefully cover much of the treatment costs. But we had burnt the bridges and were left with no option but to trust God.

Over the next couple of years, Vijaya's renal parameters (serum creatinine/serum urea) began to rise, and the prospect of dialysis loomed large. Transplants were very rare, and were prohibitively expensive. We did some research on the financial outlay of renal failure treatment and were appalled at the figures that jumped at us through the results of Google searches. We continued to pray and seek the Lord in all this. Time and again God would encourage us through Phil 4:6, 7, 4:13, and 4:19. We had a wonderful nephrologist and friend Dr. Dakshina Murthy, who was very supportive and positive, an extended family that was loving and reassuring, and our own family that was ready to face anything along with us, with the Lord going on before. All of Vijaya's four sisters and their families deserve a mention for the great emotional, physical and prayer support they have been in our most difficult days. Yet another couple that has been a tremendous blessing in this difficult period was Dr. Sudhir and Dr. Madhulatha, his wife. There were many others too who stood by us. What more could we ask for?! By the year 2006, Vijaya's renal parameters had begun to steadily rise, and because kidney failure leads to compromised production of erythropoietin that is essential for the manufacture of hemoglobin, she had to be put on injections of erythropoietin, without which hemoglobin would fall to alarmingly low levels. We had our first taste of the costs of treatment, as this injection was very expensive (Rs.1800/- each then) and she had to take two per week without fail. She was also prescribed steroids, resulting in her developing what is known as "moon face," the puffing up of the face.

Vijaya's energy levels would drop with her falling hemoglobin levels, tiring her easily, yet she would never miss a single ministry engagement that the Lord gave. Even during the worst of days, she would never give an inkling of what was transpiring within her. She always had a smiling face, a caring heart and a helping hand to extend to anyone who needed her comfort, counsel and help. Her constant answer to people enquiring about her health was, "I am fine, praise God!" There were times when she would feel so weak and yet had to go to preach/teach, and she would strengthen herself in the Lord and say, "His grace is sufficient for me." She had every legitimate reason to feel depressed or grumble, yet never once in her entire battle with sickness did she ever grumble or question God. Her faith was unshakeable and infectious. Even till today, people talk about her faith, happy demeanor and uncomplaining service.

It was in January 2010, soon after Sruti's marriage that Vijaya began to throw up non-stop, and her nephrologist discovered that her serum creatinine level was standing at 12.5, necessitating immediate commencement of dialysis. We discovered that we would need to spend approximately Rs. 25,000 to 30,000 a month. Thankfully, she was put on peritoneal dialysis, which had to be done three times a day at home. She was trained to do it herself. She had to take in 2 liters of dialysate every eight hours expelling it after 8 hours of a dwell time in her peritoneum, together with excess body fluids built up and not excreted by the kidneys, thereby preventing the dangerous buildup of fluids in the body. This was a better option for us over hemodialysis, which would require her to visit a hospital every alternate day and undergo a procedure for almost four to five hours, each time. Amazingly, God gave us grace to travel everywhere and perform peritoneal dialysis even during our travels. She performed this dialysis herself not only in India but in Europe as well! This allowed her to continue with the ministry both in Hyderabad and also during her travels, whether in India or overseas. We had to order the dialysis fluid in advance and have it sent to the place of our travel if the stay was an extended one. We would carry our own dialysis fluid for shorter durations of travel. Anyone who understood what was involved would be amazed, and it would become an occasion to glorify God for his mercy.

Peritoneal dialysis also allowed Vijaya to be able to travel to UK in November 2011 to witness the arrival of our first grandson, Bolu. She and Sruti had the joy of taking care of him when he was born. During September 2012, soon after our return from Europe, she came down with peritonitis, a severe life-threatening infection. This infection damaged the peritoneum, and she was hospitalized for about three months. We spent a very significant and meaningful Christmas 2012 and new year 2013 at the hospital and went around singing carols for patients in the wards. This infection proved to be the beginning of the end, when she had to undergo machine dialysis at home every night from April 2013 onwards. This was extremely expensive to the extent of costing us almost Rs.75,000 to 80,000 a month. Yet never once did we ever find Vijaya sad, depressed or anxious. She had that unshakeable faith in God, her very own personal Father, who never fails! It is for the glory of God that I need to mention, that during her entire 13 years of battling with renal failure, we would have spent an enormous amount of money on treatment and hospitalizations. Yet God did not allow us to dip into our personal resources at any time, and provided the entire cost of treatment from His overflowing and generous provision. Now, in retrospect we realize that the banks we worked for could have never covered even a fraction of the costs of treatment like the Lord did in his own way. Praise God!

In this battle with renal failure, there was a time during the mid-2000s, especially when her creatinine levels began to rise, I would become anxious at times. I remember, I woke up one night and saw Vijaya sleeping next to me. Immediately anxious thoughts began crowding my mind. I wondered what I would do without her, if something were to happen to her. Both our children had not even finished their studies and were yet to be married. The ministry was going on very well and that night, I sat there just worrying. It is then that the Lord hit me with 1 Peter 5:7 and Psalm 121. It was as if He was telling me, "Look I am enough to worry for the both of us, and please remember I am awake 24/7, 365 days of the year." He reassured me that He will never let us be "moved." What a reassurance! Then and there, I knelt down and cast all my anxieties upon Him and told Him, "God you take my anxieties, because you are adequate to handle them, all through the day and night and all through the year. So now you carry my worries, and I am going to sleep!" From that day onwards to the very last day I never ever had to worry and both Vijaya and I never had a moment of anxiety all through.

Although the Nizam's Institute of Medical Sciences, where she was treated throughout was planning to give a cadaver transplant to her, God had other plans! He wanted to heal her permanently and call her home to be safe in His arms, freed from physical suffering and pain. Finally, Vijaya was called home to be with her Saviour on the 18th of November 2013. She was in the hospital for 10 days and she left an indelible impression of faith and courage, not only on the whole family and friends, but also on the hospital staff as well, who could not stop talking about her. Even in death, she witnessed about our God who could be relied upon and was adequate for every situation of life. One month after Vijaya's home call, in December 2013, God spoke to me from Ezekiel 24:16–20, where God asked Ezekiel to preach soon after the death of his wife. God very clearly told me that He was not through with me, and there was yet a task of declaring His word to people that awaited me! Hallelujah!

Many friends and well-wishers, after Vijaya's home call, naturally presumed that I would be so grief stricken and helpless that I would stop the ministry, personal and that of Family Foundations. I must confess that the pain of losing a spouse is unimaginable; it can leave you totally shattered, confused and at times can make you angry and bitter. You can get into a tendency of just calling everything off and slide into a cocoon of self-pity and inactivity. Vijaya was my constant companion, my partner in the ministry, my best friend and advisor besides being my wife and the love of my life. The first few weeks were terrible, and I do not remember how I managed to live through those weeks. I guess I was just operating as a robot, unable to feel anything. Every time I got into the car, I would see the empty seat beside me and my heart would bleed. One time that I was driving, going out of town, I saw the empty seat beside me and just broke down. Again, the Lord gently cuddled me and brought Isaiah 54:5 to my mind like a bolt of lightning. I told the Lord that if He could be a husband for His people, He could also be a wife to His child who had just lost his earthly wife. It is amazing how His peace can come rolling over us and I experienced His presence and a reassurance that come what may, He would never leave me and He was my eternal joy and strength. From then on, I do miss my wife, but I never grieve over her, because I affirm that the Lord's plans are the best for us even through bereavement. And He has filled the void more than adequately by His presence and power.

The Lord since then, has multiplied and expanded the ministry, opened new doors, gave new zeal, new commitment, renewed health and a new vision to serve Him across the far corners of the earth. Often, the lines of Robert Frost come flitting into the mind, "I have miles to go before I sleep." So then, the underlying bedrock of our story is how God can put cracked, scarred, and sinful people to bring out His best in them despite their failings, shortcomings and weaknesses. Life is all about leaving your footprints on the sands of eternity—as Vijaya did! If He could do it for us, He can do much more for you! And it is our prayer that as you read this chapter, you will praise God with us, celebrate God's goodness with us and totally and irrevocably submit not just yourself but your whole family into His great hands for Him to transform you and empower you to be a blessing to the peoples of the earth. The Abrahamic blessing from Gen 12:3 is one that you can claim by right as heirs through faith in the Lord Jesus Christ. May all glory belong to the Triune God for ever and ever!

ENDNOTES

[i] Vance Havner, *Just a Preacher* (Chicago: Moody, 1981).
[ii] Steven J. Lawson, *Holman Old Testament Commentary* (Nashville, TN: B&H, 2006).
[iii] Corrie Ten Boom with John & Elizabeth Sherill, *The Hiding Place* (Old Tappan, NJ: Bantam Book, 1971)
[iv] Charles Dickens, A Tale of Two Cities (Jalic Inc, 2000–2015) from www.online-literature.com
[v] Martin E. Marty, *Dietrich Bonhoeffer's Letters and Papers from Prison* (New Jersey: Princeton University Press, 2011)
[vi] Matthew Henry, Matthew Henry's Commentary (Nashville, TN: HarperCollins Christian Publishing, 1706)
[vii] Emilie Barnes, *What Makes a Woman Feel Loved: Understanding What Your Wife Really Wants* (Concord, CA: Harvest House, 2007)
[viii] Stephen R. Covey, Principle Centred Leadership (New York: Simon&Schuster, 1990)
[ix] H. Norman Wright, *Quiet Times for Couples* (Eugene, OR: Harvest House, 1990)
[x] New York Times, www.nytimnes.com, October 22nd 1991
[xi] Cited by Nancy Campbell, *Woman's Daily Encouragement Blog*, 2014
[xii] Wikiquote, 2016.
[xiii] Blanchard Eades, *If Jesus Came to Your House and Other Poems* (Kansas City: Beacon Hill Press, 1957)
[xiv] Zig Ziglar, *Courtship After Marriage* (New York: Thomas Nelson, 1992)
[xv] Nate Carter, *God Never Panics: He Is the Anchor of Your Soul* (Shippensburg, PA: Destiny, 2004)
[xvi] Vance Havner and Dennis J. Hester, *When God Breaks Through: Sermons on Revival* (Grand Rapids, MI: Kregel, 2003)
[xvii] John H. Reumann, Stewardship and the Economy of God (Eugene, OR: Eerdmans, 1992)
[xviii] See https://en.wikipedia.org/wiki/Brand_(play)
[xix] https://www.ons.gov.uk/peoplepopulationandcommunity/crimeandjustice/bulletins/domesticabuseinenglandandwales/yearendingmarch2016
[xx] C. S. Lewis, The Screwtape Letters: Annotated Edition (New York: Harper, 2013)
[xxi] Vincent Thnay, Quote Worthy (Singapore: Thnay, 2015)
[xxii] The joke section quote was labelled "Anonymous" in the September 1956 issue of Readers Digest (New York City)
[xxiii] As cited by Edward Connery Lathem, "Stopping by Woods on a Snowy Evening" from *The Poetry of Robert Frost* (New York: Henry Holt, 1969)

www.ingramcontent.com/pod-product-compliance
Lightning Source LLC
Chambersburg PA
CBHW051640230426
43669CB00013B/2377